T0323401

Possessive Individualism

Possessive Individualism

A Crisis of Capitalism

DANIEL W. BROMLEY

OXFORD
UNIVERSITY PRESS

Oxford University Press is a department of the University of Oxford. It furthers
the University's objective of excellence in research, scholarship, and education
by publishing worldwide. Oxford is a registered trade mark of Oxford University
Press in the UK and certain other countries.

Published in the United States of America by Oxford University Press
198 Madison Avenue, New York, NY 10016, United States of America.

© Oxford University Press 2019

CIP data is on file at the Library of Congress
ISBN 978–0–19–006284–2

1 3 5 7 9 8 6 4 2

Printed by Integrated Books International, United States of America

To Joyce Elizabeth

Contents

Preface

In a Nutshell

The Enlightenment gave us the idea of the individual as an independent sapient being. Freed from superstition and official dogma, the individual was now in comprehensive control of her innate and acquired capabilities. Fearing the loss of moral certitude, Immanuel Kant found a substitute—it was moral to be rational and rational to be moral. The young discipline of economics embraced this newly created autonomous agent and assigned that individual the task of rendering rational—self-interested—choices. Such choices revealed true value: the rational individual could not be wrong about her choices. Individualism was now wedded to acquisitive behavior.

Max Weber's *The Protestant Ethic and the Spirit of Capitalism* provided theological gloss to the emergent culture of enterprise and striving. By the middle of the twentieth century, economics had become the *civic religion* of the modern industrial state whose purpose was to provide ever-increasing living standards for its citizens. As with daily weather updates, certain economic data came to define life under industrial capitalism. The unemployment rate, daily movements in the stock market (including those in far-off places), and the latest perturbations in the consumer price index became the contemporary equivalent of ancient astrological sightings.

By the end of the twentieth century, *industrial capitalism*—with a new global reach—had given way to *financial capitalism*. As the twenty-first century dawned, there was yet another transition underway: *managerial capitalism*. The Great Recession of 2007–2009 delivered a surprising destructive shock to large swaths of the population in western Europe and the United States. The angst and anger produced by that disruption have not abated. An abrupt loss of faith in the presumed beneficence of capitalism coincided with mounting despair—and political revolts—in the Middle East, parts of Latin America, and much of Africa. Immigrants became a threat to the comfortable social compact that had defined life since the end of World War II. The political class, regardless of party affiliation, was now bereft of ideas.

The lack of comprehension is to be expected. Governing elites have been mentally nurtured on the defining fiction of modernism. The autonomous acquisitive individual was both rational and moral. The civic religion provided the necessary benediction. The destructive paralysis was abetted by a fiction within a fiction. The civic religion had managed to insist that the economy—the "market"—is a separate and quite delicate sphere of efficiency and rectitude. When held up against the self-dealing incoherence of politics, tampering with the economy can only inflict harm. Kenneth Arrow proved that social choices were inconclusive and contradictory. Only markets offered consistent clarity. Politicians must not *interfere with* the mystical workings of the economy. Private firms, praised as "job creators," now comprise the sacred temples of modern capitalism. Government *intervention* in the market is dangerous and must be avoided. This protected realm is the fragile fount of future well-being.

Ironically, the autonomous individual is now an unwitting accomplice in his own economic marginalization. Dependent on the constellation of sanctified private firms for his precarious livelihood, he is unknowingly enlisted in the self-defeating cause of laissez faire. As politicians in western Europe and the United States quake and bluster before the alleged hordes of migrants seeking a better life, their constituents—nervous victims of the abundant caprice of managerial capitalism—exhibit behavior that further confounds the anomie and paralysis.

Possessive individualism both reigns and incapacitates.

The Journey

The sweep of history and ideas covered here suggests that a brief guide would be useful. The book is divided into three parts: The Problematic Triumph of Capitalism, The Great Unraveling, and Recovering Hope.

Part I contains three chapters. In Chapter 1, I develop the case that it is time to take a fresh look at what might reasonably be called *world disorder*—to play off of Henry Kissinger's recent book, *World Order* (Kissinger, 2014). I suggest that the primary reason for this disorder is the depth and reach of possessive individualism in contemporary life. In this first chapter I explain the role of the Enlightenment in creating the individual, I discuss the rise of industrial capitalism in eighteenth-century Britain (and a century later in Germany), and the emergence of economics as the civic religion of modern life. It is also in Chapter 1 that I spell out the general attributes of what I call *possessive individualism*. Finally, I introduce the idea of personhood, and argue that possessive individualism has undermined personhood. The promise of the Enlightenment has been hijacked by the acquisitive urge under market capitalism.

In Chapter 2, my purpose is to develop the broad outlines of how the discipline of economics—building on the created individual of the Enlightenment—has crafted a suite of concepts and practices that constitute justificationism. Here I argue that much of contemporary economics is misleading in its assumptions, willful in its presentation, and contrived in its conclusions. The central idea of rationality—the rational individual and rational choice—is circular and is thus a profound deception. Its purpose has been to situate economic calculation—maximizing utility—at the center of human behavior. To borrow from Gertrude Stein, I will show that there is no there there.

The popularity of contemporary economic concepts and the acquired habits of mind based on those concepts will be exposed as the perverse contamination that has undermined the aspirations of the Enlightenment. Freed from the chains of ancient superstition, the individual was soon reenslaved in the service of industrial capitalism and its offspring. Today the liberated individual is a nervous striver seeking something that relentless acquisitiveness cannot provide.

Chapter 2 is essential in yet another way. Most of the accounts of world disorder—the political anger, the rise of authoritarian xenophobic leaders, the alienated pro-Brexit voter, the forgotten rural resident of the great American Midwest—tend to be circular. It will be claimed that there is political unrest because the political system is broken. Partisan politics has become the reason for the political dysfunction, while political dysfunction is offered up as the reason for partisan politics. Yet the real explanation is found elsewhere, outside of this bizarre circle. The political class—those whose task it is to help the rest of us figure out where we wish to go—is immobilized by its many failures to understand the perverse workings of contemporary capitalism. Having accepted the promise of a world organized along the lines of a striving consumer maximizing his or her utility, yet emasculated by the associated deceit that a market economy is some inviolate parallel universe ruled by wise entrepreneurs who bring forth marvelous products and necessary employment, it seems that there is no place to turn.

If the subject of stagnant incomes does arise, inequality will be seen as a political problem rather than a problem with the economic system. And if inequality is somehow recognized as a systems problem, the durable cultural commitment to capitalism will divert any possible conversation about how to correct the reasons for the obvious problem. Fragile employment prospects—and defective earnings—will be blamed on endless political fights over international trade, immigrants, or taxation and regulations of businesses. Accepted economic verities lurk behind each of these issues, but their central role is misunderstood. And so the prevailing narrative becomes preoccupied with a failure of political will. It is often claimed that if only there could be a return to the good-old days of bipartisan compromise, these problems would be fixed. However, the root of the current despair is economic, not political, and therefore no amount of bipartisan comity will fix the problems under consideration.

The central message of Chapter 2—standing apart from the theoretical details therein—is that contemporary economics continues to provide a defective and misleading account of how a market economy actually does its work. In more practical terms, the culturally agreeable economic message accepted by the population at large, but especially in the political class, is one of a benevolent signaling system that guides the rational individual toward utility-maximizing transactions. After all, isn't exchange natural to the human system? The origin of this beneficent account of market capitalism is no surprise. As I note in Chapter 1, it was as recent as 1991 that Soviet communism collapsed of its own internal incoherence. The giddy triumphalism following that momentous event solidified in the public mind the idea that capitalism was the best of all possible systems. Economics as taught and practiced in the capitalist world provided the theoretical justification for why that was the case. Think of it as apologetics. Chapter 2 exposes the nature and extent of this deceit.

The purpose of Chapter 3 is to explain the evolutionary trajectory of the household from precapitalist provisioning, then into merchant capitalism, evolving into industrial capitalism at the end of the eighteenth century, next into financial capitalism, and finally, as the twenty-first century got underway, being transformed into managerial capitalism. We will see that each stage in this evolutionary pathway has rendered the household increasingly marginalized and precarious. Coincident with this difficult journey for the household, the increasingly atomized individual within the household has become more isolated and tenuously engaged with a meaningful livelihood.

The possessive individual is now seen to be the victim of her own liberation wrought by the Enlightenment.

The evident anger and alienation that mark much of the forgotten class in western Europe and the nonmetropolitan reaches of rural America are misplaced. The cultural embeddedness of the possessive individual, a creature of the acquired economic spirit of our time, blinds each of us to the underlying source of our perplexity. We have so much to be thankful for—just look at our material abundance. Why are we so haggard and jumpy?

Part II contains two chapters. In Chapter 4, I present a brief window into the evidence and associated accounts that suggest just how precarious life now is under the attentive financial wranglers of managerial capitalism. We are introduced to the ancient tale of foxes and hedgehogs. In today's wealthy countries—but especially in western Europe and the United States—daily life for many individuals is a precarious and peripatetic quest for reliable employment, a "livable wage," and financial security. The modern household now resembles, in many respects, the wily fox who must know many things and who must have a portfolio of survival strategies available for the wielding. Gone are the days when a household with one income earner could hope to achieve a plausible "middle-class" lifestyle. Many households contain multiple earners engaged in more than a single job. So-called full-time work is now a remote dream when considered against the daily scramble of juggling children, schooling, aging parents, unreliable (and often unaffordable) child care, flawed urban transportation, and the many other aspects of modern life.

Meanwhile, a class of individuals (in earlier versions of capitalism they were called the "captains of industry") now sits astride massive accumulations of liquid assets easily deployed to capture the immediate attention of sweatshop clothing manufacturers in Bangladesh, Cambodia, or Vietnam, electronic device assemblers in East Asia, or corporate flower farmers in East Africa. Global commerce is now orchestrated by a class of financial wranglers, hedge-fund conjurers, and private equity tormentors who—like the reliable hedgehog—need to know only one big thing. And the one thing they know is that they can render low-wage workers unemployed at the click of a button on their computer. They bear no responsibility for their actions because they are from Thomas Nagel's *nowhere*. They are divorced from place and the attachments thereof.

Chapter 5 represents a profound turn in our story in terms of both geography and economic circumstances. We come to the other side of the world in more ways than one. If daily life in the metropolitan core is characterized by a growing realization of stagnant livelihoods and financial anxiety, life in the periphery has always been precarious and problematic. Here we see just how difficult life has been for those countries that missed out on the Industrial Revolution. In fact, that enduring misery can be traced to the growth and spread of capitalism in the metropolitan core. In that sense, this chapter is the logical companion to Chapter 4.

Chapter 5 introduces us to a yet more profound distinction between the harried life under managerial capitalism and meager existence in the poor periphery. Where political life in the metropolitan core is stabilized by a reasonable though paralyzed democracy, the problematic periphery is littered with ineffective *notional states*. By a notional state, I mean political jurisdictions in which the *mask of citizenship* precludes coherent govern-ance. The mask of citizenship can be thought of as a grand deceit in which individuals reside *in* a particular political jurisdiction—a nation-state—but they are not *of* that jurisdiction. The central element in the mask of citizen-ship is the absence of the tax bargain.

The modern nation-state in the wealthy metropole is characterized by a historic and secure tax bargain. Citizens are part of a social compact in which they understand that the payment of a certain suite of taxes represents their commitment to the larger public good, but it also represents something much more profound. It acknowledges that in exchange for those tax receipts, the government of the day recognizes the reciprocal obligation to provide a suite of goods and services that could not be made available otherwise—national defense, roads and bridges, schooling, local police services, garbage collec-tion, and the provision of reasonably safe drinking water, to name just a few. The payment of taxes not only funds those necessary *collective consumption* goods and services, it provides the citizen a plausible claim on the attention of government agents when the quality of those services fails to live up to the expectations of those who are paying for their provision. The tax bargain is an essential "binding agent" of the citizenship exchange that characterizes the modern nation-state.

By way of contrast, many countries in the poor periphery do not levy taxes on their citizens. They rely, instead, on excise taxes levied on exports to the rich metropole. Government income is thus derived from timber, minerals, oil, and perhaps a few agricultural products that bring revenues directly into the central treasury. Notice that these excise tax receipts are divorced from any accountability to the citizens. In fact, they often work to the detriment of those citizens when local forest and mineral re-sources are made available to international corporations for export to global centers of manufacturing. Furthering the problem, with no revenue available to local units of government—states, counties, provinces, towns, cities, villages—these political entities must beg the central government for funds to pay for schools, roads, communications facilities, libraries, water supplies, etc. And in this necessity to solicit the central government for funds, we find yet another mechanism for political graft and dubious transactions.

This political reality of revenue mobilization in the poor periphery epitomizes the perverse mask of citizenship we find in much of the developing world. Central governments pretend to care about all of their citizens scattered across the impecunious countryside, but in fact, receiving nothing from them in the way of tax payments, they have scant incentive to pay attention to their needs and aspirations. To the extent that economic progress has long required a collaborative and focused effort by most citizens across the geographic reach of a nation-state, the absence of a citizenship exchange in the poor periphery sentences those countries and their populations to persistent want and despair.

We cannot leave the material of Chapter 5 without noting that the situation just described, a world of politically dysfunctional notional states, is the plausible result of colonialism throughout Africa, South and Southeast Asia, and the Middle East—and to a lesser extent in South and Central America. This long period of external control—one that was not eliminated in many places until after World War II—was motivated by the logic of *surplus extraction*. Colonial powers were motivated to establish administrative structures and processes in their colonial possessions in order to facilitate the extraction of desired raw materials to the metropolitan core. Included in these desired imports were oil, tropical timber, precious minerals (diamonds, gold, silver), tasty spices and condiments (salt, pepper, chilies), comforting beverages (tea, coffee), and—most despicably—slaves.

The point of colonialism was not to improve tax collections or to create enhanced governance. Christian missionaries were there to convert souls, and colonial administrators were there to collect materials and convert them into new income streams in the metropole. Those colonial possessions were mere supply depots for industrial capitalism, and their defective governance today is the inevitable result of that unpleasant history. Possessive individualism shaped their past, and it continues to undermine their future.

Part III turns the emphasis away from an explanation for the current state of affairs and shifts our attention to a discussion of how we might work our way out of the current predicament. Chapter 6 brings us to a practical account—a theory—of how human systems are continually undergoing adaptation and accommodation to new stresses and strains. It is offered as a reminder that all human systems are constantly in the process of becoming. The accounts in Chapters 1 through 5 reflect this continual transformation from precapitalist provisioning to merchant capitalism, then to industrial capitalism, on into financial capitalism, and now into the early stages of managerial capitalism. The life span of an individual is too short to perceive these profound transitions in economic and political structures. Our attention span is too attenuated to fix on the details of what is going on around us. The news of the day is focused on the latest tax reform, on the gradual emergence of commercial giants such as Apple or Amazon, on slow reforms in the health care system. But over a decade or more, important transformations have been taking place.

In Chapter 6, I explore these changes as the inevitable result of new, unwelcome problems in the *status quo ante*. These unwanted settings and circumstances motivate problem solving. Change is difficult. I introduce the concept of the habituated mind, which is resistant to new ideas and does not easily accommodate change. John Dewey (1859–1952) insisted that we do not adopt or take on new habits. Rather, we *are* our habits. But some problems demand our attention, and change cannot always be avoided. These persistent problems are the animating spring of human action. I introduce the idea of human systems as purposeful evolutionary constructs, and I develop the argument that this gradual evolution in social structures and processes can be thought of in three phases: (1) animation; (2) adjustment; and (3) adaptation. This process of change and adaptation is one of the most difficult undertakings for the human psyche. We come to love and revere what has become familiar to us. We like our "ruts," or most of them anyway. The human mind adapts itself to familiar routines, and once those routines become normal, they also become right, correct, and worth defending.

But of course change is both inevitable and necessary. I draw on Dewey's Arc as an essential component of what I call *volitional pragmatism* and the development of a theory of change in human systems.

Chapter 7 concerns the decisive institutional change that is necessary to rescue managerial capitalism from its flawed state. The prevailing demarcationist notion that regards the economy as a separate autonomous realm standing distinct from politics and civic activity by governments must be abandoned. Believing in the sanctity of the private firm destroys any opportunity to rescue contemporary life from the ravages of possessive individualism. I argue in this chapter that the private firm is, necessarily, a *public trust*. This recognition would clear the way to rectify the manifold damages being wrought by managerial capitalism.

In Chapter 8, I elaborate the reasons why possessive individualism must be overcome. Here I document the extent of the persistent economic inequality between the metropole and the problematic periphery. I show once again how possessive individualism undermines plausible livelihoods across the globe. And I conclude by introducing an idea that has gone missing under the conceits of the Enlightenment, the emergence of neoclassical economics, and the full flowering of possessive individualism. That idea, so jarring to the modern citizen of the global economy, is *obligation*. Modernity has brought us a profusion of claimed rights, and in that abundance of self-interested claims to special standing, the idea of obligations has fallen away. Can it be any mystery why the angry occupants of rural America, or eastern Germany, or the north of England are so worked up over immigrants? The selfish citizen is the social and economic manifestation of what Richard Dawkins likes to call the "selfish gene." The profound difference is that genes are inanimate biological constructs. Humans are sentient creative beings. All they lack is good reasons.

Chapter 9 brings us to an idea by which personhood might be rescued from the comprehensive ravages of possessive individualism. Here I draw on an idea from Josiah Royce (1855–1916) who was writing during the height of the crushing and dehumanizing Industrial Revolution and its heartless barons. Royce wished to advance the profound idea of *loyalty*. Loyalty seems more congenial to most of us than obligation. Royce liked to talk of loyalty to loyalty and of *burdened loyalty*. The point was to ask us to consider "burdened loyalty to community." I show that in this simple and quaint notion of loyalty we might just find the key to rescue the future from the perverse ravages of possessive individualism.

~~~~~~~~~~~~~~~~~~~~~~

Reflection

This book is a project of renewal. It is a detailed account of the political and economic implications of what seems to be a spent force. My purpose is an appeal to start over. The spent force of interest here is capitalism, which now is so involuted, disfigured, and encrusted that it has ceased to be a source of hope. The burst of material plentitude that began in the mid-nineteenth century in Europe seemed to offer a better life all around. Instead, it has bred a culture of acquisitiveness and self-centered hedonism. It also has become an excuse for realization of the worst of human instincts—social differentiation and exclusion.

We here confront the essential flaw in a meritocracy. That flaw is the evolutionary tendency toward exclusionary webs of advantage that resist penetration. There is an endogenous process at work that tends to reinforce a narrowing trajectory toward the commanding heights. There is nothing in democratic systems that can assure modulation of that tendency.

This is also a diagnostic undertaking. I stress the need to search for reasons as distinct from symptoms. Pragmatism insists on a relentless quest for reasons. The most important phrase in the English language is quite straightforward: "Please tell me again why you think that would be a good idea." The speaker is eager for reasons.

Imagine just how disarming—how humbling—that can be to someone intent on imposing some new imperative on a homeless person, a corporate executive, a welfare recipient, a neighborhood association, a small shopkeeper, a school superintendent, a police chief, or a local mayor. All assertions about what it would be good to do must be held up to the pragmatist's insistence concerning the asking for and giving of reasons. Democracy is not about voting. *Democracy is about reason giving.* It is only in the cold hard stare of a calm query about one's reasons that humans work out what it seems we would like to have as we struggle with what it seems possible for us to have. Asking for and giving reasons is a diagnostic activity. The reason we reason is to generate reasons for why it would be reasonable to do this rather than that. And the judgment of what is reasonable is not an individual gift. Reasonableness is a collective benediction.

In today's fraught political and economic climate, it seems the world is full of people who are seldom right but never in doubt. Doubt is the first step in the quest for reasons. Good reasons defeat doubt.

D.W.B.

Madison, Wisconsin
June 2019

Acknowledgments

The genesis of this book dates from November 2009 when I had the honor to present the prestigious Helmholtz Lecture at Humboldt University-Berlin. I had just begun what would turn out to be a five-year research and teaching appointment at Humboldt. Each autumn I taught an intensive 10-week version of my standard graduate course—"Institutional Economics"—at the University of Wisconsin-Madison. The title of my Helmholtz Lecture that November evening was: "Hunger, Poverty and Financial Crisis: Are We Trapped in an Obsolete Economic Order?"

The year 2009 was momentous in several respects. It would mark the official end of the Great Recession (2007-2009)—an event of unimagined severity for millions of unsuspecting households. The constant discussion throughout that period had been the alleged role of contemporary economics—with its emphasis on individual acquisitiveness. Also implicated was the extreme mathematical approach to our work that somehow pushed "real live" individuals aside for the sake of formal elegance. Were "we" to blame for this disaster? Were our models avoiding important issues?

The year was also profound in a larger sense. My lecture was just ten days after the twentieth anniversary of the breach of the Berlin Wall on November 9, 1989. The city had recently been awash in celebrations and self-satisfaction that the hated Wall had finally been rendered impertinent. A mere 200 meters from the large lecture hall, just across Unter den Linden, loomed *Bebelplatz*—the shameful scene of the Nazi book burnings of that famous university's library collection on the night of May 10, 1933. In 2009, the good people of Berlin certainly had much to celebrate, and yet here—in the heart of what was once East Berlin—I was offering caution and concern. I still recall the vague sense that the audience saw me as much too pessimistic. After all, many students and faculty in attendance had recently been liberated from the severe version of East German Soviet fealty. Now they were free and learning to love a market economy. I felt like an uninvited guest at a picnic.

I had been developing the philosophical grounding of my concerns for several years. My 2006 book <u>Sufficient Reason: Volitional Pragmatism</u> <u>and</u> <u>The Meaning of Economic Institutions</u> (Princeton) had allowed me to work out a way to look at economic systems from a deep ideational perspective. That book had also opened up a number of opportunities to present my ideas on *volitional pragmatism* to a generally receptive German academic audience. This was a valuable reminder that American economists differ from German (and European) economists in profound ways. It seems that social views mirror—in some general way—academic views. As the reader will see, this should not surprise us.

Prior to my appointment at Humboldt University, I had benefitted from valuable feedback to my 2006 book at a number of German universities—Freiburg, Göttingen, Heidelberg, Marburg, Greifswald, Jena, Halle-Wittenberg, and the Max Planck Institute for Human Development in Berlin. I also encountered an encouraging audience at the University of Geneva. These valuable interactions stimulated my commitment to keep pressing ahead. In 2011, I was fortunate to receive the marvelous Reimar Lüst Prize from the Alexander von Humboldt Foundation. Proceeds from that Prize enabled me to extend my stay in Berlin for several more years—and to remain engaged with an academic community that seems more open-minded about economics than what one often encounters in the typical American research university intent on reproducing graduate students in a narrow and formalistic mode.

Several years after returning from Germany, a presidential election loomed on the horizon. As 2016 evolved it became clear that the Republican Party had been expropriated by a new sort of candidate—one who eagerly preached suspicion, anger, xenophobia, class division, and most importantly, celebrated his innocence and incuriosity concerning the complexities of modern life. Then, as this crescendo was building, the British people succumbed to a simplistic and equally spiteful urge—fueled by lies and illusions of long-lost British imperial grandeur—to quit the European Union.

Something deep and troubling was going on. It was around this time that millions of migrants began working their way north out of the Middle East and North Africa. Problems of poverty and civil strife became standard newspaper stories. The expected calm world of post-Soviet peace and prosperity was now coming apart. I knew it was time to get to work. The original version of the book was called <u>World Disorder</u>. But that focused on symptoms. The anonymous reviewers disliked the title. I then reflected on my 2009 Helmholtz lecture concerning the possibility of an "obsolete economic order." And that brought me to diagnosis—and thus to *possessive individualism*.

This long gestation period renders it impossible to acknowledge all of those individuals who have helped me craft, work out, and clarify my ever-evolving views of the world around us—and how we navigate that world. I must be content to express my special gratitude to three anonymous reviewers for finding enough here to urge Oxford University Press to engage this project. And that brings me to Economics Editor David Pervin and his colleague Macey Fairchild—both of whom have been supportive, fair, tough, encouraging, and wonderful. Unlike journal editors—who imagine themselves to be the world's ultimate guardians of ever-lasting truth who must stand firm against any thought of open-mindedness (I know, I was a journal editor for 44 years)—book editors are a special breed. They indulge our ideas, seek incisive yet fair reviewers, deal with the inevitable differences of opinion that arise, consult the stars, and then they make the difficult calls.

This book challenges deep and firmly held beliefs. I am grateful to David for his faith in the notion that despite all of the attention to social media and digital hoopla, the world still moves forward when individuals hold a precious collection of ideas in their hands and slowly turn the page—pausing, reflecting, going back, then going forward. May the human race never abandon Johannes Gutenberg's Gift.

PART I
THE PROBLEMATIC TRIUMPH
OF CAPITALISM

The Enlightenment created the individual,
thereby liberating us to engage reason.

The emergence of the individual authorized
the charming pursuit of self-interest.

Economic theory offered convenient
justification for our unleashed acquisitiveness.

~~~~~~~~~~~~~~~~

Possessive individualism imprisons.

1

The Crisis of Capitalism

Why are the richest and most advanced economies facing political turmoil? Why have so many poor countries in the agrarian periphery continued to languish under defective governance that yields livelihoods of despair and vulnerability? Possessive individualism—a joint phenomenon growing out of the Enlightenment and the emergence of contemporary economics as the civic religion of modern life—is at the core of the emerging world disorder. The evolutionary pathway of capitalism has undermined the idea of personhood and left the modern household dependent on a fickle world of managerial capitalism in which money managers exercise profound control over the life prospects of millions. Possessive individualism thrives in a world of ubiquitous assertions about individual rights. Meanwhile, notions of civic obligations are considered quaint and impertinent. This is the crisis of capitalism, and it offers clarity about the reasons for the current world disorder.

I. World Disorder

It was not supposed to be this way. With the end of the long Cold War in 1991—itself the result of a devastating world war that ended in 1945—life was expected to return to normal. No longer would we live in fear that the world's two superpowers would risk mutually assured destruction. Early optimism was certainly justified. Gradually, a number of former satellite states of the Soviet Union—Poland, the Czech Republic, Slovakia, Hungary, Bulgaria, Romania, and the newly independent nations that had been part of Yugoslavia—became members of the European Union. This expanded political community, whose defining purpose was to prevent future wars on the continent—now numbering 28 independent nations—comprised the most populous unified bloc of independent countries in the world. It seemed destined to become a political and economic rival to the United States. That was the new Europe in early January 2007. Less than one year later, the world suffered the greatest financial disruption since the Great Depression of the 1930s. And then, late in 2010 and continuing into 2011, a series of political revolts in the Middle East—named the "Arab Spring" in a spasm of unjustified optimism—accelerated the regional turmoil that had been brewing since the Iran–Iraq War of 1980–1988, Iraq's invasion of Kuwait in August 1990, and then the U.S. invasion of Iraq in March 2003.

By 2015, the future seemed settled—and it would not be as we had expected. There is persistent sectarian warfare and turmoil in the Middle East, of which Yemen and Syria loom as the most vexing. The havoc being wrought by the Islamic State of Iraq and Syria (ISIS) must also be noted. Waves of desperate migrants have streamed out of the Middle East and northern Africa headed for a Europe that is itself in a crisis largely of its own making. The influx of migrants simply compounds several endemic problems. We see a newly aggressive China spreading its military intentions in the South China Sea and an increasingly belligerent Russia under the authoritarian leadership of a former *Komitet Gosudarstvennoy Bezopasnosti* (KGB or Committee for State Security) agent who spent his formative years in the severe Soviet satellite state of East Germany. The decision by the United Kingdom to withdraw from the European Union and the 2016 election of an American president from the angry fringe suggest that the emerging situation is far from placid. Right-wing parties are on the ascendency in much of Europe. Is this the 1930s all over again?

The emerging scene begs for understanding. How is it possible that many of the successful democratic market economies—all with very high per capita incomes—are experiencing economic malaise and political revolt? Is there a relation between these surprising events in the metropole and similar events occurring in the periphery? What do these unexpected events tell us about the robustness of democratic market economies? At a deeper level, if democracy and market economies are mutually supportive and conduce to human well-being, why are most countries in South Asia and Africa so poor and generally dysfunctional? Most of them are clearly irrelevant to global capitalism. Why are so many countries in the more comfortable periphery plagued by economic dysfunction and political chaos? I have in mind here many countries in the Middle East and Latin America, most recently Brazil and Venezuela.

To ask such questions is to receive back a long list of rather standard vacuous "explanations"—the abundant political failures around the globe give rise to market failures that then produce poverty and dysfunction. This explanation will not do.

If democracy and a market economy are so salubrious for the human condition, then they should gradually produce political leaders and administrators who will fix problems and get their countries on a promising trajectory. In other words, it is not acceptable to praise democracy and ubiquitous markets as the way to future prosperity and political stability, and then to turn around and blame imperfect democracy and flawed markets for allowing the very incoherencies that are now on such vivid display around the world. Nor is it acceptable to praise democratic market economies as ideal *if only* their leaders were more honest and acted with better information. These political-economic systems of such constant acclaim cannot be so ideal if, year after year—often for a century or more—they continue to languish in debilitating dysfunction.

Political economic systems are revered precisely because they manage to solve their various problems by producing their own honest and competent leaders in both politics and commercial affairs. It simply will not do to defend democratic market economies as the best of all possible worlds, and then retreat behind the façade of ". . . if only they weren't so corrupt and dysfunctional." Worthwhile credible systems earn their accolades precisely because they are self-correcting. Like Neurath's Mariner, all nations are required to repair their ship (of state) while at sea. No safe harbor—with a dry dock—is available. Countries must repair themselves while "on the run" as it were. If they do not—if they cannot—then all of the extravagant claims for democratic market systems are empty boasting.

Too often, the many problems on display are blamed on political flaws, leading to what is now called "failed states." Books have begun to appear to tell us why nations fail (Acemoglu and Robinson, 2012; Fukuyama, 2014). These particular dueling blockbusters—running to 500–600 pages each—are sweeping in their coverage. But they also are circular; problems (symptoms) are confused with reasons. We are told that nations fail because of political weakness. Weak states cannot manage to carry out the necessary tasks of governance as well as strong states do, and thus weak states are hampered by political dysfunction. But what is cause and what is result? What are symptoms and what are reasons?

My purpose in this book is to break into this pernicious circularity of so-called failed states in a serious quest for reasons. We must know *why*, in modern times, the historic ideal of independent and reasonably functional nation-states so very often get it wrong. Of course, these mistakes are not confined to recent times. Both world wars and persistent civic conflicts around the globe offer evidence that turmoil and strife just might be the normal human condition. But there is also ample evidence that humans are capable of the hard work of securing domestic peace and tolerable prosperity, while also managing to avoid constant warfare with neighbors. The dividing line between these two circumstances seems to justify careful thought.

II. The Idea

I am concerned with the modern idea of the sanctity of individual choice. It is time to confront ideational modernity, meaning that we must explore the full extent of the Enlightenment's main idea—the *creation of the individual* as a sapient, discerning, and choosing agent, whether that agent is choosing sundry commodities, various services, alternative employment possibilities, or political leaders. Our task is to inquire into the full flowering of the created individual freed from superstition and command. The creation of individual agency is our challenge. It is time to comprehend what the Enlightenment has wrought.

A. The Created Individual

It has long been argued that freeing humans from the iron grip of fate and superstition would bring about an orderly world in which reason would deliver humanity to a calm and stable future—one based on rationality rather than fear and emotion. Empowering individual sapience, discernment, and reason would, it was thought, eliminate parasitic monarchs and religious warfare. The ensuing state of affairs would then bring about needed improvements in the human condition. Progress on this front is undeniable. The growth in living standards since the beginning of the eighteenth century in much of the world is an achievement of enormous magnitude. But this happy condition has not been uniformly experienced in all places. Indeed, this optimistic promise seems to have been undermined in a number of nations. It seems that the emergence and spread of what the philosopher C. B. Macpherson calls *possessive individualism* has stymied the full realization of the promise of the Enlightenment (Macpherson, 1962). Specifically, with individuals now liberated to pursue their own self-interest, it seems that they have developed an overarching affinity for doing precisely that, very often showing precious little regard for the interests of others. Should we be surprised?

Is it possible that persistent emphasis on—indeed, the celebration of—the rights of the individual has gradually undermined the emergence of reciprocal obligations that are necessary to a sense of what might be called a shared *community of interests* within, and among, individual nations? Is there a defect in the Enlightenment project that has led us to presume that the liberated individual would, by some *deus ex machina*, necessarily be concerned about the interests of others? Why, it is tempting to ask, would seventeenth- and eighteenth-century thinkers suppose that the liberation of individuals to do precisely as they wished would lead to a future in which individuals would fail to become charmed by the appealing idea of doing precisely as they wished? This quite unsurprising outcome has necessarily required elaborate governing machinery and processes in order to rein in the inevitable self-interested individual. But what are we to do if those mechanisms and procedures are not quite up to the task? Did Enlightenment thinkers underestimate the nature and scope of the self-interest they so optimistically enabled and nurtured?

As if recognizing the problem, the French Declaration of the Rights of Man and the Citizen of 1789—despite its narrow title—clearly recognized correlated duties and obligations that accompany these much-revered rights. On this view, being a full person—and thus a proper citizen—entails duties. This French manifesto, much influenced by Thomas Jefferson, differed from the earlier American Declaration of Independence, which placed exclusive emphasis on individual rights. And so "rights talk" has flourished in America. Mary Ann Glendon cites a 1958 U.S. Supreme Court decision that regards citizenship as "the right to have rights." By way of contrast, she calls attention to the granting of citizenship in Canada in which great emphasis is placed on "the importance of participation in the political life of a multicultural society" (1991, pp. 12–13). Even the United Nations Universal Declaration of Human Rights notes that "Everyone has duties to the community" (Glendon, 1991, p. 13).

Notice that declarations of individual rights are incoherent in the absence of some attention to correlated obligations. When someone claims to have a right to smoke in an airplane or a restaurant, what of the claimed right of others to clean air? A world in which every individual insists on the importance and sanctity of his or her alleged rights is not very different from that which concerned Thomas Hobbes (1588–1679) in the opening years of the seventeenth century—his "war of all against all." Glendon reminds us that the language of the United Nations' Declaration of Human Rights

> is a melding of the Anglo-American rights tradition with the more nuanced dialect of rights and responsibility associated with the Romano-Germanic legal traditions. These traditions in turn are informed by a somewhat different amalgam of Enlightenment political philosophy from that which inspired the American founders. It made a considerable difference, for example, that natural rights theories were elaborated for us principally by Hobbes and Locke, without the glosses added within the continental tradition by Rousseau and Kant. (Glendon, 1991, p. 13)

Instead of obligations, Hobbes conjured Leviathan to harness the inevitable conflict. But what if Leviathan fails? Or what if highly concentrated economic interests manage to enlist Leviathan to their narrow cause? Gradually, the paradox is coming into focus. If governments and democratic processes are unable to hold unbridled self-interest in check, does the presence of a market economy add to the difficulty of that challenge? The point here is to ponder the potential confounding influence of a market economy embedded in—indeed often central to—a democratic political system. Recall that market economies are celebrated precisely because they are said to give individuals exactly what they desire in the way of goods and services constrained only by their income. A market economy reinforces the idea that individuals can have exactly what they wish to have. This means that a market economy plays into the idea of democracy in its emphasis on choice and the freedom to choose. Notice that there are no obligations in a market economy. There are only tempting choices—individuals can have exactly what they want, with the only condition being that they must pay for it. But this is not an obligation or duty toward others; rather, it is merely a quite expected condition of living in a market culture. Of course, we must pay for what we wish to acquire. But the individual consumer *owes* nothing to others; he or she bears no market-related duties.

We see that autonomy as a consumer in the market is supportive of, and coincident with, autonomy in the political arena where elections are instances of our celebrated political freedom. A market economy is a further encouragement to pervasive rights talk because a market is considered instrumental to individuals having exactly what they want, rather than having to settle for what some authoritarian planner decides they will get. We have now brought together the individual autonomy of the Enlightenment with the individual autonomy of a market economy. What has this convergence given us?

B. The Idea of Progress

By the middle of the eighteenth century, profound economic changes had begun to emerge, first in Britain—but very soon throughout Europe—that would transform the pecuniary aspects of everyday life. The Industrial Revolution, with its emergence of large impersonal factories and the rise of sweatshops and deep coal mining, brought a new form of violence bearing down on the individual. Now, domestic tranquility was not threatened by physical harm from assaulting neighbors and strangers. Rather, it was the power of a nascent industrial system and the associated working conditions that became of great concern. Charles Dickens (1812–1870) and Karl Marx (1818–1883) became famous for their accounts of the horrors of this emerging economic system. Soon, aggregations of workers arose to replace the easily dispensable *individual* worker with an indispensable *group* of workers—a union of all workers—so that there would be a semblance of countervailing power between those who owned capital and those who owned only their labor.

Eventually, the industrialized workplace could be characterized as a microcosm of larger society in which workers were protected from abuse by other workers and owners of factories and firms, like nations, were obligated to respect the emerging rights of their employees. This protection had a physical dimension (working hours and conditions) and a pecuniary dimension (pay and associated benefits). What we call *horizontal violence* and *vertical violence* were gradually brought under control in the name of individual rights enshrined in the ideas of the Enlightenment.

Before the emergence of a strong central state, horizontal violence was the norm. Personal slights or physical violence among individuals or families were traditionally seen as requiring retribution administered by victims or their allies. The point was to save face by exacting revenge. The story line of many famous operas captures this common practice. One of the early obligations of the modern state, intent on securing domestic peace, was to gain a monopoly on this tradition of reciprocated retribution. A strong police force and a credible judicial system gradually combined to eliminate this perverse behavior. What had formerly been privatized violence became an essential aspect of the public sector's purpose. Individuals soon enjoyed a right to protection from the state, and victims of crimes began to expect justice at the hands of the state rather than through their own dangerous exertions against perpetrators. A second development, more important in terms of individual liberty, was the gradual establishment of protection against abuse at the hands of governments. It is here that we encounter the significance of declarations of the "rights of man."

The granting of rights to individuals against the predatory behavior of their government addressed the problem of vertical violence—that visited on individuals by increasingly powerful governments. The earlier horizontal Hobbesian war of "all against all" had been tamed by strong governments, and then John Locke (1632–1704) inspired the creation of protections against vertical violence. The sanctity—autonomy—of the individual was gradually secured. Individual lives were increasingly protected from physical violence by other citizens and from the coercive power of their government.

The new industrial system, increasingly constrained by the same social norms that began in the seventeenth century, gradually gave rise to personal incomes that enabled the consumption of all manner of novel commodities. Massive factories and distribution systems transformed entire sectors—clothing, printing, food production and distribution, housing, and automobiles. This new economic regime triggered the demographic transition in England. There were three phases in this transition: Phase I, characterized by high rates of births and deaths; Phase II, marked by falling death rates as diet and public health improved—yet still consisting of high birth rates as fertility behavior lagged behind technical change; and Phase III in which social change began to reduce fertility so that births and deaths were brought into a new balance at a much reduced level. This process began around 1750 in England and was completed around 1900.

Because the twentieth century was dominated by two world wars, the evolving industrial system was primarily devoted to the production of war materiel. But with the end of World War II in 1945, the massive system of well-organized production was now available to focus on consumer goods. A large fleet of military transports was soon repurposed to play a major role in the international transportation of oil from the Middle East and other parts of the world and to carry other goods in an increasingly globalized marketplace. Consumers, exhibiting a substantial pent-up demand for all manner of goods and services after six years of war, were only too happy to oblige. Factories turned to the production of gaudy automobiles with fins and threatening grills. Suburban homes quickly emerged across the landscape, and their modern kitchens and bathrooms implied a massive market for an impressive variety of new labor-saving gadgets.

The 1950s and 1960s were a consumer's paradise. Grocery stores became palaces of color and temptation as entire aisles were devoted to hundreds of different breakfast cereals, countless varieties of bread and canned goods, and dairy cases stuffed with a bewildering variety of cheeses, yogurt, sour cream, and soy milk. In keeping with Enlightenment ideals, the individual was certainly free to choose—and the emerging postwar market economy was devoted to offering as much choice as possible. In fact, many psychologists began to focus their research on the debilitating effects of discerning consumers facing too much choice. Were over 200 types of breakfast cereal really a sign of progress?

C. The Irritation of Doubt

This profusion of material objects mirrors a related development in the emergence of new ways to make money in a flourishing market economy. Exotic financial instruments and associated firms appeared. Private equity firms bought underperforming businesses and, after necessary restructuring and notable employee dismissals, sold them at impressive financial gains. Increasingly, the modern economy came to be defined as *financial capitalism* in which factories and firms making objects for consumption—the earlier phase of industrial capitalism—were replaced by firms specializing in the ownership of those firms that made objects. The accelerating pace of mergers and acquisitions is consistent with trends of consolidation and concentration throughout the economy.

Coincident with this blossoming of economic concentration fostered by financial capitalism, there emerged a long period—beginning in the 1980s—of economic stagnation for many families. In the two or three decades prior to 2008, median household incomes in America, corrected for inflation, had been generally stagnant. Everyone knew that the top of the income distribution was doing well but that the majority of families were treading water. For many households this was unpleasant but tolerable. American families are notoriously deficient in saving for retirement and old age. But they have a profound ace-in-the-hole—their home. The loss of a job was often offset by the large number of two-income households. According to the Pew Research Center, over 60 percent of households had two earners in 2012. Often, one of those workers was in the labor market to gain access to family health insurance. These individuals were most often employed in the public sector. If a husband lost his job, his wife might still have employment (and health insurance) at the local library, school, police department, hospital, or county courthouse. But the crisis struck the asset base (savings) of many households.

In many respects, the financial disaster of 2007–2009 was more of a *wealth* crisis than an *income* crisis. Over 7 million U.S. families lost their home through foreclosure—often precipitated by a somewhat ravenous mortgage market liberated from culturally defined "burdensome" regulations. By 2009, it is estimated that approximately 12 percent of homeowners were technically "under water"; that is, their mortgage debt was greater than the appraised value of their home. Just two years earlier, in 2007, the comparable figure had been 4.7 percent (Carter & Gottschalck, 2011). The difference over just two years is striking. Suddenly, treading water was profoundly troubling. As millions of families wondered, would the next wave wash over them? The loss of wealth and fear of the future were exacerbated by the enormous growth in the share of income being received—note that I did not say *earned*—by the very wealthiest individuals.

A central component of a market economy is that rewards to labor and management (often this means owners) are considered to be justified. In simple terms, people are paid what they are worth, and that worth is determined by the very same process that guides efficient production. A market economy gains its hold on our affections because it is presumed to solve several vexing problems at once. A market economy provides us with the goods and services we want, and it does so at the lowest possible cost (thus saving consumers money). It then distributes the presumably correct rewards (incomes) of that efficient production system in the correct (unbiased) manner. This is what motivational speakers and other conveners of feel-good seminars would call "win–win–win."

However, the fact that a quarterback in the National Football League is paid $22 million per year, while an elementary school teacher is paid $33,000 per year (and often must use her own funds to purchase necessary school supplies for her students), often causes reflection on the overall performance of the American market economy. Are employees *really* paid what they are worth? And here I do not mean worth to their employer, but *worth* in the larger sense of value to society. The point here is not to pick on superstar athletes, or entertainers, or even hedge fund gurus. The salient point is that much of the basis for a sense that there are "two Americas" arises because many people notice disparities such as this and wonder whether or not the market economy brings about incomes that can be called fair. Of course, the word *fair* invites reflection. And that reflection will always bring us back to one single question: is the market economy *working* well for me (and my family and those I care about)?

If this question is answered in the affirmative, that individual is happy with the market economy and its current outcomes. If the answer to this question is negative, then the market economy (and its outcomes) is somehow flawed. Now the judgment of good outcomes shifts from what economists might say and becomes a judgment rendered by the citizenry. And that judgment is rendered not just by the winners in the metropolitan growth centers of America but in all corners of the country where those less well served can be found. The 2016 election revealed a very large number of such individuals.

It seems that many rural voters have suddenly come face to face with the flaws in the American version of a market economy. They are sensitive to it because it has left them in the economic hinterland. We have here not just a political problem; rather, it is first a profound economic problem. The market economy works wondrously for those living in the hot spots of metropolitan America, especially if they have the mobility, the near-perfect information, and the confidence to follow the money. The American version of capitalism is tailor-made for them. But a market economy must be held to a standard of *fairness* that is sustainable and agreed to by all, not just the winners.

The philosopher John Rawls had a compelling thought experiment (Rawls, 1971). The relevant Rawlsian question is as follows: what sort of a market economy would you defend from behind a Veil of Ignorance that prevented you from seeing beyond the Veil, but that, once removed, would place you in a metropolitan hub of economic vitality, or in a rural town in the middle of a stunning prairie? Your economic prospects are profoundly different, but not because of any personal flaws on your part. The difference comes from the failure of current American capitalism—the only market economy available—to offer hope for too many people in too many places.

But what is this thing called a "market economy"? It is useful to think of a market economy the way we think of meatloaf. There is not a single meatloaf (or a single market economy)—there are hundreds of varieties. Swedes are aghast at the American version of a market economy, and many Americans cannot possibly imagine living with the Danish version. But what about the very successful German version? We have a tendency to love the meatloaf we grew up on. Once the honeymoon is over, serious discussion gets underway—your mother's meatloaf or my mother's meatloaf? Some couples take turns, with every other Sunday one of them getting the "proper" version. But here the similarity ends. Within individual countries, there can be only one version of meatloaf. And so when we talk of a (or the) market economy, it is necessary to keep in mind the problem of meatloaf—every country has its own version. Recently, it seems that the American "meatloaf" does not satisfy.

We can now begin to connect the pronounced individual autonomy brought on by the Enlightenment with the stark possessive autonomy enabled and encouraged by the market culture and the economic system it justifies. Macpherson's *possessive individualism* captures this profound conjunction.

III. Possessive Individualism

> Inequality has the natural and necessary effect, under the present circumstances, of materializing our upper class, vulgarizing our middle class, and brutalizing our lower class. (Matthew Arnold, 1879)

The dominant idea and practice of democratic market economies have inherent tendencies toward extreme individualism. It cannot be a surprise since that is the defining purpose—the intent—of these two mutually reinforcing ideas. The liberated discerning individual endowed with certain inalienable rights is regarded as the defining triumph of the Enlightenment. The full flowering of a globalized market economy following the 1991 collapse of the Soviet Union, which was generally coincident with the sweeping market reforms in China that began in the late 1980s, reinforced the sanctity of the individual not only as a political agent but as a sapient consumer intent on (and entitled to) acquiring exactly what is most desired at the moment. This newly enabled global consumer is endowed with rights and yet bears few, if any, obligations to others. Meritocratic triumphs in the economic sphere lead to agreeable incomes and wealth that then reinforce the presumed social and political worth of those so endowed. With such pecuniary advantages gained in the economic sphere, the cultural hegemony of financial success leads to a sense of political entitlement. The evolving system tends in the direction of furthering the current advantage of those who have mastered the system.

There are very few reliable checks on the tendency toward economic and political knighthood. Possessive individualism reigns.

Paradoxically, the culture of possessive individualism leaves the individual exposed to the self-regarding tendencies of everyone else. In a fully atomized world, the flowering of meritocratic processes then tends to threaten political coherence and a shared sense of purpose within a community. Meritocracies reward merit, but they also begin to generate institutional arrangements—public policies—that tend to reinforce such self-interested inclinations. Sooner rather than later, self-regarding behavior gives rise to particular basins of attraction—others with approximately similar interests. Much of the Marxian legacy is framed around just such polarized entities—workers and capitalists. However, history reminds us that it is a mistake to presume that workers are necessarily united in their interests. Too many workers are either willing or forced to toil under conditions that other workers find unacceptable. The recent contention over union representation among American automobile workers reminds us of the absence of deeply shared interests among those on the assembly line. Possessive individualism undermines collective action.

But we may also notice that the spread and depth of possessive individualism in market capitalism do not prevent some small groups of individuals from having very pronounced and stringent singular interests. These individuals just might be owners of capital. It goes without saying that capitalists are united in their opposition to labor unions, to virtually all taxes, and to so-called intrusive government regulations. There are exceptions to be sure. But a certain unity of purpose serves to unite those individuals who are, to use a current popular term-of-art, "job creators." That shared idea of political-economic solidarity among a relatively small group of individuals in a democratic market economy provides a new window into the idea of societies organized along meritocratic lines. Market capitalism has a particular idea of the indicators of merit—and mature market economies are not in doubt about those indicators. Nor is there much timidity in organizing political affairs in accord with those culturally defined norms. Wealth is revered, while poverty is a correctible condition if only the poor would apply themselves with the necessary discipline. Unions impede efficiency in the factory as well as in schools. Regulations stifle innovation and profits.

The connective tissue running through this account is straightforward. Specifically, possessive individualism will be exposed as a surprising threat to the economic security of the household. In market capitalism, only two organizational entities warrant scrutiny—households and firms. Possessive individualism advantages firms and stands as the defining threat to the well-being of most working households. Like the famous account of the fox and the hedgehog, the household (and its members) are foxes: their survival requires them to know many things.[1] Firms in market capitalism are hedgehogs: they thrive by knowing one very big thing. It is no contest.

A. What We Owe to Each Other

The abiding challenge of our time concerns finding an answer to the timeless question of what, exactly, we owe to each other (Scanlon, 1998). Possessive individualism, an acquired habit of mind, offers a clear and definitive answer: not much. As Matthew Arnold (1822–1888) reminds us, the idea of possessive individualism is not a recent phenomenon. Indeed, in 1826, Parson Thomas Malthus (1766–1834) was moved to suggest that

> I cannot help believing that if the poor in this country were convinced that they had no claim of *right* to support . . . the bond which unites the rich with the poor would be drawn much closer than at present, and the lower classes of society . . . would have less . . . reason for irritation and discontent. (Thomas Robert Malthus, 1826. Essay Book IV, Chapter VII, p. 528. From Smith, 2013, p. 66)

It seems that the good Parson Malthus was quite sure that if the poor would but relinquish their right to relief under the Poor Laws—thereby absolving the government and British taxpayers of an obligation to provide such relief—they (the poor) would be much happier. While Britain's upper classes would surely have been eager to praise the poor for their refusal to accept necessary food and housing, it seems unlikely that this noble forbearance would have led to measurable interclass bonding. The rich have rarely shown much affinity for the poor, and the poor have returned that disregard with an equal measure of disdain. Perhaps this explains why the quite specific legal mandates of the Elizabethan Poor Laws were found necessary in the face of the rather unreliable voluntary charity of the rich. It is an old problem, and it therefore invites puzzlement over why it persists today. Aren't we moderns beyond such historic loathing of the poor among us?

The views of Malthus may seem curious, especially because the legacy of his writings, especially among environmentalists, is that he was driven by a concern for overpopulation. After all, his name is central to hundreds of studies seeking to determine whether or not particular societies were (or are) facing so-called Malthusian pressure. It may surprise many current admirers of the famous Parson to learn that he did not care one way or the other about population growth. What Malthus did care very deeply about was the prodigious breeding habits of the poor—and only the poor. Here he was particularly clear in his thoughts. To Malthus, the poor were undeserving predators on the private finances of the wealthy. When the Poor Laws finally legislated the expenditure of government tax proceeds to support the poor, the extent of individual charity and compassion among the better-off British was revealed to be vanishingly small. How quaint it is, therefore, to see Malthus talk of the "bond which unites the rich with the poor." What sort of bond might this have been in the early phases of the Industrial Revolution? Few historians can locate such unity of purpose during Malthus's lifetime. Nor was it strong either before or after Malthus.

The earlier quote from Matthew Arnold, reflecting on the full flowering of Britain's Industrial Revolution, captured prevailing public sentiment. A short time later, the English historian R. H. Tawney (1920) wrote that Britain had become a "grotesque acquisitive society." These strands of acquisitiveness and vulgar materialism were woven together by the political philosopher C. B. Macpherson (1911–1987), who coined the phrase *possessive individualism* (Macpherson, 1962). Macpherson's writings suggest that possessive individualism comprised the dominant unifying assumption—the primary organizing idea—of British society as far back as the seventeenth century. However, it seems that the seeds of that idea were planted much earlier. Alan Macfarlane argues that individualism and the culture of capitalism date back to at least the fifteenth century—shortly after the ravages of the Great Plague of 1348 (Macfarlane, 1978, 1987).

We therefore must inquire into what, exactly, Arnold had in mind when he wrote of the new wealth—and growing inequality—materializing the upper classes? For assistance in that regard, we can turn with good effect to the writings of Thorstein Veblen (1857–1929), author of the well-known *The Theory of the Leisure Class*.[2] Veblen observed that the rich were usually motivated by the pursuit of "conspicuous consumption." Consumption was considered conspicuous when its main purpose was to impress others, but also to demonstrate the gratuitousness of it all—high-heeled shoes minimally capable of being walked in, ostentatious homes and automobiles, and other baubles that were often seen as being in bad taste but just *avant garde* enough to be endearing to others. Members of the upper class were "materialized" by their preoccupation with showy consumption, most of which had no purpose other than to demonstrate just how rich they were.

When Arnold talked of "vulgarizing the middle class," he captured the idea that mindless emulation of the consumption habits of the rich (necessarily by more affordable knock-offs) constituted the essence of vulgarity. The middle class was drawn to its crass mimicry of the rich by the hope that doing so would signal to others that they too were rich. It rarely worked. In addition to conspicuous consumption, Veblen gave us the famous "bandwagon effect" to capture this notion of consumptive mimicry. Since the social function of the rich has always been to serve as trendsetters, those individuals with less income and wealth will always seek to buy what the rich tend to be consuming, even though such consumption requires spending above their means. As above, the rich are materializing the middle class. The "snob effect" is another Veblen phrase to explain the pronounced aversion by the rich to consumption patterns that might be popular among the poor. In other words, the rich will gladly pay more for certain goods and services to make sure that they cannot be copied by the less well-off.

Finally, Arnold insisted that the lower classes were brutalized by the social pressure of their economic betters to consume because it was these workers—servants, drivers, gardeners, nannies, all-around laborers—who, by virtue of their minimal wages and long hours, helped to keep the upper class in their comfort. The lower class was further brutalized by the middle class—who stood barely above the poor—in its evident desire to keep the poor a safe social and economic distance below them. While the rich were not in doubt as to their social station, the middle class needed to exert constant effort to keep the laboring poor in their place. The precarious middle class made sure that the poor were not in doubt about this essential aspect of capitalism.

B. Fragmentation and Alienation

Macpherson suggests that in the early days of the possessive market society, beginning in Britain around 1700, individualist impulses were somewhat kept in check by the realization that all individuals were subject to the same forces of a competitive market. The ubiquity of these pressures suggested that such circumstances were inevitable and perhaps they were "natural." Even exceptions to this sense of consumptive solidarity, exemplified by the aristocratic class, were excused—rationalized—under the premise that it was part of God's plan. The perception that fate ruled the world meant that the poor who had nothing understood that situation to be part of some larger scheme of things. Low prices for things being sold, high prices for things being purchased, and hungry times from drought, crop failure, disease, marauding soldiers, and cold wet winters wreaked havoc on one and all in rather equal measure. That was life, and it was hard all around. And it had been that way since time out of mind.

Not only were all individuals subjected to the same ubiquitous discomfort, there was a certain cohesion of self-interest in which the inherent centrifugal forces of a competitive and hurly-burly market society could be meliorated and constrained. As possessive individualism slowly gained momentum, political voice had previously been restricted to what Macpherson calls the *possessing class*. This small group of families held most of the material wealth, and it retained exclusive control over the selection of a succession of rather unpleasant sovereign authorities. These ruling elites perceived their material and political entitlements as reciprocated in their political obligations. We may notice that at this time there was a relation between perceived rights and expected obligations, which is not to say that the scale was always in agreeable balance. But the wealthy clearly understood that they were seriously outnumbered by the common man on whose arduous labor they led relatively agreeable lives.

As the nineteenth century progressed, and as the Industrial Revolution produced both profound wealth and stark despair, this historic coincidence of interests began to dissipate under the assault of an advancing modern state in which the franchise began to spread downward. As Arnold observed, the emergence of a distinct class consciousness—central to the writings of Karl Marx—was profoundly corrosive of both the political and material cohesion of British society. Marx exposed the emerging deceit of a unified and cohesive population. At the same time, the gathering inevitability of competitive market relations—and an emerging bitter awareness of unequal outcomes from that competition—added weight to the gradual disintegration that was now coming into view. It was not long until the old social order began to corrode from within. And then, when a newly enfranchised working class became aware of possible alternatives, the former tight cohesion of British society was destroyed forever. Democracy had gradually delivered what democracy is—a voice for all. With the gradual spread of political voice, the ancient cohesion was irreparably sundered. Soon, historic market relations were no longer accepted as natural or morally compelling. Not surprisingly, the increasingly unacceptable economic divide further undermined former notions of a unified political and economic community.

This dissolution of social cohesion in Britain coincided with the early years of the emerging public order in the United States. While political elites drew on the confident certitudes of Locke and various Enlightenment writers, daily life was forged not by those high-sounding ideals but by the rough and tumble of a new economy and new political machinery that had to be constructed, de novo, in a land defined by Frederick Jackson Turner's frontier. The newly emerging and unfettered market economy with its crude materialism, in concert with emerging political processes that often recapitulated the excesses of industrial Britain, are as much a part of U.S. history as are the ideals of Locke and Condorcet and Rousseau. What is unmistakable is just how destabilizing, how threatening, democracy can be to narrow economic and political privilege. As we saw, that was certainly the case in Britain.

Yet, there is nothing internal to democracy that precludes a reemergence of distinct social hierarchies. Active political interests, which are easier to mobilize in the urban centers of wealth and influence, can gradually work to dampen egalitarian (so-called democratic) concerns. If such tendencies are allowed to persist unchecked, there can emerge an ossified setting of extreme privilege and correlated alienation. This volatile tendency depends on how democratic societies address the tension between an emphasis on individualism and the rights which fuel that notion, and the broader ideas of civic obligation. A mature democracy cannot be understood merely in terms of the affirmation of the *rights* of individuals for the simple reason that at the core of a fully developed democracy must be found the concept of certain *duties*—obligations—that inhere to all individuals.

A society bears many similarities to a family, where all members have secure expectations, but also clear commitments. Infants must be brought into an understanding of this necessary balance between presumed rights and expected obligations. Two-year-olds understand demands, while adults understand obligations. Grown-up democracy entails a constant weighing of these two ideas. As Mary Ann Glendon argues, American society is still struggling with the ubiquitous "rights talk" of preadolescence. Not only did John Locke inform the general political philosophy of our founders, his ideas of property rights played a role in the emergence of a unique American phenomenon—a culture of rights talk (Glendon, 1991). We must understand this balancing of rights and obligations as central to the notion of personhood.

IV. Lost Personhood

As the evolution of a market economy progressed from merchant capitalism toward a possessive market society under industrial capitalism, the idea of personhood attained great importance. In a society—a culture—where belonging is measured by one's participation in the activity of gaining a liveli-hood, the absence of that ability must be understood as subtracting from one's personhood. There is little doubt that in a contemporary market society, the burden of providing a livelihood is part of the cultural expectations largely borne by men. When racial discrimination precludes participation in gainful employment, it can be no surprise that black males suffer an extraordinary burden. Forced and unwilling absence from meaningful work is destructive of the ability to form enduring family relationships. The cycle of poverty that results is a cancer that pervades the American market economy. The abrupt and quite widespread disemployment of *black* males that accompanied the decline of manufacturing jobs in the U.S. Rust Belt in the 1960s and 1970s was an ominous precursor of the job losses for *white* males that was an im-portant part of the Great Recession of 2007–2009. Consider the anger that this outcome seems to have spawned.

The prevailing idea is that the central purpose of modern society is to offer the widest possible scope for individuals to achieve their maximum satisfac-tion through their consumptive choices. Standing against this rather simple utilitarian vision, an alternative idea insists that individuals are defined by their ability to use and develop their unique human capacities. This view derives from the idea that the essence of humans is

> not as a consumer of utilities but as a doer, a creator, an enjoyer of human attributes. These attributes may be variously listed and assessed; they may be taken to include the capacity for rational understanding, for moral judge-ment and action, for aesthetic creation or contemplation, for the emotional activities of friendship and love, and, sometimes, for religious experience. Whatever the uniquely human attributes are taken to be, . . . their exertion and development are seen as ends in themselves, a satisfaction in themselves, not simply a means to consumer satisfactions. It is better to travel than to

arrive. Man is not a bundle of appetites seeking satisfaction but a bundle of conscious energies seeking to be exerted. (Macpherson, 1973, pp. 4–5)

To clarify the concept of personhood, Macpherson develops a sequence of propositions that inform the extent to which a possessive market society coheres. In this sense, coherence means that such a society offers each individual the full complement of protections that comprise what we might call full personhood. However, these conditions are not easily realized. Possessive individualism undermines that necessary coherence and gives rise to what might be called "the isolation paradox" (Box 1.1).

Text Box 1.1 The New Isolation Paradox

In the 1960s, Amartya Sen and Stephen Marglin were concerned that individuals, acting in "isolation," would leave too little to their heirs. This was called the isolation paradox (Lecomber, 1977). Possessive individualism has now bequeathed to us a new version of the isolation paradox.

A relentless commitment to the self has made it difficult for governments to raise the necessary tax revenues for collective consumption goods and services—education, health care, mass transportation, job retraining programs, unemployment protection, homeless assistance, community centers, public spaces, parks, etc. Most politicians, also afflicted with possessive individualism, gained public office by eagerly promising to keep taxes low so that individualized consumptive gratification might not be impaired. Nothing must stand in the way of autonomous acquisitiveness.

The Great Recession of 2007–2009 seems to have shocked the isolated individual into a belated realization that the "the system" did not work very well. Ironically, having rewarded politicians for their fealty to individualism, they now realize that governments lack the funds, interest, and capacity to be of any help. Late in 2018, France was paralyzed over the government's plan to raise gasoline taxes by about $0.11 per gallon (more on diesel) to help wean the country from its dependence on nuclear power. Widespread destruction soon materialized. The proud French citizen—wrong about the idea of Liberté, fixated on Égalité, and ignorant of the meaning of Fraternité—came face to face with the isolation paradox. We cannot be surprised.

Source: Lecomber, Richard. 1977. "The Isolation Paradox," *Quarterly Journal of Economics,* 91(3):495–504.

The fundamental political dilemma of a possessive market society is the inevitable impairment of full personhood for those who must sell their labor power to owners of capital. A possessive market society transforms labor power from being an endowment into being a marketable commodity (or asset). This situation forces the democratic sovereign to make a profound choice: does the sovereign align with owners of capital or with those who have only their own labor power to buffet them against deprivation and dispossession? Since the owners of labor power certainly outnumber those who own productive capital, wise sovereigns must be careful. A sovereign's recognition of an obligation to full personhood needs to be grounded on moral considerations. Prudential logic should be sufficient to convince an alert sovereign that ignoring the expectations of those who must labor in order that they might eat can be dangerous and destabilizing. If a stubborn sovereign requires any instruction in this regard, the 2016 political problems in the United Kingdom (Brexit), the rising tide of right-wing populist movements elsewhere in Europe, and the rise of a uniquely angry and incurious U.S. president in 2017 might be noticed.

The central problem in a possessive market society is that owners of capital—job creators—receive a variety of protections that are not available to those who own only their labor power. A grant of legitimacy for unlimited accumulation in a possessive market society bestows on owners of capital a wealth trajectory that is not available to those who own only their labor power. There is no moral sanction for this difference. Nor is there any economic reason for such differential accumulation.

V. Capitalism on Trial

Possessive individualism is the reigning idea of our time. It is the accepted spirit of our age and the cultural legacy of capitalism. We are now well into the fourth phase of capitalism—one symbolized by a new adjective, "managerial." Managerial capitalism is the inevitable successor to financial capitalism because it allows a severe concentration by the controllers of capital on the only thing that really matters, the one big idea. Surprisingly, that idea is not the relentless pursuit of profit. It cannot be because profit is an unknown and fickle accounting effect of manifold causes. The big idea—what the hedgehog knows—is to stay focused on *reducing costs*. That is what comptrollers do. This imperative reveals itself in various forms, all of which redound to the benefit of those with the highly specialized skills of micromanagement and political artifice.

The spirit of managerial capitalism has been given intellectual legitimacy by the evolution of microeconomic theory into a device for the pursuit of efficient markets. The quest for efficient markets is informed by the further conjuring of transaction costs: the costs of gaining information about potential arbitrage opportunities; the costs of writing contracts to exploit those precious opportunities; and the costs of enforcing those contracts once they have been struck. Each of these cost-reducing imperatives privileges those trained and acculturated into the arcane world of *the deal*. These well-honed habits of mind go far in explaining the great divergence of livelihoods in the metropolitan core of western Europe and the so-called New World, as opposed to the periphery. Or as Jeffrey Williamson phrased it: "when the third world fell behind" (Williamson, 2011).

Which brings us to a spatial (geographic) version of possessive individualism. The world is now profoundly divided into winners and losers. We see regular news accounts of the losers—the struggling citizens of South Sudan, Syria, Iraq, Venezuela, Nigeria, Somalia, Libya, Yemen, Morocco, Uganda, the Central African Republic, Afghanistan, and countless other problematic settings and circumstances. Most of these places have not been ignored by the experts who advise on how to bring about economic development. But these experts' advice has been confidently predicated on the possessive individualism of their metropolitan upbringing and their training in economics, replete with notions of efficient markets and the imperative of reducing transaction costs. The resulting idea of pervasive free markets has been visited upon (often imposed upon) weak societies and weaker governments throughout the world. In the 1980s, this cadre of development experts imposed structural adjustment programs on struggling economies. So-called market-friendly reforms were the order of the day. Then the Ten Commandments of the Washington Consensus solidified those structures, and conditionality became the term-of-art to impose even more market-based conditions. The imposed deal was: "If you want our help, get your markets working the way we say they ought to work. When you have them fixed, give us a ring."

Unfortunately, this prescriptive catechism of market capitalism was imposed on economies and societies that resemble the merchant capitalism of Britain in the early 1700s. The idea was to force many poor countries to leap over 200 years of gradual economic innovation, vaulting from merchant capitalism directly to financial capitalism. Political backlash was profound. Indeed, the emergence of the *nonaligned nations movement* in the 1970s was precisely designed to resist the neo-colonialism of the time that forced countries to stand firm against communism and aggressively embrace Western capitalism. If such countries wished to be our friends, they were required to adopt our economic ideology.

And so the crisis of capitalism is not confined to the rural counties of the United States. Nor does it reside only in the forgotten industrial towns of northern England, where Brexit voters are thick on the ground. It is not confined to northeast France or to the devastated coal regions of Belgium or West Virginia. The crisis of capitalism is now a universal phenomenon. The beleaguered household throughout the world is now facing a problematic existence.

Notes

1. Some writers trace the tale of foxes and hedgehogs to Archilochus. There is evidence, however, that the story started with Homer (Bowra, 1940).
2. John Kenneth Galbraith notes that Veblen's famous work is one of only two books by American economists working in the nineteenth century that are still read. The other is Henry George's *Progress and Poverty* (Galbraith, 2001).

References

Acemoglu, Daron, and James Robinson. 2012. *Why Nations Fail: The Origins of Power, Prosperity, and Poverty*, New York: Random House.

Arnold, Matthew. 1879. "Equality," in *Mixed Essays*, London: Smith, Elder.

Bowra, C. M. 1940. "The Fox and the Hedgehog," *The Classical Quarterly*, 34(1/2): 26–29.

Carter, G. R., III, and A. O. Gottschalck. 2011. *Drowning in Debt: Housing and Households with Underwater Mortgages*, Washington, DC: U.S. Census Bureau, Working paper, June. Available online: https://www.census.gov/programs-surveys/ahs/research/working-papers/Drowning_in_Debt.html

Fukuyama, Francis. 2014. *Political Order and Political Decay*, New York: Farrar, Straus, and Giroux.

Galbraith, John Kenneth. 2001. *The Essential Galbraith*, New York: Houghton Mifflin.

George, Henry. 1955 (1905). *Progress and Poverty*, New York: Doubleday, Page & Co.

Glendon, Mary Ann. 1991. *Rights Talk*, Cambridge, MA: Harvard University Press.

Lecomber, Richard. 1977. "The Isolation Paradox," *Quarterly Journal of Economics*, 91(3): 495–504.

Macfarlane, Alan. 1978. *The Origins of English Individualism*, Oxford: Blackwell.

Macfarlane, Alan. 1987. *The Culture of Capitalism*, Oxford: Blackwell.

Macpherson, C. B. 1962. *The Political Theory of Possessive Individualism*, Oxford: Clarendon Press.

Macpherson, C. B. 1973. *Democratic Theory: Essays in Retrieval*, Oxford: Oxford University Press.

Rawls, John. 1971. *A Theory of Justice*, Cambridge, MA: Harvard University Press.

Scanlon, T. M. 1998. *What We Owe to Each Other*, Cambridge, MA: Belknap Press.

Smith, Kenneth. 2013. *The Malthusian Controversy*, London: Routledge.

Tawney, R. H. 1933. *The Acquisitive Society*, New York: Harcourt, Brace, and World.

Veblen, Thorstein. 2007. *The Theory of the Leisure Class*, Oxford: Oxford University Press.

Williamson, Jeffrey G. 2011. *Trade and Poverty: When the Third World Fell Behind*, Cambridge, MA: MIT Press.

2

Economics

The Dubious Enabler

Possessive individualism has acquired a profound grip on contemporary political thought and action—on daily life—because it relies on a number of economic notions that now constitute our civic religion. Central concepts of that creed—efficiency, rational choice, market exchange as an arena of liberty and autonomy, consumer sovereignty, price as a measure of value, assertions of aggregate well-being—are accepted as irrefutable truths that insulate them from serious challenge. These core attributes of contemporary economics are misleading and generally false. Recent efforts to attribute civic virtues to markets are incoherent.

I. Apologetics

The most famous American economist of the twentieth century, Nobel Prizewinner Paul A. Samuelson, is said to have remarked that, given the choice of writing a nation's laws or authoring the most popular undergraduate economics textbook ever published, he would, of course, choose the latter. Not only did his famous book—with the grand title *Economics*—make Samuelson a millionaire several times over, it offered him an enduring platform to create a durable set of beliefs among millions of young (and not so young) people throughout the world. Samuelson's book went through 19 editions in 40 languages and has reportedly sold over four million copies. Economists everywhere glory in the wide public acclaim. The Swedish National Bank's Prize in Economic Sciences in Memory of Alfred Nobel (the economics "Nobel") was established in 1969, and in 1970 Samuelson became the first American winner—after the Norwegian Ragnar Frisch and the Dutch Jan Tinbergen. Economics now ranks right up there with physics, chemistry, and medicine/

physiology as a serious science. Samuelson and Milton Friedman carried on a series of dueling editorial columns in *Newsweek* magazine during the 1970s. The reading public was both entertained and confused. Economics, it turns out, is just political ideology in disguise.

Economists generally identify what we do as neoclassical economics. That is false advertising. We are Samuelsonians. Paul Samuelson, married to a mathematically adept economist who helped him along, eagerly made mathematics the language of economics, and today no serious economist could possible start to think about a problem without the acquired instinct to "write down a model." That model, inspired by the constrained optimization algorithms of physics, informs how the world is seen by economists, and it informs how individuals in that world ought to behave. They ought to behave as rational utility maximizers, and now we will show them exactly what they must do in order to fulfil that obligation. We want them to "know the model."

The exquisite irony here must not go unnoticed. Economists insist that we are objective—value-neutral—scientists who would never tell individuals or governments what they *ought to do*. These standard boasts about avoiding normative prescriptions—*ought* statements—are dishonest (MacIntyre, 1959). While economists refuse to suggest what ought to be done, we are quite confident in telling individuals how they *ought to* decide what *ought to* be done. We then hedge our normative advocacy with an artful dodge. It will be claimed that our advice of how they ought to behave is "contingently normative." That is, on the one hand, individuals or firms or governments should only follow our advice if they wish to do what is *efficient*. If, on the other hand, they wish to do what is *inefficient*, then they are free to ignore our advice.

But who could possibly aspire to be inefficient? This excuse is thought to save us from being accused of advocating some value-laden behavioral prescriptions. Actually, the tactic simply shifts the normativity up one level from the individual economist to the allegedly neutral scientific artifice of contemporary economics. That prized theoretical structure simply reifies the normative commitments that underpin what many economists imagine to be objective scientific practice. That deception is not necessarily willful: it arises from scientific hubris, disciplinary conceit, and intellectual lassitude.

The quest for an understanding of the consequences of possessive individualism must start with an inquiry into how modern economics became both a cause and an effect of what I call a prevailing *cultural echo*. Economics is a cultural echo because, as Samuelson figured out very early on, there is enormous power in being able to explain to a population why they would be well advised to see the world as Paul Samuelson imagined it to be. And once they have apprehended that selective vision, they would then become forceful disciples of a new received truth as it worked its way into everyday public discourse. What adult has not heard of laissez-faire economics, of "free markets," and of the abundant advantages of free trade? Some individuals, quite innocent of economic theory, have been heard to complain of the insidious trade balance and the manifold dangers of a budget deficit—as if pondering their monthly bank statement. Who among the adult population cannot warn us that increasing the minimum wage will cause unemployment? That is a false claim right out of the pages of Samuelson's political nemesis Milton Friedman.

Another claim that is now firmly entrenched in the political firmament is that government regulations impose a burden on firms that undermines their efficient operation. Who could possibly deny that government interference in the so-called free market is a bad thing? Can there be any doubt that teachers' unions impede the efficient operation of our schools? And isn't it marvelous that school vouchers—allowing parents to shop around for schools the way they shop around for a new car—will bring efficiency and quality improvements to otherwise desultory public schools? Recently, voucher advocates have started referring to public schools as "government" schools—an apparent smear that anything associated with governments is automatically to be despised. It is well understood that America's health care system requires a dose of free-market discipline to make sure that costs are driven down to the lowest possible level. Who could possibly abide the socialized medicine that has ruined health care in Britain, Germany, Sweden, Denmark, France, Canada, Finland, and Norway?

These alleged truths, reflecting the cultural echo of economics as it is now understood by the general population, are mostly false. Nonetheless, they are firmly held and eagerly advanced by a citizenry that is, in general, economically illiterate. But few individuals admit to being wrong about their false economic truths. All of this takes place while many economists insist that economics is free of political ideology. The existence of such contrasting views as those of Milton Friedman and Paul Samuelson is the clearest possible evidence that economics is ideological to the core. Right-wing and left-wing economists use this exquisite conceptual apparatus to disguise—dress up— our personal values in a scientific costume.

Samuelson's magisterial textbook and others like it gave many citizens a shallow and dangerous *linguistic* grasp of economics that remains completely unhitched from any plausible connection with the larger complex theoretical apparatus within which those linguistic artifacts reside and do their work. Many citizens imagine themselves to be experts in economics in the same way they are experts about their favorite sports team. Some opinions, such as about which movie should be awarded the Palme d'Or at the Cannes Film Festival, are idle and quite harmless. Other opinions, about minimum wages, the cause of unemployment, the benefits of international trade, the salutary effects of school vouchers, or the size of the budget deficit, are quite dangerous when they become widely held by a number of people who are less clever than they suppose. Again, popular ideas from economics, superficially grasped and eagerly deployed, are mostly wrong and therefore dangerous.

When politicians and their committed adherents provide their own ersatz economic diagnosis, and then insist on their own bogus policy solution, millions of lives can be harmed. Current fights over raising the minimum wage are not really fights about economic theory since most of the combatants have no idea what economic theory and empirical research have to say about the matter. These political players do not care what the evidence has to offer. Owners of business firms are opposed to raising the minimum wage for obvious reasons. Their political allies are compliant parrots.

The realization that economic policy is a favorite topic of conversation for the economic illiterate has a deleterious influence on the body politic. After the 2007–2009 recession, there was much angst and self-criticism among many economists for our alleged role in that meltdown. Graduate education was to blame. Our overly mathematical models were to blame. Greed, surely central to economics, was to blame. No one blamed Paul Samuelson or Milton Friedman. On the other hand, two economists *were* often implicated: Eugene Fama and Michael Jensen, whose pathbreaking theoretical work on principal–agent models and incentive problems were sometimes singled out. Or Myron Scholes, Fisher Black, and Robert Merton were fingered for their work on options-pricing models. This was unfair.

These intricate theoretical refinements could not possibly carry any significance in economic affairs unless there were already a pervasive political culture regarding regulations that had made its peace with a world dedicated to economic efficiency. That is, for the most part, the zeitgeist of the metropolitan core. Differences surely exist, but they are mere refinements of the fundamental beliefs of market capitalism. Options-pricing models, like

Ibuprofen and Aspirin, are wonderful creations for specific problems. In the hands of financial wizards (called "quants"), and unregulated on the shared belief that regulations impair the pursuit of efficiency, such instruments can produce great mischief. In the case of unregulated financial machinations by large banks and investment houses leading up to 2007, that mischief destroyed many lives throughout the world.

The question we must now address is how this shared spirit of our age has come to hold such sway over two distinct and disparate realms of life—not just the metropolitan core, but also the isolated periphery. Is it possible that daily life in such different places is shaped by this single organizing principle of efficiency in unregulated markets?

II. The Problematic Efficiency

There is not a single concept of greater importance—and mischief—in economics than that of efficiency. Here is our lodestar: that by which we instruct individuals, and firms, perhaps even government agencies, in how they ought to navigate through the manifold complexities of daily life. Efficiency is our Archimedean implement by which we leverage the world, bending it to our vision of how things ought to be arranged. Economics gives us the theoretical grounding to offer descriptions, prescriptions, and predictions. Description is the act of writing sentences that appear to fit the world out there. Prescription is the act of getting the world out there to fit the sentences we wish to write about it. Prediction is the act of writing promising sentences about the prescriptions we offer. Efficiency underpins our prescriptions and predictions about the world. Much of economics consists in justificationism—the act of explaining why, exactly, the world out there *ought to* coincide with our prescriptions for it.

Many economists just wish the world would follow the model. Given the cultural embrace of managerial capitalism, efficiency is the foundation on which economists construct the impressive monument to our indispensability. Who cannot be interested in efficiency? The concept is akin to a world of divine blessings—weightlessness and a perfect vacuum in which gravity and friction have been vanquished. Efficiency authorizes us to assure everyone of how the world could work if only there were no gravity and no friction to contend with. Government interference in market capitalism is friction. Regulations represent the dead weight of gravity.

Unfortunately, efficiency is a flawed guide. Constrained optimization of physics is the yeast of this potion. The requisite idea of the scientific objectivity—the ethical neutrality—of economics emerged late in the nineteenth century under the influence of Nassau Senior (1836), John Cairnes (1874 [1965]), and Walter Bagehot (1885). These writers were united in the belief that economics was, to quote John Neville Keynes (1852–1949), "positive as distinguished from ethical or practical, and in its method abstract and deductive" (1917, p. 75).

Keynes, building on August Comte's defective logical positivism, seems to have popularized the now-familiar distinction between *positive* and *normative*, with positive being synonymous with scientific objectivity and normative connoting value-laden arguments that comprise metaphysics. To state what every economist holds dear, positive economics speaks to *what is* or what might be and normative economics speaks to *what ought to be*. At that time, Keynes had defined economics as the study

> of those human activities that direct themselves towards the creation, appropriation, and accumulation of wealth; and by economic customs and institutions . . . of human society in regard to wealth. . . . Political economy or economics is a body of doctrine relating to economic phenomena in the above sense. (Keynes, 1917, p. 70)

Here is an open and encompassing definition of our discipline. Notice as well how this view is consistent with my earlier assertion about the importance of the well-being of households and nation-states consisting of such households. At the time Keynes was writing, political economy and economics were synonymous, and he saw them as providing information as to the probable consequences of given lines of action, but not offering judgments or pronouncements about what ought to be done. At the same time, however, Keynes argued that

> the greatest value is attached to the practical applications of economic science; and . . . the economist ought . . . to turn his attention to them—not, however, in his character as a pure economist, but rather as a social philosopher, who, because he is an economist, is in possession of the necessary theoretical knowledge. . . . [I]f this distinction is drawn, the social and ethical aspects of practical problems—which may be of vital importance—are less likely to be overlooked or subordinated." (1917, p. 76)

At the end of the nineteenth century, economics was under growing pressure to be taken seriously as a science. Alfred Marshall at Cambridge University had managed to convince the University to offer a prestigious qualifying examination in economics, a move that was strongly resisted by the physicists, chemists, and other "real" scientists then ruling Cambridge. At that time, economics was dismissed as but a branch of moral philosophy and certainly unworthy of the status bestowed by the passing of the famous Cambridge tripos—named for the three-legged stool on which students sat to write their exams. Marshall's eventual victory signaled that Cambridge had finally accepted economics as a science, and in those days, as Cambridge economics went, so went the rest of the English-speaking world. Now it became doubly important to prove the case—economics could be as rigorous and precise as physics. However, the discipline would need to reform itself to meet those exacting standards.

A little over a decade after Keynes's writing, Lionel Robbins published his most influential book entitled *An Essay on the Nature and Significance of Economic Science* (1932). Robbins had been much influenced by the logical positivists of the Vienna Circle, and he drew upon their ideas to stress several methodological points that survive today. Of foremost pertinence here, Robbins took from logical positivism the idea that there were only two kinds of propositions that could be countenanced in a science: those that were true by definition (tautologies), called *analytical* statements ($2 + 2 = 4$), and those that were empirical propositions, called *synthetic* statements (that tree, over there, is a conifer). Propositions that did not fit these two classes were said to be lacking truth content and hence were value laden. It is usually held that since the scientific part of economics consists exclusively of descriptive statements—either tautologies or empirical propositions that can be tested—economics cannot have any ethical entailments and is therefore value-free.

Unlike the enabling and creative definition of economics from Neville Keynes before him, Robbins insisted that economics concerned the study of the allocation of scarce means among competing ends. Such ends were beyond question to the economist, "Being neutral, the argument proceeds, economics does not choose between or pronounce value-judgments on different ends, and it is implied that no value-judgments are involved in recommending 'means' to given 'ends'" (Hutchison, 1964, pp. 110–11). In other words, to remain objective, economists should not comment on different ends but must restrict themselves to recommending means so as to accomplish those ends. A close reading of Robbins reveals that he used the word *means* to refer to factors of production or financial resources that could be allocated to alternative employments—or to alternative bundles of consumer goods. This is precisely the consumer's problem of striving to reach a bliss point of maximum utility.

It is necessary to consider just what the methodological turn under the Robbins manifesto has meant to the discipline of economics. The clearest indication is to recall how students are taught to think about the individual in standard microeconomic theory. Importantly, this introduction to the individual does not regard the person as being engaged in the complex matters of life—the individual's embeddedness in a household with other loved ones, the individual's participation in the social aspects of a neighborhood, or in the civic activities of a political community. The individual—*Homo economicus*—is none of these things. The individual is a mere *consumer* of goods and services, the acquisition of which will enhance her level of utility. Why was it decided to treat the individual, who plays many roles in life— parent, wife, husband, protector, nurturer, provider—as a mere consumer? Is consumption the only human activity that brings satisfaction? Why do we measure the happiness of the individual only in terms of what can be consumed?

Economics decided to embrace individual consumption because this is the sole activity where real money is spent. Inspired by Lionel Robbins, economists began to see spending money as allocating scarce resources to attain some desired end. And of course spending scarce money is a constrained maximization problem—how best to maximize utility through the allocation of scarce resources. Moreover, spending money in a market economy carries important information: it reveals value, and revealed value is at the core of the wonders of a market economy.

We see an example of this standard framing of the individual (*Homo economicus*) in a well-regarded microeconomics graduate text: "The central figure in microeconomic theory is the consumer, and the first step is almost always to provide a model of the consumer's *behavior*" (emphasis in original) (Kreps, 1990, p. 17). The student is then introduced to a simple diagram in which two commodities are arrayed—one on the horizontal axis, the other on the vertical axis—and a budget set marks off the zone of consumption possibilities that will allow the individual to reach the highest possible level of preference satisfaction (utility) as she chooses between the two consumption possibilities.

If the consumer's budget set expands—perhaps she receives a pay increase—then greater utility is attainable because she can consume more of both commodities. The hedonistic individual is now declared to be better off. Similarly, if the price of one or both of the commodities should fall, then again the budget set will expand and the consumer will be able to attain higher utility. Again, the individual is declared to be better off. If the price of one of these two commodities should drop, while the price of the other remains unchanged, then the alert and agile individual will quickly adjust her consumption bundle—effortlessly sliding along her highest possible indifference curve until, once again, she arrives at the marvelous bliss point. The point of the theory of individual behavior is to reach the highest possible level of preference satisfaction. Utility is thereby maximized.

This depiction of the individual led Thorstein Veblen, deploying his classic cynicism, to observe that

[t]he hedonistic conception of man is that of a lighting calculator of pleasures and pains, who oscillates like a homogeneous globule of desire of happiness under the impulse of stimuli that shift him about the area, but leave him intact. He has neither antecedent nor consequent. He is an isolated, definitive human datum, in stable equilibrium except for the buffets of the impinging forces that displace him in one direction or another. Self-imposed in elemental space, he spins symmetrically about his own spiritual axis until the parallelogram of forces bears down upon him, whereupon he follows the line of the resultant. When the force of the impact is spent, he comes to rest, a self-contained globule of desire as before. Spiritually, the hedonistic man is not a prime mover. He is not the seat of a process of living, except in the sense that he is subject to a series of permutations enforced upon him by circumstances external and alien to him. (Veblen, 1990, pp. 73–74)

We will see just how closely this cynical account matches up with the concept of possessive individualism.

Aside from trivializing the individual as a mere price-obsessed consuming automaton, the fundamental flaw concerns how to demarcate the scientific part of economics from the value-laden part. Robbins relied on the dubious and unreliable distinction between means and ends to draw this demarcation. However, to make a clear differentiation between ends and means, it is necessary to locate and then invoke some *external* criterion so that the distinction—and the linkage—between the two is placed in context. At the most abstract level, it may seem that an end is something that enters into an individual's utility function, while a means would not be found there. However, this is simply a definition; it fits the positivist idea of an analytical statement—a tautology. But having thus differentiated means from ends, what has been accomplished? In one sense, it seems that ends are those things that individuals care about, whereas means are mere instruments, of no special notice, for accomplishing desired ends.

As above, however, we are no better off. This distinction is not drawn by an external observer who can ascertain whether or not something is found in the utility function of an individual, or a group of individuals. It cannot be our determination, for that is to impose the value system of the investigator onto the analysis. Hence, the dichotomy on which Robbins based his edifice of scientific objectivity against the insidious effects of metaphysics is nothing more than a convenient assumption. It is a self-serving stipulation.

Despite this, Milton Friedman, convinced that such models of constrained choice could be relied upon for the widest possible application to contentious issues, was moved to claim:

> I venture the judgment, however, that currently in the Western world, and especially in the United States, differences about economic policy among disinterested citizens derive predominantly from different predictions about the economic consequences of taking action—differences that in principle can be eliminated by the progress of positive economics—rather than from fundamental differences in basic values, differences about which men can ultimately only fight. (Friedman, 1953, p. 5)

The obvious question in response to this confident assertion is, where, exactly, might we find individuals who can honestly be said to be disinterested citizens? Who is not interested in public policy concerning immigration, poverty, environmental degradation, wage rates, or international trade? A society consisting of disinterested citizens is a community of social eunuchs. And, in fact, that is precisely how economics models the individual.

Had economics persisted with the program spelled out by Neville Keynes, we might now have in hand conceptual and empirical protocols that would allow economists to assess and diagnose the constituents of well-being of the individual—and of the household of which that individual is a central part. In Veblen's phrasing, this would have entailed an intellectual program that considers the individual as a "seat of a process of living." This agenda would enable economic theory to complement the approaches common in sociology, psychology, public health, and, to some extent, anthropology. In other words, economics would lend some of its profound analytical approaches to other social sciences that are rich in descriptive and interpretive methods.

On that more promising path, we would now have a discipline that understood the individual and the household as they coevolved from precapitalist centers of provisioning, through the long period of role differentiation under merchant capitalism, and on to the troubled and fraught phase of bringing the rather independent individual into the demanding and inflexible structure of the factory system under industrial capitalism. That intellectual history would also have prepared economics to understand the individual who now finds himself aloof and alienated from the full flowering of managerial capitalism as it moves money around the world in response to the slightest perturbations in economic signals. In such a world, the individual—as a highly dispensable supplier of labor power—finds himself precariously engaged *in the world of work*, but he is clearly not *of the world of work*. He is therefore quite unsure of what might come next. The recent history of an assured place in a nation's workplace seems to be a quaint remnant of yesterday.

So complete was the break with the other social sciences that some economists sought to encapsulate those other approaches into the choice-theoretic models of economics. The work of Gary Becker on crime, the family, and schooling fits this pattern, confirming the impression that economists have imperialistic ambitions. In some corners of the discipline, it is not enough to bring economic insights to bear on new problems. Rather, it was thought better to bring the other social sciences under the theoretical machinery of economics so that they might thereby become mere specialized appendages of microeconomic theory. Indeed, the idea that economics might revolutionize public policy—institutional change—led Douglass North to insist that

> [b]uilding a theory of institutions on the foundation of individual choice is a step toward reconciling differences between economics and the other social sciences. The choice theoretic approach is essential because a logically consistent, potentially testable set of hypotheses must be built on a theory of human behavior. The strength of microeconomic theory is that it is constructed on the basis of assumptions about individual human behavior. (North, 1990, p. 5)

We can only speculate how these other social scientists might react to this imperialist project. Despite his Nobel Prize, North seems unaware of the conceptual flaws in that standard theoretical approach. We will now see that economic theory offers nothing of value to a plausible theory of individual choice. It cannot explain choice because standard theory lacks the ability for individuals to offer reasons for choices. Utility is not a reason.

III. The Problematic Concept of Choice

> Conventional economics is not about choice, but about acting according to necessity. Economic man obeys the dictates of reason, follows the logic of choice. To call his conduct choice is surely a misuse of words, when we suppose that to him the ends amongst which he can select, and the criteria of selection are given, and the means to each end are known. . . . Choice in such a theory is empty, and conventional economics should abandon the word. (Shackle, 1961, pp. 272–73)

Since the early days of the twentieth century, economics has prided itself on being the science of choice. This confidence is unwarranted. The central problem is that, as Shackle suggests, the idea of choice in economics leaves individuals with no choices to make. In such models, humans are but passive automata—"homogeneous globules" in Veblen's caustic phrase—responding without thinking to external stimuli. It seems that if this is choice, then the word has lost any plausible meaning. Notice that individuals have but one choice to make—the one that maximizes utility at that moment. This is not choice for the same reason that if you cannot move then you are not *choosing* to stand still.

The fundamental problem of human choice is that actions that can still be chosen or rejected on the basis of their plausible implications for the future have no objective outcomes associated with those available actions. The only outcomes that such actions can have merely exist in the mind—the imagination—of the individual. This means, quite simply, that outcomes of available actions are not *ascertained* (or discovered) but *created*. Specifically, *outcomes of available actions are only imaginable, and in the process of imagining them we do not ascertain those outcomes; rather, we create those outcomes.* This distinction between *discovering* (ascertaining) and *making* (creating) lies at the heart of the current struggle in philosophy between adherents to the classic dyads—facts versus values, mind versus body—and those who reject the demarcationist program so central to Plato, Kant, and Descartes (Rorty, 1979, 1982, 1999). This is what G.L.S. Shackle (1961) has termed *created imaginings*.

> Outcomes of <u>available</u> actions are not ascertained but created. We are not speaking . . . of the objective recorded outcomes of actions which have been performed. Those actions are not "available." An action which can still be chosen or rejected <u>has no objective outcome</u>. The only kind of outcome which it can have exists in the imagination of the decision-maker. (Shackle, 1961, p. 143)

Growing evidence concerning the incoherence of rational choice models represents a serious challenge to the notion of rational individuals seeking their best advantage by first consulting their preferences and then picking those actions that maximize their utility defined over those preferences (Akerlof and Dickens, 1982; Ariely, 2009; Bowles, 1998; Camerer and Weber, 1992; Kahneman, 2011; Lawson, 1997; Rabin, 1998; Sen, 1977, 1982; Shackle, 1961, 1992; Thaler, 2015). The implications of this conceptual flaw are profound when the model of rational choice is transported into the contested realm of public policy. When action in the legislature or the courts is, by definition, an arena of contending and conflicting individual notions of what is best to do, appeals to rational choice models are of little value (Bromley, 2006).

To get a start on this problem, consider the following scene in which I say to my dining companion at a fine French restaurant: "Gee, why did you order snails?"—to which she responds: "In order to maximize my utility." Wrong. Utility does not—and cannot—constitute a reason for action. Utility maximization cannot be a reason for ordering snails because utility maximization could be offered as a reason for any possible choice, including deciding not to order anything at all. When one is asked why he or she did something, the questioner is seeking reasons, not justifications. The questioner wishes to know *why* snails were ordered rather than something else.

This reminds us that "a reason makes an action intelligible by redescribing it" (Davidson, 1963, p. 695). What sentences, what possible redescriptions, might count as reasons? Possibilities include: (1) because I spent six months in France, and eating snails gives rise to such fond memories; (2) because

I read somewhere that snails contain high levels of Omega 67 (or some number), and it is good for us to consume as much of that as possible; (3) because snails are farmed on a sustainable basis and I am into sustainability; (4) because my grandfather always ate snails, and I so much loved my grandfather (he is dead now); (5) because snails are the most expensive thing on the menu—and since you are buying I thought I would enjoy myself; (6) because nothing else on the menu appeals to me; or finally (7) because I love snails. As Joseph Raz would say, deliberation is not a process of discovering what we want, but a process of reflecting upon what there is the most reason to want. Specifically:

> When we reason about what we want most, we reason about what we have most reason to want. Since the value or the goodness of things and options constitutes the reason for having them or doing them, their value or goodness is also the reason for wanting to have them or to do them, Normally when we deliberate about what we want most, we deliberate about what it would be best for us to want because it would be best for us to have or to do. (Raz, 1997, p. 115)

When we ask "why," we seek to move from doubt to belief. When others offer up their reasons, we make a move in the right direction. Did my dining companion offer good reasons? Is she rational? And here it is important to point out that *every possible* action is both rational and reasonable under some description. Notice that an explanation of an action is simply a re-description of the reasons for that action. When we say "why," we are really saying, for what reasons. "For what reasons did you order snails tonight? I ordered snails because. . . . " My dinner companion has explained herself—her choice—to me. Only someone taught to believe that utility explains choice and action would—or could—respond: "Because eating snails increased my utility over all other possible choices I could have made."

The notion of choice—or rational choice—is seen to be problematic. The escape is to consider the connection between reasons and explanations in a diagnostic mode. Notice that the conversation started with an expression of surprise: "Gee, why did you order snails?" An event has occurred, and the questioner seeks an explanation—a reason for the surprise. Ordering snails was a surprise that begged for reasons. The various possibilities on offer make clear that the diagnostic challenge is to avoid simplistic justificationism—utility—and keep searching until we locate a plausible explanation for the surprising choice. Utility is not a reason for doing anything.

IV. The Dubious Virtues

It is widely believed that freedom of choice in markets enables maximum utility, and the inevitable efficiency of market exchange reveals that once obtained, no possible gains remain unexploited. Individuals, and the economy in general, have arrived at a bliss point from which any move, in any direction, threatens a loss of overall welfare. The exercise of free choice is of the very highest virtue. Freedom of choice is a marvelous thing, whether in the political arena or in the market. How could individuals hope for more?

There is one more alleged justification for markets as arenas of free choice: participation in markets makes us more virtuous than we would otherwise be.

> On the supposition that the *telos* of the market is mutual benefit, a market virtue in the sense of virtue ethics is an acquired character trait with two properties: possession of the trait makes an individual better able to play a part in the creation of mutual benefit through market transactions; and the trait expresses an intentional orientation towards and a respect for mutual benefit. (Bruni and Sugden, 2013, p. 153)

This aspirational boast captures the significance of markets to many people. The assertion here is that societies that operate as market economies gradually come to be composed of individuals who are socialized to master behavior that reinforces the inherent mutually virtuous character traits of such market societies. Moreover, those acquired character traits are manifestations of an unavoidable intention to orient one's individual actions in the direction of enhancing the mutually virtuous social outcomes that are the reason why societies decide to adopt a market system in the first place. These outcomes are said to be market virtues. The conceptual provenance of these rather extravagant claims for virtue now warrant our attention.

Deirdre McCloskey's book *The Bourgeois Virtues: Ethics for an Age of Commerce* (2006), has stimulated interest in many of the pertinent issues, and it seems to have encouraged a reawakening of ethical discourse in the economics literature. Indeed, the *Journal of Economic Perspectives* featured a special section on "economics and moral virtues" in which Michael Sandel summarized rather popular philosophical concerns about the role of ethics in economics (Sandel, 2013). In the same volume, Luigino Bruni and Robert Sugden countered with a defense of what they call *virtue ethics* in economics. According to these authors, acquired virtue ethics enables market participants to become adept at fostering mutual gains in markets. This acquired virtue in turn inspires all market participants to have respect for the mutual gains that arise from being engaged in markets. In other words, markets are arenas of virtue: they inspire virtue ethics, and they provide a harmonious arena for the instantiation of those virtues.

While the Bruni–Sugden title refers to "virtue ethics for economics," these authors have a much more limited scope in mind. They advance a case for the virtue ethics of *markets*. Even here, they are not interested in all markets. For instance, they have no interest in the market for low-priced labor in Cambodia or Vietnam. Nor are they interested in markets for outsourced labor in the call centers of India and the Philippines, for elementary school teachers, for migrant farm workers the world over, for professional athletes, or for chief executive officers of Fortune 500 companies. These labor markets, where the overwhelming majority of the world's adults (and some children) seek to make a living, are not under consideration. Instead, Bruni and Sugden are interested in a very limited class of markets. They are concerned *only* with buyers and sellers seeking to exchange some commodity (or service) in a normal market. These are the same markets earlier described by David Kreps in which the individual pursues maximum utility from engagement with the market for consumer goods.

Consider the question posed by Bruni and Sugden: "What is the characteristic end or purpose—the raison d'être—of the market? How would you describe, in the simplest and most general terms, what markets do that is valuable?" (Bruni and Sugden, 2013, p. 152). In answering their own question, they echo Friedman to argue that the "technique of the market place" is "voluntary cooperation of individuals" (Bruni and Sugden, 2013, p. 152). The word *technique* is meant to suggest the instrumental nature of markets. The second purpose of markets is said to be the opportunity for mutual gain among the participants (Buchanan and Tullock, 1962). Markets enable winners all around.

Here we see a hint of the teleological fallacy—the confusion of an *effect* with *purpose*—in this two-pronged praise for markets. Medievalists once believed that the purpose of the moon was to facilitate travel by night. The teleological fallacy confuses the effect of the moon (illumination) with its purpose—its raison d'etre. Did someone—a benevolent God?—create the moon so that travel by night would be less terrifying? A similar problem is on display in that a moral claim for a technique is then used to attribute a specific moral purpose for a process—a market economy—of which that technique is a central part.

The belief that markets arose to serve the purpose of voluntary cooperation clearly overlooks the obvious point that the necessary condition for a market is that two different parties are in possession of superfluous products. Market exchange is not animated by the desire of a number of individuals to engage cooperatively in some virtuous activity. Rather, market participation first requires that some individuals have more of particular objects than they are able to put to beneficial use. Localized abundance is a necessary condition for the emergence of the *idea*—and therefore the practice—of exchange with others.

But such abundance is not sufficient. Others must be found who have too little of the very same thing, as well as an abundance of something else of potential interest to those with a different plentitude. Lacking that, there can be no natural instinct to truck and barter. After all, any momentary excess could easily be given away or, as with many early peoples, consumed and/or burned in elaborate ceremonies of propitiation for the good fortune of episodic and fleeting abundance. Voluntary cooperation and the chance for mutual gain cannot stand as the animating *purposes* of market exchange. In other words, these circumstances cannot *explain* the emergence and persistence of market exchange.

Bruni and Sugden offer another virtue of the market—wealth creation. Appealing to Adam Smith, they argue that the primary means by which wealth is created is the division of labor and the extension of the market. In fact, empirical evidence suggests that wealth gains from competitive exchange are relatively minor (Leibenstein, 1966). These authors assert that market transactions are

valuable because individuals want to make them, because they satisfy individuals' preferences, because they create wealth, and because the opportunity to make them is a form of freedom. We therefore propose to treat the mutual benefit as the *telos* of the market. (Bruni and Sugden, 2013, p. 153).

In other words, Bruni and Sugden insist that markets arose, *ab initio*, to allow for mutual benefit. That is their purpose, the end to which they carry us. Notice here a correlated teleological fallacy—as well as a historical error—in the literature concerning the emergence of money. Economists have been quite certain that money arose to facilitate market exchange (Feldman, 1973; Galbraith, 1975; Hayashi and Matsui, 1996; Jones, 1976; Matsui and Shimizu, 2005; Menger, 1892). As with Bruni and Sugden, who apparently believe that exchange is deeply embedded in human DNA, it seemed to make sense that money was therefore invented to supplant the otherwise-difficult barter of heavy and cumbersome objects. If exchange is preternaturally human, then money and markets are the necessary institutional innovations to enable that incorrigible urge.

In fact, money first emerged *not* as an expedient for exchange, but as an instrument of debt. Clay tablets from Babylon depicted degrees of indebtedness, and this evidence clearly predates the first coins used in exchange (Innes, 1913). Moreover, money had long played a role as a measure of value in the enforcement of property rights. Since exchange requires the prior existence and social acknowledgment of property rights, it seems clear that money as a measure of value in use and holding emerged prior to exchange (Chavas and Bromley, 2008).

If individuals are able to act on the basis of their self-interest, then the moral case for the arena in which those voluntary acts takes place is justified. However, just because individuals wish to engage in a market transaction cannot, on that evidence alone, stand as sufficient grounds for the compelling virtue of that voluntary exchange. There are certain market exchanges—for opium, prostitution, and child pornography, for example—that lack moral virtues. Most importantly, and referring back to the problematic nature of choice, satisfying individual preferences need not be welfare enhancing. Hence, there is no basis for asserting that market exchange provides compelling evidence of the agreeable moral properties of markets (Cowen, 1993; Hausman and McPherson, 2009). Teenagers provide abundant evidence that some preference-satisfying behaviors are contrary to individual welfare (Hausman, 2001). Nor do all market transactions create wealth. Notice that if a set of market transactions merely reapportions income and wealth among market participants, then the wealth-creation claim for markets is not sustained. The second-hand housing market does little to create new wealth.

What is to be made of this claim that markets are arenas of virtue? Is it true that market behavior induces virtue? For the answer we need Alasdair MacIntyre.

V. After Virtue

[T]he utilitarianism of the middle and late nineteenth century and the analytical moral philosophy of the middle and late twentieth century are alike unsuccessful attempts to rescue the autonomous moral agent from the predicament in which the failure of the Enlightenment project of providing him with a secular, rational justification for his moral allegiances had left him ... the price paid for liberation from what appeared to be the external authority of traditional morality was the loss of any authoritative content from the would-be moral utterances of the newly autonomous agent. Each moral agent now spoke unconstrained by the externalities of divine law, natural teleology or hierarchical authority, but why should anyone else now listen to him? It was and is to this question that both utilitarianism and analytical moral philosophy must be understood as attempting to give cogent answers; and if my argument is correct, it is precisely this question which both fail to answer cogently. (MacIntyre, 1984, p. 68)

MacIntyre anchors his treatment of virtue and morality by noting that all assertions about what is good (ethical) must be anchored on *some external and unquestioned* source. In other words, moral assertions pertaining to specific performances cannot be conditional and contingent. This means that moral approval cannot be applied to the claimed efficacy of components of a system of which they are essential parts. For example, the separate component parts of a criminal justice system are not worthy of moral praise just because the justice system has a plausible moral purpose. Capital punishment cannot sustain a claim of moral approval by being part of a system of criminal justice. The system of which those components are a part is not merely some neutral external source of moral authority. Those components are merely doing the job that is expected of them. That they do it well is no measure of their virtue. Market exchange does what a market system expects of it. It is the system—*the market economy*—that is or is not praiseworthy.

In societies with a market culture, it necessarily follows that the market system—capitalism and competitive markets—will be deemed presumptively good. If it were not considered good, the citizenry would have replaced it with something else. The system endures and is considered good because of the collective inability to imagine an alternative. In other words, the economic system in which one is embedded comes to be regarded as normal and morally legitimate. We are born into an economic system, and, as with all aspects of our socialization into the norms and practices of that system—the only one we come to know—we thereby lack the necessary perspective to judge its qualities. Only malcontents and misfits dare to criticize the system into which they have been born. This is no different from the former Soviet Union in which central planning and state capitalism were presumptively good. It was judged good not because of political oppression but because individuals lacked a plausible reference point to assess the real merits of their unavoidable encapsulation.

Given the cultural embeddedness of either system—capitalism or socialism—no other moral judgment is possible. Any flaws that come to light must, necessarily, be of an operational nature. Those flaws are *not* flaws in the ideological grounding of the system. That is, individuals embedded in an economic system lack a logical basis for judging the morality of that system. A few thinkers are always available to do that. However, our inability to imagine life in a different system cripples us—honest assessment is impossible. Something cannot be compared to nothing. Something must inevitably be compared to a different something. And the absence of direct knowledge of an alternative economic system deprives the individual of a plausible reference point.

MacIntyre's argument is that the moral approval of any economic system is meaningless because it has no plausible referent on which that moral approval is grounded. All comparative assessments require a grounded basis for those comparisons. Citizens of each country—Denmark, France, Britain, Germany, the United States, Canada— approve of their economic system and would not think of changing it. Of course, they will complain about particular aspects of it, but to them, their economic system is morally prized. However, this prizing rests on nothing more substantive than their familiarity with it. Danes cannot imagine surviving in the American market economy, and Americans cannot imagine surviving in the Danish market economy. There is no irrefutable moral anchor—there is mere familiarity.

What is familiar is normal, and what is normal is natural and right. We tend to love the meatloaf we grew up on.

Indeed, it would be a mistake to assume that Soviet citizens disliked their economic *system*. Parts of it invited ridicule, but other parts clearly found approval—housing, medical care, schooling, vacations, child care, equal opportunity for women, etc. Only in the early 1980s, when the economy began to suffer, did frustration arise. But there was little interest in switching to another *system*—American capitalism. Soviet citizens simply wanted *their* system to work better. The same can be said for the East German economy (Bromley, 2017; Fulbrook, 1995, 2005; Major and Osmond, 2002). The point of this realization is found in the trauma associated with the collapse of the Soviet Union in 1991. Despair, alcoholism, and dislocation brought about a precipitous drop in economic output, and the social turmoil actually led to the first known decline in life expectancy in modern times. By 1999, eight years after the collapse of the Soviet Union, life expectancy for Russian men had fallen to 58 years, down from 62 years in 1980.[1]

Throughout Western history, religious doctrine provided a necessary reference point on which to anchor all moral claims. Religion was the sole source of moral authority. In the wake of the Enlightenment, that durable, unquestioned, and irrefutable lodestar fell into disrepute. The gradual dissipation of universal comprehensive faith dissolved enduring truths, with radical implications for the modernist project of Kant and others intent on finding another authority—another other. Nietzsche and Sartre undermined that program. MacIntyre observes that "[c]ontemporary moral argument is rationally interminable, because all moral, indeed all evaluative, argument is and must always be rationally interminable" (MacIntyre, 1984, p. 11). People can only fight.

MacIntyre writes that "all evaluative judgments and more specifically all moral judgments are *nothing but* expressions of preference, expressions of attitude or feeling, insofar as they are moral or evaluative in character" (MacIntyre, 1984, pp. 11–12). He shows that we use moral judgments "not only to express our own feelings and attitudes, but also precisely to produce such effects in others" (1984, p. 12). When one says "I love opera," the person is declaring what is good by her lights, and she hopes that you will agree with her. She is looking for affinity with you—"aha, I had no idea, I also love opera." And voila, they have found something that unites them—an essential aspect of being human and seeking community with others.

As MacIntyre notes, the sentence "This is good" is equivalent to "I approve of this; do so as well." If you scowl or express indifference the speaker has two options—she can change the subject, or she can declare "you should too." If the listener asserts the latter, the speaker has succeeded in making you an instrument of her desires. In economic jargon, she has altered the arguments in your utility function. In summarizing the problematic claims of virtue ethics for economics, MacIntyre notes that

> an agent can only justify a particular judgment by referring to some universal rule from which it may be logically derived, and can only justify that rule in turn by deriving it from some more general rule or principle; but on this view since every chain of reasoning must be finite, such a process of justificatory reasoning must always terminate with the assertion of some rule or principle for which no further reason can be given. (MacIntyre, 1984, p. 20)

The Bruni–Sugden case for markets as arenas that both instill and reinforce virtue rests on the claim that market exchange is voluntary, that it gives rise to mutual gains, that it conduces to wealth creation, and that it enables freedom. But of course the causal chain is tautological. If these virtuous traits constitute the *telos*—the purpose—of the market, then it is logically impossible to find that markets are other than virtuous. If voluntary action, if cooperation, if wealth creation, and if freedom are each morally good on their own terms, then any human activity that embodies those desired attributes is obviously moral. Or is it?

The problem addressed here concerned whether or not it was possible to agree that markets are arenas of rational choice and virtue. Are humans better off living in a market system compared to any other possible alternative? Since social welfare must inevitably entail moral claims, it is impossible to sustain the view that the quest for mutual gain, or free choice, or cooperation, provide evidence of any moral prizing. A claim of virtue ethics for economics requires much more work than merely extolling the virtues of volitional exchange in particular markets.

MacIntyre shows us that there can be no plausible defense of the virtue of economics (or of markets). All moral *judgments* are the linguistic survivors of classical theism which, after the Enlightenment, lost the necessary context. To utter such sentences is simply a habit of mind that is no longer underwritten by any external authorizations. In other words, moral judgments lack clear status, and the sentences in which they are expressed are meaningless. Claims from Bruni and Sugden concerning moral virtues for markets are devoid of meaning.

VI. Economics as Cultural Echo

The marginalist turn in economics has worked to deprive the discipline of a clear way to think about the fraught nexus of the capitalist firm and the vulnerable household. The exacting and elegant theoretical explanations of the rational hedonistic consumer fail to offer a complete picture of the individual as the owner of labor power exposed to the decisions of the capitalist firm. Marx predicted that workers would rise up in protest against their employers. Instead, the capitalist firm has risen up against the household and is waging a gradual long-run campaign against owners of labor power. Aggressive assaults on labor unions, the continual push for automation to drive down costs, and the enduring political power of owners of capital have combined to suggest a growing commitment against the economic interests of households. After all, what the firm regards as a cost of labor is nothing but household income.

Economic theory, by focusing attention on the utility of the consumer through allegedly rational choices at the lowest possible prices, lacks a plausible answer to the problem that households face under relentless pressure exerted by owners of capital. Economists are reluctant to admit that the concept of power is seriously undertheorized and usually dismissed as irrelevant. By implication, such work is best left to sociologists.

We must see economics as a *cultural echo*. Economic theory provides the conceptual apparatus that enables politicians to take the side of the capitalist firm in pursuit of the flawed notion of efficiency with respect to taxation, regulations, outsourcing of jobs, environmental regulations, regressive income taxes, and the movement of thousands of manufacturing jobs to foreign countries in the periphery in the name of free trade. A related problem is that politicians are open to threats of companies moving to another location if subsidies and favors are not forthcoming.

The other side of this play for favors arises when firms engage in a bidding game with local units of government to locate their firm in particular jurisdictions. In public discussions and political debates, these moves are said to be justified by the need for firms to be competitive. The justification is always in terms of job creation. Yet the evidence runs against a genuine interest in creating jobs. Owners of capitalist firms seek higher net incomes so that they can reward shareholders and their own compensation schemes. If firms are to be celebrated as "job creators," what then are we to call them when they show themselves to be "job destroyers"?

Repeated praise for the market—as a place where individual freedom is actualized by a happy consumer facing interminable choices—is related to the wonders of democracy where another form of freedom is offered up. This mutual reinforcement serves to persuade the general citizenry that a capitalist market economy is the necessary materialist analogue to their prized political apparatus. The intent is to emphasize the point that you cannot have a democracy without also having market capitalism.

It would be too easy to assume that this cultural echo—contemporary economics and the dominant political culture—is confined to the rich countries of the metropolitan core. In fact, the recent interest in diagnosing failed states in the poor periphery does so by emphasizing the desired juncture of these two ideas. Political dysfunction is blamed on flawed economic programs, and flawed economic programs are blamed on dysfunctional political structures (Acemoglu and Robinson, 2012; Fukuyama, 2014). The implication is clear. States fail because they lack the political-economic embrace—the prized mutuality—that characterizes the successful states of the metropolitan core. In the core, politics and economics are in harmony, and therefore rich states are successful.

This claim must be recognized as incoherent. In light of pronounced income inequality in the United States—which now is of unprecedented magnitude—one might look at the political fragmentation and extreme partisanship and ask just what it means to be a failed state. Likewise, the splintered political standoff in Britain, leading to a vote in 2016 to leave the European Union, is not exactly a ringing endorsement of the *status quo ante*. The rise of right-wing nationalist parties in Europe would also suggest problems with the prevailing situation.

One might even note the irony here. At a moment in history when so many things seem slightly akilter in the rich metropolitan core, it is curious to see poor countries being advised, by earnest experts, to become more like us. Do these prescriptive certitudes offer coherent advice, or is it just another version of the standard presumptive arrogance that rich countries possess the recipe for the secret sauce?

Note

1. https://www.ncbi.nlm.nih.gov/pmc/articles/PMC1116380/ (accessed September 10, 2017).

References

Acemoglu, Daron, and James Robinson. 2012. *Why Nations Fail: The Origins of Power, Prosperity, and Poverty*, New York: Random House.

Akerlof, George, and W. T. Dickens. 1982. "The Economic Consequences of Cognitive Dissonance," *American Economic Review*, 72(3): 307–19.

Ariely, Dan. 2009. *Predictably Irrational*, New York: Harper Collins.

Bowles, S. 1998. "Endogenous Preferences: The Cultural Consequences of Markets and Other Economic Institutions," *Journal of Economic Literature*, 36(March): 75–111.

Bromley, Daniel W. 2006. *Sufficient Reason: Volitional Pragmatism and the Meaning of Economic Institutions*, Princeton, NJ: Princeton University Press.

Bromley, Joyce E. 2017. *German Reunification: Unfinished Business*, London: Routledge.

Bruni, Luigino, and Robert Sugden. 2013. "Reclaiming Virtue Ethics for Economics," *Journal of Economic Perspectives*, 27(4): 141–64.

Buchanan, James M., and Gordon Tullock. 1962. *The Calculus of Consent*, Ann Arbor: University of Michigan Press.

Cairnes, J. E. 1874 (1965). *The Character and Logical Method of Political Economy*, London: Frank Cass. (Originally published in 1874 as "Some Leading Principles of Political Economy.")

Camerer, C., and M. Weber. 1992. "Recent Developments in Modeling Preferences: Uncertainty and Ambiguity," *Journal of Risk and Uncertainty* 5(4): 325–70.

Chavas, Jean-Paul, and Daniel W. Bromley. 2008. "On the Origins and Evolving Role of Money," *Journal of Institutional and Theoretical Economics*, 164(4): 624–51.

Cowen, Tyler. 1993. "The Scope and Limits of Preference Sovereignty," *Economics and Philosophy*, 9(2): 253–69.

Davidson, Donald. 1963. "Actions, Reasons, and Causes," *Journal of Philosophy* 60(23): 685–700.

Feldman, A. M. 1973. "Bilateral Trading Processes, Pairwise Optimality and Pareto Optimality," *Review of Economic Studies*, 40: 463–74.

Friedman, Milton. 1953. *Essays in Positive Economics*, Chicago: University of Chicago Press.

Fukuyama, Francis. 2014. *Political Order and Political Decay*, New York: Farrar, Straus, and Giroux.

Fulbrook, Mary. 1995. *Anatomy of a Dictatorship: Inside the GDR 1949-1989*, Oxford: Oxford University Press.

Fulbrook, Mary. 2005. *The People's State: East German Society from Hitler to Honecker*, New Haven, CT: Yale University Press.

Galbraith, J. K. 1975. *Money: Whence It Came, Where It Went*, London: André Deutsch.

Glendon, Mary Ann. 1991. *Rights Talk*, Cambridge, MA: Harvard University Press.

Hausman, Daniel M. 2001. "Explanation and Diagnosis in Economics," *Revue Internationale de Philosophie*, 217: 11–26.

Hausman, Daniel M., and Michael McPherson. 2009. "Preference Satisfaction and Welfare," *Economics and Philosophy*, 25(1): 1–25.

Hayashi, F., and A. Matsui. 1996. "A Model of Fiat Money and Barter," *Journal of Economic Theory*, 68: 111–32.

Hutchison, T. W. 1964. *"Positive" Economics and policy Objectives*, London: Allen & Unwin.

Innes, A. M. 1913. "What Is Money?" *Banking Law Journal*, May: 377–408.

Jones, R. 1976. "The Origins and Development of Media of Exchange," *Journal of Political Economy*, 84: 757–75.

Kahneman, Daniel. 2011. *Thinking Fast and Slow*, New York: Farrar, Straus, and Giroux.

Keynes, John Neville. 1917. *The Scope and Method of Political Economy*, London: Kelley.

Kreps, David M. 1990. *A Course in Microeconomic Theory*, Princeton, NJ: Princeton University Press.

Lawson, Tony. 1997. *Economics and Reality*, London: Routledge.

Leibenstein, H. 1966. "Allocative Efficiency vs. 'X-Efficiency'," *American Economic Review*, 56: 392–415.

MacIntyre, Alasdair. 1959. "Hume on 'Is' and 'Ought'," *Philosophical Review*, 68(4): 451–68.

MacIntyre, Alasdair. 1984. *After Virtue*, South Bend, IN: University of Notre Dame Press.

McCloskey, Deirdre. 2006. *The Bourgeois Virtues: Ethics for an Age of Commerce*, Chicago: University of Chicago Press.

Major, Patrick, and Jonathan Osmond (eds.). 2002. *The Workers' and Peasants' State: Communism and Society in East Germany under Ulbricht 1945–71*, Manchester, UK: Manchester University Press.

Matsui, A., and T. Shimizu. 2005. "A Theory of Money and Market Places," *International Economic Review*, 46: 35–59.

Menger, K. 1892. "On the Origins of Money," *Economic Journal*, 2: 239–55.

North, Douglass C. 1990. *Institutions, Institutional Change and Economic Performance*, Cambridge: Cambridge University Press.

Rabin, M. 1998. "Psychology and Economics," *Journal of Economic Literature*, 36: 11–46.

Raz, J. 1997. "Incommensurability and Agency," in R. Chang (ed.), *Incommensurability, Incomparability, and Practical Reason*, Cambridge, MA: Harvard University Press.

Robbins, Lionel. 1932. *An Essay on the Nature and Significance of Economic Science*, London: Macmillan.

Sandel, Michael J. 2013. "Market Reasoning as Moral Reasoning: Why Economists Should Reengage with Political Philosophy," *Journal of Economic Perspectives*, 27(4): 121–40.

Sen, A. 1977. "Rational Fools: A Critique of the Behavioral Foundations of Economic Theory," *Philosophy and Public Affairs* 6: 317–44.

Sen, Amartya. 1982. *Choice, Welfare, and Measurement*, Oxford: Blackwell.

Senior, Nassau W. 1836. *An Outline of the Science of Political Economy*, London: London School of Economics Reprints.

Shackle, G.L.S. 1961. *Decision, Order, and Time in Human Affairs*, Cambridge: Cambridge University Press.

Thaler, Richard H. 2015. *Misbehaving: The Making of Behavioral Economics*, New York: W. W. Norton.

Veblen, Thorstein, 1990 (1898). "Why Is Economics Not an Evolutionary Science?" in *The Place of Science in Modern Civilization*, New Brunswick, NJ: Transaction Publishers, pp. 56–81. (Originally published in *The Quarterly Journal of Economics*, 12(4): 373–97, July 1898.)

3

Emergence of the Isolated Household

We here explore the gradual emasculation of the household as the basic unit of provisioning during the four evolutionary phases of capitalism. This economic history reveals a gradual redefinition of the purpose of the household from the center of entrepreneurial initiative to a besieged and insecure provider of inconvenient and unwanted labor to managerial capitalism whose central imperative is to reduce labor costs in the service of greater net returns to owners of capital. This evolutionary pathway will reveal the household to be an increasingly precarious and politically vexing participant in global capitalism.

I. The Household

The Greek word *oikos*, the root of "economics," captures the idea of the household or family, often including the extended family. The discipline of economics grew out of a concern for how this basic unit of human existence continually organized its provisioning and thereby secured its future. From early days, the subject of economics has concerned the well-being of the household as it contributed to the wealth of nations—to borrow a phrase from Adam Smith. The subject matter of economics is therefore centrally concerned with *the study of how individuals and societies organize themselves for their provisioning*. Notice the important sequencing here—humans first must *organize (arrange) themselves*, and then they might be able to *organize (arrange) their provisioning*. However, that historic focus on the well-being of the household has been pushed aside by an increasing focus on individual rationality and the sanctity of the consumer.

In the preceding chapter, I showed how contemporary economics has gradually developed its central tenets as nothing but an exquisite apologetics for possessive individualism. The conceptual defects exposed in Chapter 2, unknown—and perhaps incomprehensible—to the general public, have nonetheless contributed to a shared spirit of laissez-faire market consecration. In this chapter, I trace the gradual economic isolation and fragility of the household under the growing influence of economic theory and practice.

It is essential to start here because the household is the only natural organization in human society. It is natural because it is the only entity that is reflective of—and predicated upon—biological considerations. Throughout history, families simply existed, and they did so without any official sanction from the state or its authoritative agents. We might usefully consider a family as a going concern united by the central biological imperative of reproduction, while also constrained by the necessity to provision itself so that it might continue into the future. That is its purpose. In contrast to the naturally occurring family, a firm is an artificial going concern—a contrived bringing together of individuals with no inherent connection, who then collaborate to accomplish a specific goal or purpose. Of course, there are a few family firms, but ironically, many of them fail to survive beyond the third generation. Firms can cease to exist, whereas families run into the future.

Our interest in these two social constructs—one natural, the other contrived—is justified by the empirical reality of the modern economic system. Households rely on firms for jobs and income, and they acquire desired goods and services from firms. Firms rely on households to provide labor power and to purchase what has been produced. It is a symbiotic relation fraught with mutual dependence, frequent resentment, and, very often, open conflict. It is rarely a happy mutuality. We must figure out why this is so.

With that need in mind, we will explore the increasingly fraught situation of the household through history. We start with precapitalist times and then come forward as capitalism underwent evolutionary change from: (1) merchant capitalism; to (2) industrial capitalism; to (3) financial capitalism; and finally to (4) the managerial capitalism of today. These evolutionary stages are not demarcated by sharp historical breaks. Rather, they represent gradual phases that can be characterized by the primacy of a central personified medium—the *entrepreneur* of merchant capitalism, the *engineer* of industrial capitalism, the *banker* of financial capitalism, and the *wrangler* of today's managerial capitalism. The contemporary wrangler is of the hedge fund, the private equity fund, or some other financial behemoth.

As we will see, the essential characteristic of this long history is the increasing economic irrelevance—indeed impertinence—of the household as a supplier of labor power to the capitalist firm. The profound inconvenience of hired labor, and the enticing promise of automation wherever possible, is the leitmotif of the history under consideration.

We must start at a time when the household was the only center of economic activity. This was long before the contrivance of firms as going concerns.

II. The Precapitalist Household

Precapitalist economic history is an account of the family and the household. In very early days there were no kings, no landlords, no manors, no ecclesiastical estates, and no firms. There were only families organized into a variety of entities we would recognize as households. For millions of years, the naturally occurring autonomous family was the seat of living, the motive force of our shared evolutionary trajectory, and the singular entity around which economic history would play out. Even today, in many low-income countries, the prevailing political and economic system can only be understood by comprehending the primacy of the family in civic life. This is profoundly true in those societies that remain civically underelaborated. Where the state is weak, the family remains strong. The prominence of the *Cosa Nostra* ("our thing") in Sicily attests to its emergence in the absence of an official structure of law enforcement and protection. The group provided or arranged for a variety of public goods and services that Sicilian governments were too weak to offer. The importance of the family and clan in many poor countries reflects similar functions even today.

In early days, as hominids navigated the slow evolutionary pathway to what would come to be called *Homo sapiens*—thinking man—the family was all there was. Families had few possessions, and they ranged over a vast territory where occasional encounters with other family units were either hostile or passably agreeable. Provisioning was a broad-spectrum affair, reliance being on fruits, nuts, roots, an occasional animal, and fish. While meat was a delectable luxury, the more reliable subsistence was often limited to vegetable matter. This hardscrabble existence began to improve approximately 250,000 years ago when early humans gradually emigrated out of Africa and began to take advantage of the fertile agricultural environment in the Levant. This bountiful ecosystem enabled the gradual clustering of families, the emergence of organized agriculture, and eventual sedentarism (Reed, 1977).

The growth of settled human aggregations then led to two new imperatives: (1) special arrangements for controlling access to the physical assets—dwellings, personal objects, animals, garden plots, agricultural land—belonging to individual clusters; and (2) a common defense against other groups. From these modest beginnings, and with the emergence of a variety of sovereigns, we gradually come to observe political and economic arrangements that appear as familiar aspects of European history: a strong central ruler, obligated agricultural households cultivating land that belonged to powerful lords and sublords, and a variety of institutional arrangements governing battles of aggression and defense.

The earliest phase in this emerging European provisioning program was a gradual refinement in the reciprocal relationship between individual households and those who controlled access to land. Across western Europe, several types of hierarchical relationships bound individual families in servitude to superiors of one form or another. The terminology is familiar, though the specifics of each arrangement are often unclear—serf, peasant, vassal, and villien (or vill, perhaps leading to "village"). The basic arrangement was that of superior and inferior, of reciprocated rights and obligations—largely in terms of service and dues (or fees) falling on the family in exchange for the right to inhabit some small portion of what belonged to those occupying a higher social and economic position. The essential feature in these precapitalist relations was one of obeisance and mutuality of ties. Those on the lower social and economic rung did what their betters demanded of them.

In England, that timeless precapitalist arrangement began to change early in the fourteenth century when constant rains and cold weather precipitated three years of crop failure and severe famine (1315–1317)—the "three years without summer." A serious agrarian crisis running from 1310 to 1322 took out approximately 10 percent of the population (Hinde, 2003). There was another famine in 1322. By 1325, the population had fallen from 4.7 million to slightly over 4.0 million. Thirty years later a more profound shock arrived when the Black Plague struck. Between 1348 and 1353, total population plunged by 46 percent, and it continued on a downward trajectory for another century, reaching a low of 1.9 million in 1450 (Figure 3.1). This succession of outbreaks persisted—another major one occurred in 1361–1362—until the great London Plague of 1665–1666 (coinciding with the London Fire of 1666). Death rates in 28 scattered townships on Durham Priory estates ranged between 21 and 78 percent, with an average of

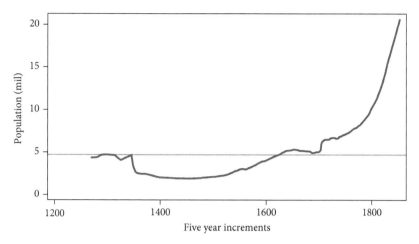

Figure 3.1. British Population, 1270–1850 (horizontal line at 1290 population of 4.75 mil.)

Source: Broadberry et al. (2015).

50 percent. The toll was over 50 percent in 16 of the 28 townships (Britnell, 1990, p. 31).

The Little Ice Age (1388–1620) overlaps with this period of severe population loss (Mann, 2002). Average temperatures fell from a long-range normal of +0.4°C in 1280 to – 0.3°C by 1650. While a swing of one-degree centigrade may not seem like much, current alarm over climate change is based on predicted increases of 0.2 degree centigrade per decade over the near future. The Plague and the continual cooling over the next 300 years combined to unleash profound disruption in livelihoods. England's population did not recover to its pre-crisis level until 1622. These changes were similar to, but more pronounced than, changes taking place throughout the Old World around this time (Campbell, 2016).

The first enclosures (which were of such controversy in economic and social history) occurred in the fourteenth century driven by severe labor shortages associated with the Plague. In the wake of the first Plague in 1348, a large farm—an estate—could absorb the death of 40 percent of its domestic household and still endure as a going concern. But it could not lose 40–45 percent of its workforce (and associated agricultural produce and income) and still expect to survive. With this new demographic reality, the delicate balance of power between landowners and those who owned only their labor power dramatically changed. As we proceed in our account of the history of the economic role of the household, it will become apparent just how alarming this profound realignment of economic advantage would turn out to be.

The loss of over 45 percent of the population—the basis of England's agricultural economy—rendered a continuation of traditional practices impossible. While a reduced population relieved the demand for food, it also reduced the supply of labor necessary to produce that food. In an age of minimal agricultural technology, the number of hands was decisive. This pronounced labor scarcity forced adjustments in land use concerning the share of arable land that could actually be sown to crops.

Now that agricultural labor was in very short supply, it is not surprising to see the beginning of rental contracts between increasingly desperate landowners and suppliers of exceedingly scarce labor power. These emerging contracts represent the earliest manifestation of the liberation of the indentured agricultural household as it gradually became the locus of actual bargaining over its embodied labor. Population shortages had rendered the household more powerful in a seller's market, and the economic nature of the traditional household was transformed forever. In hindsight, one may speculate that this was the first time that landless households gained a clear economic advantage vis-à-vis owners of land. This new relative advantage for households would be quite fleeting; it would not last beyond 1700. Indeed, the perils of the present are found in the long-run oversupply of household labor vis-à-vis the demand for labor under managerial capitalism. There is a mismatch in terms of both available skills and location (geography).

During this time, labor shortages gave rise to a new opportunity to earn a livelihood unrelated to arduous agricultural activities. This emergence of contracting over labor power within the agricultural household then began to divide family members into two groups: those who had economic opportunities (market value) outside of the home, and those who did not have such value. In other words, we see the beginnings of market-induced differentiation among individuals within a family, with the practical effect of particular individuals shedding or loosening their full-time commitments to the household as a going concern. If individual family members were now free to enter into a wage contract over access to their labor power, it became more likely that individuals might gradually leave the household entirely.

The family as a unified and tightly integrated going concern was now facing fragmentation and isolation. This emerging division of labor power would henceforth magnify the historic specialized tasks within the household—women's work, men's work, children's work—and pull those skills and aptitudes away from the hearth and out into a harsh and demanding world of organized, controlled, and monetized work. The necessity of economic survival of the household would very soon leave the family with no choice. We will see that with the passage of time, the Industrial Revolution provided just this prospect—and this necessity.

By this time, most agricultural households were not properly considered to be peasants in the classic European notion of that term. Rather, they had become quasi-independent agricultural entrepreneurs. As such, they were increasingly resentful of frequent demands for tax proceeds to underwrite the periodic wars of assorted kings. The Magna Carta of 1215 was the first such meaningful protest. While this revolt against King John was led by the several hundred major English barons of the day, the tax burden to which they objected eventually fell on their miserable tenants. And they well understood how dangerous it would be to squeeze their workers any more than they were already being weighed down by obligations. Poll taxes had been levied in 1377, 1379, and 1381 (Britnell, 1990, p. 39). Some historians imply that little came of the Peasants' Revolt (1381). However, a profound institutional innovation soon emerged—the *copyhold*.

This new land contract offered legal escape from traditional obligations (labor time on the demesne and delivery of product from "their" land to the lord) and replaced those obligations with the annual payment of rent. This new arrangement was duly recorded in the local court (manor) roll and the farmer—as head of the household—was given a copy. Land could now pass from father to son, or to whomever the parents designated, for the payment of a fee. In this institutional innovation, copyhold tenure became the equivalent of a perpetual lease between the family and the landowner. Landlords (lords) "held land of the king," while increasingly independent families "held land of the lord." Fee-simple ownership of land as we know it today was now on the horizon.

Gradually, copyhold leases gave way to what were called *beneficial leases* that could run for an extended period of years—commonly for a period of a single life (or multiples of a life). Very often, local customs discouraged landlords from raising rents during the life of such leases. The new arrangement, restricting adjustments in annual payments, predictably induced landlords to urge tenants to purchase their leases, thereby becoming freeholders of the land they had always farmed. This innovation also served to liberate rural households from exclusive dependence on agricultural labor. As above, this gentle transformation meant that for the first time in Western history, individual members of households were liberated to sell their labor power in exchange for money or other considerations. In economic terms, this was the beginning of a *market for labor* that would, in 300 years, prove to be an indispensable inducement to the emergence of the Industrial Revolution. After all, coming industrialization would have been impossible without a "reserve army" of laborers willing to work for what was on offer. As early as 1530, "20–25 percent of the [agricultural] population showed signs of belonging to landless families. By 1688 . . . two thirds of the households were landless" (Overton, 1996, p. 178). This meant that they obtained their livelihood in nonagricultural pursuits.

Throughout this post-Plague era, persistent labor shortages and high agricultural wages combined to induce important technological changes in the nature of agriculture. Newly independent farmers began to abandon labor-intensive crop production and turned to the raising of sheep—an event that fueled the emergence of fine woolens in England as well as on the Continent. The first wave of autonomous enclosures—the conversion of arable into sheep pasture—had produced a necessary realignment of land–labor ratios in agriculture. Mutton production increased significantly, as did the production of wool. Before the Plague, there were an estimated 16 million sheep. By 1500, that number had fallen to about 8 million, reflecting the correlated drop in human population. Then, after 1500, the number of sheep began a strong recovery with expected fluctuations from disease and weather conditions. By 1770, the number of sheep had recovered to its pre-Plague level and continued climbing so that by 1870 sheep numbers were approximately 28 million (Broadberry et al., 2015). Not only did the newly abundant meat improve diets, the new prevalence of spinning and weaving of wool combined to stimulate the spread of rural industrialization (cottage industry), thereby creating welcome new income to many rural households. Industrial employment in rural areas increased quite dramatically during this era (Dyer, 1994). Households were now thriving.

We see that the population crash of the late fourteenth century had unexpectedly bestowed economic agency on those with strong backs and a history of hard work. The economic chaos in the aftermath of the Plague served to re-create the traditional agricultural family—the indentured, obligated, subservient peasant—as a newly liberated *Homo economicus*. This transformation in the economic standing of the family and the individual within that family would turn out to be of profound importance as the wheel of history continued to turn.

III. The Economic Refinement of the Individual

The emergence of individualism as an idea—not in the lush salons of eighteenth-century France but embedded in the verdant agricultural landscape of fourteenth-century England—drove the gradual evolution of family-based agriculture and property relations that are with us today. By the middle of the fourteenth century, acknowledgment of the political and economic importance of the individual had begun to spread down to the lowest agricultural worker. This evidence of independence from the usual ties associated with so-called peasant agriculture coincided with the emergence of a nascent craftsman/artisan/trader mentality, and it confirmed an important role for the rise of nonagricultural economic activity in rural areas. This evolving concept of the individual as an economic agent in an agrarian economy and society was intimately related to issues of land tenure. In classical European peasant societies, land belonged to the family as a corporate entity (Macfarlane, 1978, 1987). A member of the family retained a durable claim to his or her place on that land—and to the benefits (and obligations) arising therefrom—by staying close at hand. To turn against the land was an act of self-abnegation of a commitment to the land and the family that farmed it.

As early as the thirteenth century, if not earlier—and a full two centuries before the ravages of the Black Death—individualized ownership of (and control over) land, the mode of inheritance, and an active land market had already combined to weaken peasant-like ties of the young to family land, and vice versa. Simpson (1986) traces secure inheritance of land possessed (used) by tenants to the time of Henry II in 1176. The tenant of a lord (who was, after all, a tenant of the king) could demand seisin (possession by freehold) from that lord, and this claim could not be denied. A payment of "relief" was then required. That which is held by the tenant was called a fee and can be seen as the precursor of a very contemporary legal concept (ownership by "fee-simple title").

Children were free to leave the hearth when able, or to stay and work their way into legitimate possession of the land under control of the family. Before long, land ownership had become highly individualized: "Land was bought and sold without consideration for any wider group than husband and wife. It was, in fact, treated as a commodity which belonged to individuals and not to the household" (Macfarlane, 1978, p. 80).

Central to the emergence of a labor market was the growing practice of sending children away from home at an early age—an English pattern dating from the thirteenth century (Macfarlane, 1978). On this point, there is evidence that when Adam Smith wrote (in 1776) about the nature of a market economy, he was not writing in the prospective voice of what might happen if the long-standing strictures of tradition could somehow be thrown off. Rather, he was describing what he—and others—had long observed in economic life. Adam Smith was not some exalted visionary that market fundamentalists portray him to be. He was, instead, an exceedingly adept observer and chronicler who was also able to offer conceptual explanations—theoretical insights—concerning observed practices. He was foreshadowing a similar talent displayed by Ronald Coase a century and a half later (Coase, 1937).

The percentage of "ever-married" individuals plummeted during the problematic 1600s, dropping from around 90 percent to around 70 percent by 1675. However, as that difficult century came to a close, marriage rates soared—reaching over 95 percent by around 1755. Clearly, the economy was improving. There was a predictably similar trend in swings in total fertility rates. Family formation and births seem to have risen dramatically in response to the improving economic situation of the eighteenth century. It is important to point out that this reversal of fortune for families preceded by a full century the emergence of modern industry with its massive factories and attendant urban advantages and manifold problems.

In summarizing this precapitalist period, from 1300 to 1600, we see that it was a period of profound institutional innovation in terms of: (1) individual freedom and autonomy enabled by a growing market for nonagricultural labor; (2) land tenure and the associated economic restructuring of agriculture; and (3) the gradual emergence of proto-industry and associated service activities in rural areas. Over this period, the agricultural labor force fell from nearly 60 percent of the total to less than 40 percent. The dominance of the unified family in rural households was weakened and redefined in terms of individual participation in both emerging land markets and labor markets. With this gradual fragmentation of the family in terms of income strategies, this period of economic history was of profound significance for the future economic status of the household.

Unfortunately, whatever gains were soon to be realized would not last.

IV. The Emergence of Merchant Capitalism

Very soon after 1600, a full century and a half before the acknowledged start of the Industrial Revolution, the nonagricultural labor force surpassed 50 percent (Figure 3.2). In other words, the reconstituted rural family, with its ability to engage the labor market, had given rise to a new form of rural economic activity now referred to as *merchant capitalism*. Here we see the emergence of what would come to be recognized as the *entrepreneur*. Now, members of households began to emerge as creators of specialized objects and as purveyors of those objects.

The advent of merchant capitalism in rural areas brought a much-needed infusion of cash—urgent liquidity—into many agricultural households. This new enterprise was not just the well-known cottage industry with housewives and elder daughters spinning thread, weaving small articles of fabric, baking bread, or brewing beer. Now it was husbands and sons manufacturing small wagons, agricultural implements, harnesses, wooden furniture, and assorted specialized tools. Under this evolving proto-industrialism, immediate use was made of the sporadic cash infusions into the household. This new income opportunity entailed very little fixed capital (investment). It was a mode of production—well understood by Adam Smith and David Ricardo—predicated on a small stock of *circulating capital*. Equilibrium in such an economy occurred quickly

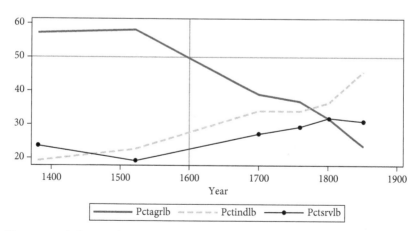

Figure 3.2. Relative Labor Shares Between Agriculture, Industry, and Services, 1381–1851

Source: Broadberry, Campbell, van Leeuwen (2013).

as demand and supply were aligned at a point determined by the productivity of labor, prevailing wages, and the inevitable leakage of money into so-called nonproductive uses—foreign campaigns, church donations, etc. But it was a profound conceptual break from what had gone before. It was *capitalism.*

We now had the mixing of labor power with the *means of labor*—capital—in a market-based system of production and remuneration. Labor was paid out of the proceeds of production made possible by that labor. Here lies the source of contention between owners of labor and owners of capital that persists to this day. As we will see, the very best way to eliminate this tension is for owners of capital to replace labor with new forms of capital—machines that automate important aspects of the workplace. Machines make no demands on the rate of pay, nor do machines care about working conditions. Machines do not get sick or expect health benefits. Vacations are of no interest to machines.

The agricultural economy until this time had been limited to the use of animals and simple tools and ploughs. Most of the output was consumed by those who brought it forth, or minimal sporadic surpluses were traded in small local markets. Now, with the advent of a new type of output from rural households, a new market channel gradually emerged. It soon became possible to purchase reliable supplies of simple household items and agricultural implements. We begin to see a profound convergence in which the limited investment possibilities in the *means of labor*—spinning wheels, small looms, simple forges, a few heavy implements, improved saws and woodworking tools, a "shopfloor"—brought new income and occupational freedom to the traditional household. Gradually, the rural family was elaborated and redefined away from the single pressing task of feeding itself. Now the rural household became a multipurpose going concern engaged in a complementary economic activity that could make good use of available labor.

For the first time in human history, there was an opportunity to break from the historic reliance on the vagaries of nature and accidents of location on a highly varied ecological landscape, and to reorganize the household into a commercial going concern. The economic possibilities meant that the rural household was increasingly faced with the most fundamental of choices in this nascent capitalism: how much of current income should be devoted to sustenance (consumption) versus how much of current income should be set aside for necessary investment to underwrite the new market-oriented capitalist enterprise. This novel dilemma must be understood as the emergence of an entirely new form of economic activity. In the long history of the agricultural family, there had of course been an obvious form of investment: how much of this year's harvest of seed must be set aside to plant next year's crops?

The most difficult time in the agricultural calendar was in the spring when food was running low and the precious seeds of last year's harvest were stored away, awaiting the obligatory task of provisioning the future. We see that abstinence—waiting—was not new to the agricultural household. This necessary delicate balance had been worked out over centuries of trial and error. The necessity of self-control in the face of such uncertainty has been traced to the emergence of the economic concept of time preference (Galor and Özak, 2016). But now the emergence of a new form of saving to allow for sustainable provisioning, the need to invest in purchased objects—a new baking oven, a new spinning wheel, a new forge—presented a different sort of challenge. A new species of uncertainty pressed in on the household. Investing in productive capital required a special ability to calculate and account for the vagaries of an unknowable future. Now, for the household to invest in the means of labor—capital assets—meant diverting scarce income away from immediate consumption.

Not only did a portion of last year's harvest have to be set aside and accounted for, now current income had to be diverted from necessary consumption and devoted to a new form of savings. Limited income had to be sent outside of the household, meaning that it was lost forever. In return, a new small stock of capital entered the household, an asset of very uncertain future value. How could the household be sure that the new asset would allow an increase in production sufficient to compensate for its sacrificed consumption? Would the painful act of saving bear sufficient rewards? History provided no lessons in this regard. The household was on its own. The central aspect of merchant capitalism, that of circulating capital, reminds us of the precarious dance that was always foremost in the mind of those who entered this brave new capitalist market. They were betting their future on the fickle mercy of a world out there, with no assurance that the world would return the favor. In economic terms, the market had succeeded in penetrating the timeless and sacred boundaries of the household. There would be no going back (Polanyi, 2001).

About a century later, shortly after the end of the Thirty Years' Wars (1618–1648), in the southeastern corner of Germany, a similar phenomenon—merchant capitalism—emerged in the Kingdom of Saxony (Tipton, 1976; Pollard, 1981). As in Britain, merchant capitalism came about as a parallel economic phenomenon alongside the historic estate-based (manorial) agriculture and the enduring influence of the guilds (Kopsidis and Bromley, 2017). In Saxony, these institutional reforms spanned the period 1650–1850 and reflect a remarkable similarity to the capitalist transition in Britain. During this period, Saxony was the most densely populated of Germany's numerous political regions, and it also enjoyed the fastest population growth. As in Britain, merchant capitalism, by stimulating rural nonagricultural economic activity, actually delayed the onset of urbanization. The reason is obvious: rural proto-industrialization was made possible by its reliance on water as the dominant power source until the 1840s when coal power became feasible. The switch from water power to coal occurred later in Germany than it had in Britain. It was actually made possible by importation of British engineers and geologists to help exploit the deep seams of coking coal found in only a few regions of Germany (Kopsidis and Bromley, 2016).

The early start in Saxony then provided the preconditions for a gradual transition after 1840 to heavier industry aided by coal and steam power. As in Britain, Saxony benefited from a long history of individualized economic activity and by a very flexible institutional framework that allowed for industrial innovation in rural areas. These conditions were reinforced by the spirit of the day. In particular, Saxony was known as Germany's "wild east" as far back as the High Middle Ages with the emergence of a settler economy based on free labor. Early capitalist mining, metal processing, and chemicals complemented the emerging textile and woodworking industries—very much aided by a vibrant cottage industry sector. The new merchant capitalists gradually transformed local craft shops into agile export industries. Soon, Saxony had become the manufacturing center in Germany, with much of the activity concentrated in the western parts of the Ore Mountains (*Erzgebirge*) south of Chemnitz, bordering the Czech Republic. The decentralized and individualistic nature of Saxon merchant capitalism helped it to flourish and be adaptive. In contrast to other emerging industrial regions in Germany, Saxon merchant capitalists ignored official regulations with impunity (Karlsch and Schäfer, 2006; Schäfer, 2016).

Officials ignored these violations because they could see for themselves the economic benefits that were beginning to emerge.

Cotton manufacturing thrived in the Vogtland and around Chemnitz. As in Britain, a large supply of landless labor was available across rural Saxony throughout the seventeenth century (Tipton, 1976). At this time, only 12 percent of the rural population was directly tied to a manorial landlord. An additional 47 percent was weakly subjugated to a manorial jurisdiction, while the remainder—40 percent—lived completely outside the manorial system. A large part of the rural population was now free to sell, mortgage, or bequeath their land as they saw fit. A diversified and stable agrarian structure emerged with the mass of the land in the hands of small and medium full-time family farmers. By 1840, with the harnessing of coal in the Ruhr basin, Germany joined Britain in the startling new venture we know today as *industrial capitalism*.

V. The Emergence of Industrial Capitalism

By the middle of the eighteenth century in Britain, and then slowly spreading to the rest of Europe, the availability of new materials (large timber, coking coal, stronger metals), and the growing scale and complexity of manufacturing—epitomized by expensive machinery and a large centralized power source—led to an eventual divorce of profound importance. Now we begin to see a gradual separation between the owners of capital—commercial land, sophisticated machines, large factories—and those who own only their labor power. Eventually, production moved out of the household, yielding to what we know as the *factory system*. This was the ultimate triumph of modern industrialization.

With these transformations, fueled by the growing need for access to credit, *industrial capitalism* gradually replaced merchant capitalism as the dominant mode of production. As employment opportunities moved out of the household and into the expanding industrial system, labor power became exclusively dependent on the *means of labor* under the control of others. Recall that under merchant capitalism, the householder owned both the necessary capital equipment that enabled his (or her) specialized trade, and the labor power that he (or she) mixed with that stock of capital. Ownership was unified and embedded in the household.

But industrial capitalism split ownership of these two essential components, moving ownership of the capital stock outside of the household. Members of households henceforth were required to find transport to those new specialized industrial locations where the means of labor now were to be found under the new ownership and control of capitalists. As a result of this profound divorce of labor from the means of labor—their agricultural land, their small machines, their baking ovens, their minor breweries and distilleries, their spinning wheels and sewing machines— owners of labor power lost control over their historic source of income. Now, the erstwhile household labor of the merchant capitalist became the estranged (disembedded) and often-remote labor of industrial capitalism. Workers were now dependent on those who owned capital for the opportunity—the good fortune—to gain access to the necessary means of labor.

The former harmony of interests inside the household of the merchant capitalist was now supplanted by a system that forced households and firms into a contentious and politically fraught embrace of necessity. Capitalists were desperate for workers, and workers were desperate for access to the means of labor—without which they would be unable to eat. The future would soon become more grim. Owners of labor power became conscious of exploitation and alienation (Box 3.1).

Text Box 3.1 The Feeling of Exploitation and Alienation

"We can now see something of the truly catastrophic nature of the Industrial Revolution. . . . people were subjected simultaneously to an intensification of two intolerable forms of relationship: those of economic exploitation and political oppression. Relations between employer and labourer were becoming both harsher and less personal; and while it is true that this increased the potential freedom of the worker . . . this "freedom" meant that he felt his *un*freedom more. But at each point where he sought to resist exploitation, he was met by the forces of employer or state, and commonly of both.

For most working people the crucial experience of the Industrial Revolution was felt in terms of changes in the nature and intensity of exploitation.

Source: E. P. Thompson. 1966. *The Making of the English Working Class*, New York: Vintage Books, pp. 198–99. (emphasis in original)

The nature and extent of this profound detachment required a radical transformation of the traditional household, and also what came to be known as the *world of work*. It was not an easy transition. There had always been some workers who, perhaps for part of the year, labored outside of the household. Local or itinerant workers might provide periodic assistance at peak times in the agricultural calendar. For the most part, these workers lived with (or very near) the family for whom they worked, and generally ate with that family. In a sense, they became part of the household for brief periods of the year. Other workers might appear from time to time to replace a leaking roof, to raise a large building, to help with some particular chore, or to provide certain necessary services. These contracts were periodic, generally for short durations, and usually transacted on a piece-work basis. Notice that these providers of occasional services were themselves integrated households in that the provider of a service often owned his own tools and means of transport. He and his family often moved through the countryside acting as an independent contractor. Transience aside, he was little different in economic structure from the integrated merchant capitalist household to whom he provided occasional services.

Industrial capitalism brought a permanent separation of the owners of capital from the owners of labor across the vast majority of the population. In Britain, by the year 1600, Figure 3.2 reveals that one-half of the population was already engaged in nonagricultural pursuits, and well into the Industrial Revolution (1800), the percentage of nonagricultural population had reached 70 percent (Broadberry, Campbell, and van Leeuwen, 2013). By this time, the massive shift to industrial capitalism was well underway, and these changes brought an increasingly contentious element to general economic relations. Indeed, the transition to industrial capitalism necessitated a redefinition of the most enduring and important component of an economy. For the first time in history, labor became a *commodity* to be bought and sold just as other factors of production—raw materials—were bought and sold in markets.

Karl Polanyi characterized this transformation by defining hired labor under industrial capitalism as a *fictitious commodity* (Polanyi, 2001). Labor is a fictitious commodity precisely because the idea of a commodity—something that is produced and then sold on markets—is not a natural or intuitive idea. Of course, the slave trade was a particularly vicious aspect of the commoditization of human labor power. But polite commerce could not endure based on slave labor, and so industrial capitalism required a dedicated and compliant labor force that was available for purchase (for "rent") by the hour or the week, but certainly not to be bought and sold.

Industrial capitalists did not wish to own their necessary labor; they were content to manage and control it. As a result, once individuals separated themselves from the household of their birth and adolescence, there was no going back. Survival depended on the sale of their labor power—12–16 hours per day, 6 days per week—to industrial capitalists. Labor power became a commodity out of necessity, and yet it was an artificial commodity—a contrivance. Labor was now merely a contrived factor of production. Used when useful—necessary or profitable—discarded otherwise.

The Industrial Revolution revealed just what this commoditization of labor would entail. It soon became apparent that the owners of capital would not willingly provide humane work conditions. It therefore fell to a reluctant Parliament—reluctant because members of Parliament were of the privileged class—to establish some semblance of decency in the dreadful work environment of the new industrial firms. In 1819, the British social reformer Robert Owen successfully persuaded Parliament to enact a law prohibiting the employment in cotton mills of children less than 9 years of age and limiting the workday for all employees under 16 years of age to 12 hours per day. In 1825 and 1831, the law was extended so that all those under 18 years of age were limited to 12-hour work days, and they could not be made to work nights until they reached the age of 21. The mill owners fought these measures so aggressively that Parliament was persuaded to refuse inspections and monitoring of compliance with the Act. There soon followed the Chimneysweeps Acts of 1834 and 1840 to protect children who were particularly vulnerable (two further acts followed in 1864 and 1875). Children were especially useful for cleaning chimneys since they could crawl into small spaces.

Following Lord Shaftesbury's Coal Mines Act of 1824, women and children were no longer permitted to be hired by coal mining companies (Checkland, 1964). Lord Sandon's Elementary Education Act of 1875 required parents to keep their children out of mines and factories and in school, and this law was followed by the 1880 Elementary Education Act extending mandatory attendance to children 5 to 10 years of age. The Elementary Education Act of 1893 raised the age of mandatory schooling to 11. The attendant drop in household income, now deprived of the pay of children, was a blow to many families. While it is anathema to modern sensibilities, child labor has always been an important source of income for poor struggling families. Even Parson Malthus failed to understand that in those difficult times, additional children contributed more to household income than they required in the way of subsistence. This pressing need of families melded well with the interests of the new capitalists who depended on cheap labor for their agreeable income.

But pressure from the emerging industrial capitalists was not about to subside. In 1844, the minimum age for entering factory work was pushed back down to 8 years of age. Finally, in a series of laws enacted between 1847 and 1853, the workday of women and children was set at 12 hours (6 a.m. to 6 p.m.) with 1½ hours for meals. The treatment of women and children in the new industrial economy moved in parallel with widespread disregard for worker safety and general working conditions. However, change was on the way. The Combination Acts, which outlawed collaboration by workers to rein in powerful mill owners, were repealed in 1824. In 1859, the Combinations of Workmen Act (the Molestation Act) made explicit the right of workers to engage in peaceful picketing (Checkland, 1964).

These legal changes, and many more, reflected new social attitudes about workers versus owners. As we have seen, the writings of both Karl Marx and Charles Dickens emphasized the growing concern about the grim prospects of the newly commoditized worker—and, as above, that often meant children and pregnant women. An emerging class of politically important industrialists had revealed itself jarringly immune to minimal concern for those who depended on access to the means of labor to fend off starvation. Slowly, the political changes mentioned above, and other related legislation, offered early signs of the shifting weight of authority as between owners of capital and owners of labor—a process that would continue into the current day.

The necessity of parliamentary prohibition of a range of horrific labor practices is a useful reminder of what it meant, at the dawn of the Industrial Revolution, for owners of capital to have at their disposal a newly commoditized worker with no legal protections. It is an illustration of what Macpherson (1962) calls the widespread exercise of *extractive powers* applied against those who would be unable to eat unless they could sell their labor to those who owned the means of labor. The eventual emergence of collective action in labor markets—unionization—slowly offered some measure of countervailing power as against that exerted by the new industrial firms.

The economic justification for collective action is straightforward. As long as there was a ready supply of workers willing to work rather than go hungry, and thus available for work at low wages, firms were free to regard any single worker as dispensable. A replacement was easy to find. The practical effect of collective action via unions was to replace the *dispensable* individual worker with a group of *indispensable* workers. That is, a firm can get by without any *particular* worker, but a firm cannot survive without *some* workers. Collective bargaining by labor unions accomplished that switch by replacing the dispensable *individual* worker with the indispensable *group* of workers. With this switch, it is no mystery why owners of capital have fought against labor unions from the earliest stages of industrial capitalism. As we will see, capitalists have managed, over the ensuing years, to destroy most labor unions. Only public-sector unions still matter, and they are now under sustained assault.

By this time, approximately 30 percent of the labor force was employed in the burgeoning service sector (Figure 3.2)—part of it under government employment, but with the majority of it in the private sector. It soon became obvious that industrial capitalism, unlike merchant capitalism, required an ever-expanding cohort of financial wizards, legal enablers, and monetary clarifiers, defenders, champions, and guardians. Indeed, the more elaborated industrial capitalism became—with its increasingly wide market penetration—the greater was the need for expert legal and financial support. This reminds us that market capitalism is an exceedingly dense and interwoven network of contractual relations. Contracts must be carefully negotiated, and most contracts eventually are breached—or the threat of breach arises along the way. Capitalism creates a demand for lawyers. We see the emerging importance of what Ronald Coase, in his classic paper on the theory of the firm (1937), would call *transaction costs*: (1) the cost of gaining information about transactional possibilities; (2) the cost of negotiating contracts concerning those transactional possibilities; and (3) the cost of enforcing those contracts once they have been consummated.

Lawyers and financial experts thrive in market capitalism where the guiding ethic is to get exactly what you want through negotiation—or with the aid of threatened litigation. As it happens, the more choices there are, the more eager participants are to pursue those choices that seem most attractive. The point is to get what you want, by whatever means necessary—through market exchange or, failing that, through the courts or the legislature.

The bulk of this early service-oriented activity was concerned with real estate acquisition and management, and with banking and financial services. As industrial capitalism gained momentum and prominence, the pace of urbanization associated with migration out of rural areas accelerated, and housing and domestic services began to emerge as important components of the burgeoning service sector. Very soon, trade and transport services became of great importance. The transformation from merchant capitalism to industrial capitalism served to follow—as well as to facilitate—the gradual move of early proto-industrial activity out of the agricultural household and into slowly urbanizing locations where the use of a central power source such as coal-fired steam could be used to good effect. This was also consistent with where the increasingly proletarianized labor force could be found and put to use.

The movement of nonagricultural activity out of the rural household into dedicated buildings and associated facilities introduced one obvious difference: a labor force that was now required to travel to and from their place of work. In Medieval Europe, indentured workers could purchase their freedom from obligated labor services to landlords for a payment of dues. This process was called *commutation*. Once liberated, the commuted labor was free to work where it could strike the best bargain. Such workers became the first "commuters." But a more profound transformation was accompanying this trend—and it persisted in those firms that had remained in rural areas, even as they began to expand and specialize. This important change concerned the nature of investment capital available to the firm. No longer could the capitalist firm rely exclusively on sporadic infusions of income to meet the needs of acquiring raw materials. Moreover, the lumpy investment needs of the growing industrial firm required access to large tranches of external finance. These requirements opened the way to what is called the *fixed capital* mode of production that was the defining essence of the new industrial economy.

In this new system, a single long-run equilibrium required the exquisite matching of supply and demand throughout the production cycle. Competition among firms drove each to make the fullest possible use of capital, now consisting of both the necessary machinery and equipment, but also the borrowed liquid capital used for payroll and other operational needs. Often these operational expenses would be covered by open lines of credit resting with external lenders. The new industrial model also brought the emerging need for flexibility in labor use—a task made more difficult by the imperative to adjust production so as to satisfy fluctuating demand, while also meeting the expectations of investors.

We see that in contrast to necessary operating capital being provided by the firm as in merchant capitalism, industrial capitalism began to require large infusions of liquidity by commercial creditors or by external investors. Borrowing, or bringing in outside investors, introduced a dramatic fissure in the industrial firm between the imperatives of agile and attentive management, and the presumed oversight prerogatives of ownership (Fama and Jensen, 1983). This is obvious when we realize that creditors have always demanded an owner's interest in the assets of the firm as collateral. Of equal importance, major equity investors have long expected a voice in the operation of the firm.

Gradually, officers of the firm—those who showed up every day to manage the enterprise—found themselves answerable not only to their carefully selected coterie of engineers, accountants, product-design experts, human resource experts, and shopfloor supervisors, but increasingly to those who had provided funding for the necessary productive assets and operational liquidity that kept the enterprise running. The triumph of the engineer that brought us the Industrial Revolution was gradually being overruled by those with control over money. One might be a president, or a chairman, or a chief operating officer, but this new industrial model meant that there was always someone else monitoring the firm's financial vital signs. And that obtrusive monitor was increasingly an external party. The industrial firm was now on a "knife's edge."

In Germany, Saxony's agrarian transformation was nearly finished when manufacturing really became industrialized—again, defined as the predominance of factory production resting on a centralized power source (coal) and using new technology and related machinery. All of these components had been known and experimented with at the beginning of the nineteenth century, but they were not widespread on a large scale until the introduction of borrowed British coal technology gained momentum after 1840–1850. The coincidental advent of rail transport accelerated the modernization of Saxon coal mining and its industrial technology. The quite decentralized nature of existing Saxon merchant capitalism had impeded initial progress, but gradually this problem was overcome.

Compared to Britain's rather centralized industrialization, the process in Saxony continued to be much more scattered. It also remained relatively diversified. Textiles had long represented the major industrial activity, but engineering and specialized manufactured products gradually came to dominate Saxon industry. Rural areas remained industrialized, and there followed the emergence of industrial villages (*Industriedörfer*) in line with the widely scattered rural population. As in Britain, these developments led to the emergence of an important class of rural resident—the industrial farmer (*Industriebauern*).

Grasping the advantages of the earlier merchant capitalism, early German industrialization remained and thrived in the countryside as it benefited from ready access to a large supply of industrious skilled labor willing to work for low wages (Schäfer, 2016). By the end of the eighteenth century, intensified British competition threatened Saxony's flourishing textile industry—largely consisting of cotton spinning and the production of fine cotton cloth. Pressure to protect the industry from British competition failed out of fear that this would threaten the prominence of the all-important Leipzig trade fair. In addition, Leipzig merchants had already beaten out British suppliers of machine yarn.

In summarizing the emergence of industrial capitalism in Europe, these two global powers—one starting in the mid-1700s, the other getting going in the mid-1800s—would together define what industrial capitalism would become. Ironically, the German Karl Marx would perfect and elaborate his biting critique of industrial capitalism from the elegant comfort of the circular Reading Room of the original British Library. He is buried in London's Highgate Cemetery. He would enjoy the irony.

VI. The Flowering of Financial Capitalism

From the beginning of industrial capitalism, there had been an acute need for very substantial tranches of financial intermediation in the operation of the industrial enterprise. The massive scale of modern industry—steel, railroads, automobiles, and trucks—would have been impossible without large infusions of borrowed capital. By the turn of the twentieth century, most industrial production was becoming focused on automobiles, clothing, household appliances that offered convenience, and electronics (radios, television, music players). These trends were somewhat suppressed during the two world wars that scarred the twentieth century, but by 1950 the capitalist production machinery swung into high gear. John R. Commons writes:

> The term "financial capitalism" is used to indicate a third stage of the capitalist system. It followed "merchant capitalism" and "industrial capitalism." The above three terms indicate, not clear historical divisions between one and the other, but indicate the relative predominance of the merchant, the

industrialist, or the banker in the evolution of capitalism. These three stages all exist at the same time in different American industries, but their historical development grows out of the capitalist evolution of western civilization. (Commons, 1970, p. 61)

And at the center of that evolution was the modern corporation—the limited liability company (LLC). The corporation would make it possible for companies to attract massive infusions of cash. In the early 1930s, the economists Adolf A. Berle and Gardiner C. Means (1932) noted that the corporate form of capitalism introduced and perfected a degree of concentrated economic power that enabled the corporation to *contend* with— notice the verb—the political power of the modern nation. Perhaps it is better to put the matter the other way around: the modern nation-state now had to *contend with* the modern corporation. That is quite a claim, but it points out that the modern corporation very soon posed a governance challenge to the modern nation-state. The assertion is doubly profound and prophetic in light of the early date of this observation in the early 1930s, long before the emergence and exponential growth of the truly multinational corporations such as Royal Dutch Shell, ExxonMobil, Toyota, General Motors, General Electric, Samsung, Apple, Volkswagen, BP, Berkshire Hathaway, and Microsoft. The ability of such financial behemoths to overwhelm governments in most countries where they operate is a phenomenon to behold. The issue is not just that these corporations are too big to fail. The proper concern is that they are perhaps too big to abide. Indeed, Berle and Means observed that "[t]he law of corporations, accordingly, might well be considered as a potential constitutional law for the new economic state; while business practise assumes many of the aspects of administrative government" (Berle and Means, 1932, p. 59).

To grasp the enormity of financial capitalism, consider the sector breakdown of the 50 largest global corporations in 2016. Leaving aside the 12 that are state-owned enterprises—10 in China, one in Japan, and the American Federal National Mortgage Association (Fannie Mae)—seven firms concern financial services, six of them are automotive firms, five are in oil and gas, five are in electronics and telecommunications, five are retail (including Amazon), and three are in health care and pharmaceuticals. If we include the five financial firms that are state-owned enterprises, we see that 12 of the world's largest 50 corporations, including Berkshire Hathaway (which is classified as a conglomerate), brings the number of financial services firms to

13—26 percent of the 50 largest corporations in the world. No other classification comes close.[1]

As if the large size of these international corporations is not suggestive of their political heft, they and their lesser colleagues leave little to chance. In 2010, there were 92,000 trade and professional associations in America, of which over 2,500 have selected Washington, D.C., as their base of operation.[2] The proximity to congressional deliberations cannot be accidental. We need not dwell long on the profound role of corporate money in politics to understand that in 1932 Berle and Means grasped an important point about the modern corporation as a core component of financial capitalism. It would be difficult to imagine that very many of these 92,000 trade and professional associations are organized for the purpose of advancing—or merely protecting—the interests of either workers or consumers (households).

The financial crisis of 2007–2009, fueled by excessive leverage and a blossoming of new exotic financial devices and ploys, may appear as the simple result of recent trends in the perverse financialization of global capitalism. However, the meltdown—now referred to as the Great Recession—was actually the delayed effect of events that began in the 1980s. It was then that the world

> saw the emergence of international capital movement as a dominant feature of the economic relations among nation-states. The resulting pressures on exchange rates, balances of payments, and trade patterns have disconcerted all participants—those who make national economic policy, as well as international financiers and ordinary citizens. Perhaps the most striking episode was the collapse of the world's stock markets during the week of 19 October 1987, the suddenness, sharpness, and inclusiveness of which took all observers by surprise. (Neal, 1993, p. 1)

Almost a decade later, the Asian financial crisis of 1997 started in Thailand, which was then suffering under unsustainable debt. The animating event was an attack by international currency traders on the Thai baht. Soon, a number of rather fragile countries were made more vulnerable by this event, especially Indonesia, Laos, Malaysia, the Philippines, Brunei, and Vietnam. The more stalwart economies of South Korea, Hong Kong, China, Singapore, Japan, and Taiwan also suffered. The International Monetary Fund was required to step in to rescue South Korea, Thailand, and Indonesia with $40 billion in loans. The president of Indonesia was forced to resign. A similar fate struck down the prime minister of Thailand. Other governments in the region survived, though much weakened. It would seem that Berle and Means were profoundly alert to what the future was to hold.

We are now firmly in the era of financial capitalism—a system of massive corporations dependent on the rapid movement of liquidity around the world. As we watch the residue of the Great Recession and reflect on the Asian financial crisis of 1997, there is growing evidence that global capitalism may indeed pose a serious threat to the political stability of the modern nation-state.

VII. The Advent of Managerial Capitalism

The fundamental economic challenge is often thought to be one of scarcity—of land, of raw materials, of energy, of skilled labor, of capital, and of managerial skill. However, it would be a mistake to assume that scarcity is the essential economic problem. The fundamental economic problem is what to believe about what is the best action to take in a specific choice situation. In other words, the core economic problem is our ability as discerning humans to grasp and process *data* from the world so that it becomes *information* that can then be harnessed in the service of our next move. Humans are smart and clever problem solvers, but we are not perfect because our grasp of the world is never all it should be. Note that this is not a complaint about human stupidity. It is an observation about the idiosyncratic and inscrutable world in which we live, and the reality of our cognitive limits with respect to what can be apprehended, retained, processed, and acted upon. As Nietzsche observed, we are, after all, "human, all too human."

This implies that all economic activity is a learning and experimental task. Actually, *living* is a learning and experimental task. We are back to the Greek idea that economics is about managing the household. Notice that there are two dimensions to this problem of fixing our belief about what ought to be done in that managerial imperative.

The first aspect of this challenge is knowing which data about the world—and our place in it—must be processed and turned into information so that it is possible to figure out what ought to be done at the moment. We may consider this to be a problem of the individual. The hunter-gatherer, the early agriculturalist, and the merchant capitalist were all rather solitary decision makers confronted with an abundance of data ("facts") about the world and their limited capacity to master that world as they went about securing a livelihood. They each faced the problem of arriving at settled belief about what would be best to do in specific situations. Their world—and their experiences—were varied and often quite unexpected, but they confronted that world and those lived experiences, and they adapted. They could focus, and they were generally able to reach plausible decisions that kept their respective going concerns indeed going.

The second aspect of this problem of fixing belief began to manifest itself only when merchant capitalism gradually gave way to industrial capitalism. With the arrival of large-scale industrial activity, the solitary hunter-gatherer, or early agriculturalist, or indeed the dedicated merchant capitalist, soon realized that survival in the new economy was impossible without a little help from others. The somewhat "unitary" going concern of the past was forced to give way to the behaviorally fragmented factory, the large commercial enterprise, and eventually the global corporation. Now it seems that a large number of people needed to arrive at a rather coherent and shared fixed belief. After all, too many cooks spoil the broth.

In 2014, there were over 19,000 firms in the United States each of which employed more than 500 people, with the average number of employees per firm standing at 3,312 (U.S. Bureau of Labor Statistics, 2017). Effectively managing over 3,000 employees presents severe information problems. As these new commercial firms continued to grow in size and scope, it was necessary that elaborate governance (managerial) arrangements be created, refined, and sustained. This introduction of various forms of hierarchy introduced yet another new impediment to clarity and accountability inside of the going concern. We encounter the problem of agency. Specifically, how can a large, complex organization be structured so that once the authorized decision makers have made up their minds, all others in the organization can be enlisted in the quite specific behaviors that will ensure that the wishes of these decision makers—called principals—will be properly carried out by those whose job it is to do precisely that?

This challenge has occupied some of the best minds in economics, particularly Oliver Williamson (1985, 2002, 2005). These agents of the principals—called employees—require watching, encouragement, sanctioning, and perhaps dismissal. The second-order information problem concerns incentives (Fama and Jensen, 1983; Laffont and Martimort, 2002). In plain terms, contemporary capitalism is trapped by the vexing challenge of managing delegation. As the scope and enormity of delegation increase, the burden of control and coordination—of coherent firm governance—is magnified. And with consistent growth of the precarious nature of financial manipulation within and among firms—exemplified by the predatory inclinations of hedge funds and private equity funds—it is now appropriate to suggest that we have entered the fourth phase of capitalism.

I call it *managerial capitalism*. Here, the *wrangler* rules. The entrepreneur of merchant capitalism surrendered his autonomy to the engineer of industrial capitalism. The engineer was soon pushed aside by the money managers and bankers of financial capitalism. Now, it seems reasonable to suggest that the financial wizards are answerable to the wrangler. Someone very meticulous is now minding the store. Recall that the accounting firm of Arthur Andersen was allegedly playing the role of watchdog (comptroller) to the scandal-ridden energy operation known as Enron. The fallout of that arrangement destroyed Arthur Andersen. Large firms now find good reason to keep their wrangler close at hand—and accountable. In the aftermath, U.S. laws placed corporate officials under legal liability for the veracity of the financial dealings of the firms they managed. This public scrutiny of financial dealings, and the associated single-minded commitment inside of the large corporation to financial probity, implies a further narrowing of the core commitment bearing down on the global corporation. It might be characterized as watching every single penny.

It should not be assumed that this pecuniary obsession is confined to the very large international corporations. Since the Great Recession, a large number of firms find themselves under severe financial pressure. Many large retail firms are closing outlets—Sears and J. C. Penney come to mind. Online retailers—most prominently Amazon—are pressing in on conventional retailers with a vengeance. It seems that no sector is safe. Something as personal and domestic as grocery shopping is now under the extraordinary threat signaled by Amazon's acquisition of Whole Foods. Is nothing sacred? The disrupters are on the move. Who is watching these forces of disorder?

VIII. How Stands the Household?

It seems that the economic history of the Western world is an ongoing process of displacing owners of labor power from their necessary access to the means of labor. In precapitalist times, the essential means of labor was natural capital—open land, wild animals and plants, water resources—freely available for beneficial use by hunter-gatherers. When land and forests became the exclusive domain of a small class of individuals, ownership emerged and with it the right to exclude. Private property is celebrated for what it allows fortunate owners to accomplish. One of those accomplishments is to shut out everyone else. Those who are landless are at the mercy of those who own land. Henry George captured what that exclusion meant in practice:

> Place one hundred men on an island from which there is no escape, and whether you make one of those men the absolute owner of the other ninety-nine or the absolute owner of the soil of the island, will make no difference either to him or to them. (George, 1955, p. 347)

Some economists celebrate this power to exclude as the beginning of civilization (North and Thomas, 1970, 1977). Jean-Jacques Rousseau insisted that this was the beginning of a tyranny of private avarice (Rousseau, 1994). In the seventeenth century, individuals previously at the mercy of landlords gradually gained ownership rights to the land they farmed. Soon the emerging merchant capitalist became the owner of the minimal stock of capital that allowed him or her to generate a new income stream from their labors on their own capital. But industrialism then emerged to destroy that historic nexus. From that time forward, nonagricultural labor would lose the opportunity to retain control of the means of labor.

As industrial capitalism transmogrified into financial capitalism, and then eventually into managerial capitalism, the tenuous access to the means of labor would become increasingly precarious. We have now reached the point where it seems reasonable to ask whether or not workers ought to have a right of access to the means of labor—a guaranteed job. Others will quickly counter that such questions are inappropriate under capitalism. Therein lies the essential tension.

Notes

1. https://en.wikipedia.org/wiki/List_of_largest_companies_by_revenue. Accessed July 16, 2017.
2. http://www.npr.org/2011/05/25/136646070/time-for-associations-to-trade-in-their-past. Accessed July 15, 2017.

References

Berle, Adolf A., and Gardiner C. Means. 1932. *The Modern Corporation and Private Property*, New York: Macmillan.

Britnell, R. H. 1990. "Feudal Reaction after the Black Death in the Palatinate of Durham," *Past and Present*, 128(1): 28–47.

Broadberry, Stephen, Bruce M. S. Campbell, and Bas van Leeuwen. 2013. "When Did Britain Industrialise? The Sectoral Distribution of the Labour Force and Labour Productivity in Britain, 1381–1851," *Explorations in Economic History*, 50: 16–27.

Broadberry, Stephen, Bruce M. S. Campbell, Alexander Klein, Mark Overton, and Bas van Leeuwen. 2015. *British Economic Growth: 1270–1870*, Cambridge: Cambridge University Press.

Bureau of Labor Statistics. 2017. U.S. Government.

Campbell, Bruce M. S. 2016. *The Great Transition: Climate, Disease and Society in the Late-Medieval World*, Cambridge: Cambridge University Press.

Checkland, S. G. 1964. *The Rise of Industrial Society in England: 1815–1885*, London: Longmans.

Coase, Ronald. 1937. "The Nature of the Firm," *Economica* 4: 386–405.

Commons, John R. 1970. *The Economics of Collective Action*, Madison: University of Wisconsin Press.

Dyer, Christopher. 1994. *Standards of Living in the Later Middle Ages*, Cambridge: Cambridge University Press.

Fama, Eugene F., and Michael C. Jensen. 1983, "Separation of Ownership and Control," *Journal of Law and Economics* 26: 301–25.

Galor, Oded, and Ömer Özak, 2016. "The Agricultural Origins of Time Preference," *American Economic Review*, 106(10): 3064–103.

George, Henry. 1955 (1905). *Progress and Poverty*, New York: Doubleday, Page & Co.

Hinde, Andrew. 2003. *England's Population*, London: Arnold.

Karlsch, R., and M. Schäfer. 2006. *Wirtschaftsgeschichte Sachsens im Industriezeitalter*, Leipzig: Edition Leipzig.

Kopsidis, Michael, and Daniel W. Bromley. 2016. "The French Revolution and German Industrialization: Dubious Models and Doubtful Causality," *Journal of Institutional Economics*, 12(1): 161–90.

Kopsidis, Michael, and Daniel W. Bromley. 2017. "Expliquer la modernisation économique allemande: La Révolution française, les réformes prussiennes et l'inévitable continuité du changement," *Annales. Histoire, Sciences Sociales*, 72(4): 1117–56.

Laffont, Jean-Jacques, and David Martimort. 2002. *The Theory of Incentives*, Princeton, NJ: Princeton University Press.

Macfarlane, Alan. 1978. *The Origins of English Individualism*, Oxford: Blackwell.

Macfarlane, Alan. 1987. *The Culture of Capitalism*, Oxford: Blackwell.

Macpherson, C. B. 1962. *The Political Theory of Possessive Individualism*, Oxford: Oxford University Press.

Mann, Michael. 2002. "Little Ice Age," in Michael MacCracken and John Perry (eds.), *Encyclopedia of Global Environmental Change*, Chichester, UK: Wiley.

Neal, Larry. 1993. *The Rise of Financial Capitalism: International Capital Markets in the Age of Reason*, Cambridge: Cambridge University Press.

North, Douglass, and Robert P. Thomas. 1970. "An Economic Theory of the Growth of the Western World," *Economic History Review*, 23(1): 1–17.

North, Douglass C., and Robert P. Thomas. 1977. "The First Economic Revolution," *Economic History Review*, 30: 229–41.

Overton, Mark. 1996. *Agricultural Revolution in England*, Cambridge: Cambridge University Press.

Polanyi, Karl. 2001. *The Great Transformation*, Boston: Beacon Press.

Pollard, S. 1981. *Peaceful Conquest. The Industrialization of Europe 1760–1970*, Oxford: Oxford University Press.

Reed, Charles A. 1977. *Origins of Agriculture*, The Hague: Mouton.

Rousseau, Jean-Jacques. 1994. *Discourse on Inequality*, Oxford: Oxford University Press.

Schäfer, M. 2016. *Eine andere Industrialisierung. Die Transformation der sächsischen Textilexportgewerbe 1790–1890*, Stuttgart: Franz Steiner.

Simpson, A. W. B. 1986. *A History of the Land Law*, Oxford: Clarendon Press.

Tipton, F. B. 1976. *Regional Variations in the Economic Development of Germany During the Nineteenth Century*, Middletown: Wesleyan University Press.

Williamson, Oliver E. 1985. "Assessing Contract," *Journal of Law, Economics, and Organization* 1: 177–208.

Williamson, Oliver E. 2002. "The Theory of the Firm as Governance Structure: from choice to contract," *Journal of Economic Perspectives*, 16(3): 171–95.

Williamson, Oliver. 2005. "The Economics of Governance," *American Economic Review*, 95(2): 1–18.

PART II
THE GREAT UNRAVELING

Managerial capitalism exposes the fatal
defect in societies organized as meritocracies.

Whether in the metropolitan core,
or in the isolated periphery,
the optimistic promise of the Enlightenment
is now understood to have been a false hope.

~~~~~~~~~~~~~~~~

Possessive individualism is destructive of personhood.

4

The Cleaved Core

The evolutionary trajectory of capitalism has now rendered the household precarious, economically disadvantaged, and vulnerable to the whims of firms under the authoritarian grip of the wrangler. Stagnant living standards for the vast majority of households in the metropolitan core is evidence that most households have been reduced to peripatetic hustlers in order to survive. Job loss haunts many areas within the core. Worker protections have been reduced to a minimum and political alienation is on the rise. The Brexit decision in Britain, the election of an angry outsider to the presidency of the United States, and the rise of right-wing parties in Europe signal the extent to which households have become marginalized and angry.

I. The Hedgehog and the Fox

[T]here exists a great chasm between those, on the one side, who relate everything to a single central vision, one system, less or more coherent or articulate, in terms of which they understand, think and feel—a single, universal organizing principle in terms of which alone all that they are and say has significance—and, on the other side, those who pursue many ends, often unrelated and even contradictory, connected if at all, only in some de facto way, for some psychological or physiological cause, related to no moral or aesthetic principle. These last lead lives, perform acts and entertain ideas that are centrifugal rather than centripetal; their thought is scattered or diffused, moving on many levels, seizing upon the essence of a vast variety of experiences and objects for what they are in themselves, without, consciously or unconsciously, seeking to fit them into, or exclude them from, any one unchanging, all-embracing, sometimes self-contradictory and incomplete, at times fanatical, unitary inner vision. (Berlin, 1953, p. 2)

Isaiah Berlin's rather belabored phrasing in this statement comes from his classic "The Hedgehog and the Fox." His story was inspired by claims attributed to Homer—and popularized by Archilochus—that some individuals are hedgehogs, while others are foxes (Bowra, 1940). The first individual described by Berlin is the hedgehog—focused, driven, centripetal, and motivated by a single dominant organizing principle. The second individual is the fox—a multipurpose, wily, broad-spectrum opportunist, and a centrifugal pursuer of a number of tasks. The peripatetic fox knows many things—the hedgehog knows one big thing.

I invoke this quaint imagery because it seems promising as we ponder the workings of managerial capitalism now unfolding in parts of the metropolitan core. Of course, there are variations across these different nations, so perhaps the account is most relevant to those countries that have evolved further down the path of managerial capitalism, primarily the United States and Britain. We can think of the story of the fox and the hedgehog as a conceptual device (Northrop, 1967). Concepts are diagnostic aids—metaphors—that help us to answer the "why" question. Concepts gain currency if they are "good to think with." Perhaps this zoological allusion from Homer will be a useful conceptual device when we seek to assess and diagnose the behavior of households and firms in the early stages of *managerial capitalism.*

In the previous chapter, I suggested that the defining trait of managerial capitalism is personified by the *wrangler.* As the successor of financial capitalism, managerial capitalism necessarily inherited a stark and demanding commitment—an internal behavioral imperative—to careful financial management. After all, if the financial fundamentals of the firm become misaligned, aggressive and predatory private equity funds (PEFs) and hedge funds (HFs)—recent creatures of financial capitalism—will swoop in to acquire and then resell or "rationalize" the mismanaged firm. The existence of these financial sharks is the inevitable manifestation of financial capitalism, and they define the reason for a transition into managerial capitalism. Private equity funds and hedge funds produce nothing. Their sole purpose is to generate earnings for investors in such funds through the buying and selling of existing firms.

Hedge funds accumulate large tranches of investment capital from "ultra-high-net-worth" individual subscriptions and then move that holding of bundled money around in pursuit of firms (assets) that will yield an immediate return. Such funds will invest in almost anything. They are not making things or serving customers; rather, they are making money from firms that do that. The best hedge funds pick an early target, overwhelm resistance with their financial heft, and then resell their acquisitions for a quick financial gain. The immediate gain allows these funds to continue preying down a hierarchy of investment possibilities, magnifying their financial clout as they go. The recent ravages of the U.S. retail sector—notably Sears—has been exacerbated by the financial machinations of a hedge fund.[1] Sophisticated computer programs and readily available data allow a highly granular analysis of a large number of investment possibilities. Mining those data is the hedge fund's métier.

By way of contrast, private equity funds exist to create longer-term gains through purchasing underperforming firms (bundles of assets and their management) and subjecting them to the harsh discipline of what is called the "deal funnel." Managers of private equity funds often have specialized knowledge of particular types of firms, and so their predatory initiatives are informed by the set of technical and sector skills unique to each fund. We might think of this activity as somewhat like boot camp—not for young recruits, but for seasoned owners and managers who have become inattentive to the pennies. In essence, bloated firms are slimmed down through ruthless "scrunching" until their new, leaner management structure and cost profile make them attractive to investors. Private equity funds rehabilitate underperforming going concerns so that they are attractive to a new array of buyers. But they very often saddle these reconstituted firms with enormous debt—the better to reward the individuals who are responsible for the scrunching and layoffs.

Theorists who specialize in principal–agent models and incentive alignment assure us that the presence of these economic remodelers is beneficial because they purge the economic gene pool of firms that are unfit to survive. In a dynamic sense, ridding the economy of such firms prevents them from passing on their flawed behavioral practices—their defective business model—into the future. The animating idea here is that the economy is better off with them gone because their sloth prevented consumer prices from sinking to yet unimagined lows. Such firms would eventually die off anyway, so it's better to buy them, rationalize them, and then sell them to others for a nice financial gain. Since the individuals applying the necessary economizing discipline have no historic commitment to the firm, their radical surgery is easily imposed. As Joseph Schumpeter reminds us, capitalism eats its children. "Creative destruction" is the common phrase for this process.

This is all well and good for the future of capitalism—or is it? What of the workers in this imposed Darwinian contest? It can be no surprise that a high-cost and perhaps bloated labor force is often the first place where savings can be achieved. Older workers are often paid more than younger workers, and so they can be discarded as part of necessary downsizing—employers being careful not to make it seem like there is discrimination against older workers. Launching *labor-saving* technical change is another popular move. The artful language would suggest that the "saved labor" is being held in a special bank until it can be redeployed in some future employment opportunity. In fact, saved labor is just put out on the street—free to find work, if it can, elsewhere. That this prospect is made more difficult by the ongoing rationalization of all underperforming firms under widespread managerial capitalism actually means that labor which has been shed by firms undergoing scrunching and the funnel treatment usually remains on the sidelines. Alternative employment can be difficult for many victims of the deal funnel. And we wonder why some voters are angry.

Notice that individual firms under managerial capitalism do not themselves need to be acquired by the predatory PEF/HF sector. The mere existence of such funds, whose defining purpose is to prey on suboptimal—inefficient—going concerns, sends a strong signal to all firms that they had better get things right or they too will be cannibalized by these predatory surgical specialists. The credible threat is sufficient to send a strong signal throughout the capitalist market economy. Get lean or be eaten. Managerial capitalism is now animated by the carefully monitored discipline of the comptroller, and the assiduous whip hand of the wrangler. Shareholders applaud every move as labor costs and other alleged inefficiencies are squeezed out of the cumbersome firm. Workers are easily dispensed with.

There is little acknowledgment that this quest for efficiency inside firms is, at the same time, a war on households. Resistance to labor costs began with the advent of industrial capitalism in the mid-eighteenth century. Labor–management disputes were the earliest manifestation of the gradual transition away from merchant capitalism as it was being replaced by industrial capitalism. In fact, such disputes likely date from the first time a merchant capitalist found it necessary to take on an apprentice or helper. Such tension is at the core of principal–agent relations. It was this conflict that precipitated the emergence of collective action by workers, and it continues today as workers seek the support of unions. Indeed, the brief history of capitalism—400 years at most—is marked by little else.

In the United States, there is no national legislation to legitimize and establish unions, or to require labor participation in corporate affairs. Rather, things are made to *look* democratic. Union representation must be approved by a vote of all workers in a particular "bargaining unit." Notice the gloss of democracy by requiring workers to decide if they want to be represented by a union. Looked at differently, it is a vote as to whether workers will stand united or whether they will continue to compete against each other for jobs, higher wages, and improved work conditions.

Firms are not in doubt that they prefer workers to compete against each other. Such certification elections are often contentious, hard fought, and in recent times have produced outcomes that owners of capital much prefer. Such elections inevitably divide a firm's workforce into contending camps. It does not take much thought to realize just how unpleasant such elections can be. Commercial firms are never silent participants in these elections. Owners and managers are clear in their statements about what is at stake. They are likewise not subtle about threats of what just might happen if the vote to unionize is favorable.[2]

The advent of managerial capitalism has put the historically fraught provisioning imperative of households at the exquisite mercy of comptrollers and financial wranglers. Most firms now behave like hedgehogs, with all attention focused on one big thing. That big thing is market valuation in the eyes of shareholders or potential buyers. Nothing else matters. The officers of such firms, whose compensation contracts abound with performance incentives tied to market share, growth, and market valuation, understand very well this intense unitary focus and therefore adjust their management strategies accordingly. Costs are necessarily reduced with ruthless pressure on suppliers. And of course, growth in the sheer size of firms renders them extraordinarily exacting and forceful in their pursuit of cost reductions. Walmart and Amazon are notorious belligerents in this regard. They are too big to resist. Relentless pressure on labor costs becomes even more sustained and thorough. So-called burdensome regulations and taxes become prime targets in this multifront war on costs. Political allies are crucial in this program of cost reduction.

A new front has opened up in this regard, led by corporate giants Walmart, Home Depot, Target, Kohl's, Lowe's, Nordstrom, Best Buy, Menards, and Walgreens. The argument that arises is how to assess their stores for local property taxes. Rather than being taxed on the basis of their revenue, these corporations want their property taxes to be based on the value of nearby vacant lots and similar abandoned structures. These so-called dark-store lawsuits now plague a number of municipalities. In Michigan, such dark-store appeals reduced local revenue over a four-year period by $100 million. In Texas, it is estimated that these lawsuits, if successful, could cost local governments over $2.5 billion annually. And since necessary local government services are not reduced by these legal maneuvers, the existing property tax burden will be shifted to—you guessed it—households. Hedgehogs know one big thing, and the harried foxes are encumbered by the artful cost-shifting game now underway.[3]

Recall that on the demand side of the market, firms can only appeal to customers to purchase what they hope to sell. Constant attention to product quality, to advertising, and to promotional campaigns are standard aspects of this necessary work on the demand side. But all such efforts are mere pleadings. Things are different on the supply (cost) side. Owners of firms can work strategically to influence politicians about the need for lower taxes and to lobby against so-called regulatory interference in the internal workings of the private firm. As above, firms can keep up focused hostility to any initiative that will raise wage rates or their total payroll. Firms will threaten to relocate where the business climate is more favorable. Politicians cower. The game of "Venue Shopping" is a central aspect of such threats (Box 4.1).

Text Box 4.1 Enticements and Venue-Shopping

In the late summer of 2017, the Taiwanese technology giant Foxconn signed a tentative agreement with the state of Wisconsin to create a large electronics factory in the state. The promise from Foxconn implied that it would create 35,000 jobs—13,000 in the installation and an additional 22,000 in related activities elsewhere in the state. The facility, covering 20 million square feet, would create a campus consisting of approximately 1,000 acres. The states of Michigan, Illinois, Indiana, Ohio, Pennsylvania, and Texas were also in the competition for this commercial prize. A major announcement from the White House declared that American manufacturing was coming back. President Donald Trump was puffed up with pride. Governor Scott Walker—more so.

Why did Foxconn pick Wisconsin over six other states? First, the state of Wisconsin promised $3 billion in taxpayer-funded subsidies. With 5.9 million residents (2.3 million households), each household in the state will be subsidizing Foxconn to the tune of $1,304. Each of the promised 13,000 Foxconn jobs will cost Wisconsin taxpayers $136,364. The company will be excused from complying with existing state environmental regulations. Foxconn will be allowed to reroute streams, to construct new artificial waterways that will connect to natural streams, and then to discharge materials into wetlands without review by the state's Department of Natural Resource. Foxconn will also be exempt from a requirement that it obtain approval from the Public Service Commission before building and relocating transmission lines. Existing rules for projects under the state's Tax-Increment Financing program will also be waived. The state also promised major freeway modifications in the immediate area that the governor now wishes to call "Wisconn (not Silicon) Valley." Total subsidies for the Foxconn operation will amount to $15,000– $19,000 per job—annually. This compares to an annual average for such inducement packages of $2,457 per job (Nelson D. Schwartz, Patricia Cohen, and Julie Hirschfeld Davis, *New York Times*, July 27, 2017).

When early reactions to the Foxconn arrangement began to surface, the governor sniped that the skeptics could "go suck on lemons" (Molly Beck, *Wisconsin State Journal*, July 29, 2017).

But wait, in late January 2019, Foxconn made the stunning announcement that "[i]n Wisconsin we're not building a factory." They may hire a few researchers and engineers. So much for the promised blue-collar jobs. The state of Wisconsin has already spent money to build necessary roads, some facilities, and necessary compensation to families forced to move out of the way. This is not the first time Foxconn has misled gullible politicians (Danielle Paquette, "Foxconn's Plan for a Giant Wisconsin Factory Now Looks Uncertain," *The Washington Post*, January 30, 2019).

There is much talk about firms that are "too big to fail." We see here the idea that global corporations are too big to ignore. When such firms approach governments—whether national or local—their ability to exert political pressure as a price for creating jobs, renders politicians helpless. And, in many instances, they are left looking foolish.

Large corporations will go to extraordinary lengths to extract financial inducements and concessions from federal and local governments. A recent survey reveals that American states, counties, and cities hand over $80 billion each year to private companies in such deals.[4] They expect side-payments to bless a particular location with their jobs and supply chains, and they expect side-payments to remain in place once they learn of a more promising prospect elsewhere. It resembles extortion. In early November 2018, Amazon—the world's most valuable brand (at $151 billion)—managed to wrest approximately $2 billion in subsidies and tax breaks to locate new headquarters facilities in northern Virginia and New York City.[5] Subsequent publicity led Amazon to withdraw from New York City. It seems that over 230 cities had been pursuing this prize, with the state of Maryland offering approximately $6.5 billion in financial inducements, and another $2 billion in upgrades to local infrastructure. Columbus, Ohio, agreed to waive all property taxes for 15 years.[6]

While corporate giants succeed in gaining generous financial inducements from local and state government coffers, millions of households are forced to behave like foxes, constantly scavenging for plausible livelihood prospects. Like the wily fox, individual households must become opportunistic. The reality of Marx's reserve army of unemployed hovers as a large horde of competitors—all seeking access to the ever diminishing supply of gainful employment. With this competitive climate among households, it cannot be a surprise that the presence of immigrants and the prospect of more of them become perceived among many workers as an existential threat. The apocryphal "Polish plumber" is at the core of stories of frustration throughout western Europe.

The 2016 British vote to leave the European Union was driven, in the main, by the fear of immigrants. But clarity is required. The immigrants of concern in Britain were not "the other" from Syria, Libya, and Senegal. Britain, like all member states of the European Union, has complete control over that alleged menace from outside of the European Community. That is why the so-called Calais Jungle exists just across the Channel from England. The immigrants of potential nuisance to British workers are the citizens of other European Union members—Bulgaria, Romania, and, yes, Poland. Once again, the prevailing mental state of workers in managerial capitalism—now like wary foxes—seems to be that of deep abiding anxiety about what the future will bring. The life of a scavenger and opportunist is a life of uncertainty and dread. It is too easy to imagine all manner of looming threats. The nervous fox rarely sleeps; he is always in pursuit of fleeting sustenance.

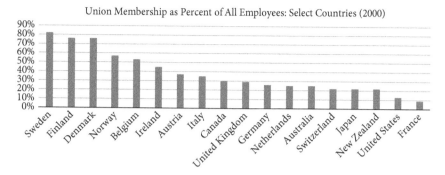

Figure 4.1. Union Membership as Percent of All Employees

Source: NationMaster http://www.nationmaster.com/country-info/stats/Labor/Trade-union-membership#, accessed December 12, 2016.

Today, fewer than 12 percent of all U.S. workers are protected by unions. Comparable shares for selected other countries are seen in Figure 4.1. In the United States, the year 2015 saw public-sector union membership at 35.2 percent of the total workforce, while in the private sector, union membership had been driven down to 6.7 percent.[7] In 1979, there were over 20 million unionized workers, and by 2013 that number had dropped by 28 percent to 14.5 million workers.[8] Much of the decline is due to the precipitous drop in U.S. manufacturing employment. But the rest of the decline came from the shifting public view of unionization against the current political worldview of "free" labor markets versus those with unions. Wage stagnation over the past several decades is often attributed to this decline in the presence of unionized workers. Capitalists are pleased, while workers are increasingly sullen. It seems that possessive individualism has turned workers into their own adversaries.

With weakened worker protection and the growth in part-time work, fragmented labor markets—individuals working several jobs, each of which might entail 16–20 hours per week—now seem to be the norm in many service industries. These conditions tend to atomize the workforce, thereby making collective action even more difficult to arrange and sustain. As above, this new "world of work" keeps many workers insecure and on edge. It is especially pronounced in the services sector.

In Figure 4.2, we see that the level of *involuntary* part-time work fluctuates along with the unemployment rate. Both seem somewhat cyclical. Following the Great Recession (2007–2009), both were quite high. Since the Recession,

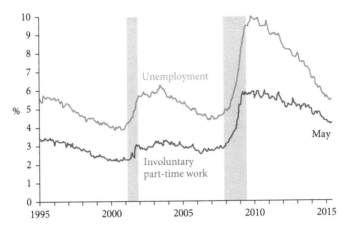

Figure 4.2. Unemployment and Involuntary Part-Time Work, 1995–2015
Source: FRBSF Economic Letter, 2015–2019, June 8, 2015, "Involuntary Part-Time Work: Here to Stay?" Rob Valletta and Catherine van der List.

the decline in unemployment has been more rapid than the decline in involuntary part-time work. But the rate of involuntary unemployment is 30–40 percent above its level during previous recoveries.

In 2014, slightly over 80 percent of total U.S. employment was in the services sector. Of that share, slightly under 13 percent was in the professional and business services, with an equal share in state and local government. Third in importance came health care and social assistance. These job categories were followed by retail trade, and jobs in the leisure and hospitality industry. These last three categories—health care and social assistance, retail, and leisure and hospitality—account for over 40 percent of all service-sector employment.[9] And it is here that fragmented labor markets tend to dominate. As for the traditional work of an "industrial" economy, in 2014 only 9.9 percent of the U.S. workforce was engaged in manufacturing, less than 5 percent in construction, and 0.4 percent in mining. Agriculture, forestry, fishing, and hunting accounted for 1.5 percent.

The United States, like most developed nations, is now a service economy. These employment categories are depicted in Figure 4.3. For those politicians and commentators who place so much faith in the revival of manufacturing, the proportion of employment in manufacturing fails to offer much encouragement. Consider Figure 4.4. Here we see an index of manufacturing output compared to total employment in manufacturing. The answer to this obvious

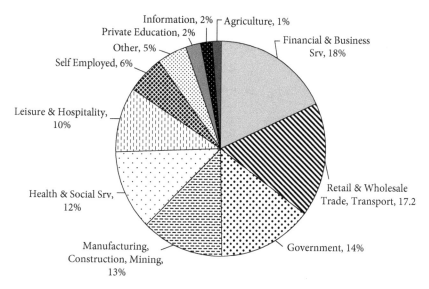

Figure 4.3. Share of U.S. Employment by Sector, 2014

Source: U.S. Bureau of Labor Statistics, 2017.

Figure 4.4. U.S. Manufacturing Employment and Index of Manufacturing Output, 1985–2016

Source: Thomson Data Stream: Business Insider, chart-2016-12.

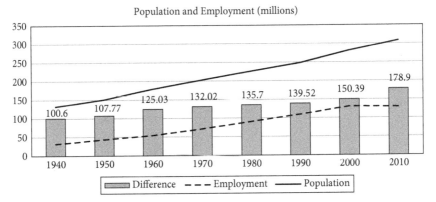

Figure 4.5. Trajectory of Population and Employment
Source: https://www.bls.gov/ces, accessed June 24, 2017.

puzzle is that automation and other imposed economies, spurred by the discipline of the wrangler, now yield enhanced manufacturing output with fewer workers.

If manufacturing employment will not deliver the imagined blessings one encounters in political discussions, are there other promising signs for harried households? Consider Figure 4.5. Here we see an interesting trend since 1940. The top line traces total U.S. population over a 70-year period (1940–2010), while the dashed line traces the total number of people employed. Of course, no one expects the total population to be employed; that is usually confined to what we call the working-age population, those between 15 and 64 years of age. The size of the total working population has varied slightly over time. In 1960, it was 60 percent of total U.S. population, rising to 67.2 percent in 2010, and dropping to 66.2 percent in 2015 (World Development Indicators).

For our purposes, the broad numbers of employed individuals and total population are sufficient. The vertical bars are simply the difference between the two historic lines. Demographers consider the total dependency ratio to be the number of individuals under 15 and over 64 years of age divided by the total population. In Figure 4.5, we are interested in the broader idea of total population being supported by those who are working—regardless of age. The issue of interest is not that of how many people in a population are dependent on those who are working. Rather, the issue concerns the reality of access to employment in the total U.S. population, regardless of age.

We see that in 1940, the difference between total population (132.2 million) and the employed population (31.6 million) was 100.6 million individuals. On this comparison, the dependent population in 1940 was 4.2 individuals per every employed person. Notice that around 1960, as more women entered the world of *paid* (rather than unpaid household chores) work, the dashed line begins a slow upward trajectory. Total population began a slight upward trend around 1990, but the year 2000 represents a profound break in the employed population. Whether or not this stark inflection point is reversible will not be known for another 10–15 years.

By 2010, however, the ratio of population to employed persons was 2.4 (population = 308.7 million; employed population = 129.8). The percentage of total population that was working had increased from 24 to 42 percent. But the actual number of *dependent* persons—those reliant on the working population—had increased significantly to 178.9 million. The pronounced jump in the vertical bars between 2000 and 2010 is suggestive of an ominous change in the labor market. This change is certainly attributable to the Great Recession. And this is worrying because that economic crisis presented an opportunity for many firms to reconstitute their business model (Sivy, 2012). We see that between 2000 and 2010, there was an increase of 28.5 million individuals who fell out of the category of employed—a jump of 19 percent.

If job losses of this sort endure into the future, one obvious question concerns whether or not there is relief from the appearance of new firms. Might the new economy—exemplified by the so-called disrupters (Uber, Lyft, Airbnb)—offer some relief? A moment's reflection suggests that these disrupters are not the employment engines they might seem. Airbnb is the easy case: it could even be a job killer. The model is one of homeowners renting out part or all of their dwelling. No obvious jobs are thereby created, especially if homeowners perform maid service once guests depart. And if Airbnb undermines regular lodging—hotels and motels where actual jobs exist—then this particular disrupter might actually be a job killer. As for Uber and Lyft, the evidence seems to be that most drivers are simply filling up their spare time; evidently, one-half of Uber's drivers work less than 10 hours per week.[10] Notice that a city flooded by hundreds of part-time Uber/Lyft drivers seems to pose a serious threat to established taxi drivers who tend to be full-time workers. The city of New York is now plagued by a crisis in the livery sector. Moreover, increased traffic gridlock is a related result of so many Uber and Lyft cars cruising the streets of Manhattan.

This question is pertinent because many politicians express an affinity for policies that will foster the creation of new firms as a promising landscape for meaningful careers and economic recovery in areas suffering from the loss of manufacturing employment. Sadly, the staying power of start-ups is not encouraging. The U.S. Bureau of Labor Statistics reports that in March 2018, only 50.7 percent of the firms that had opened five-years earlier (March 2013) had survived.[11] It seems that the promise of new firms is quite problematic.

For instance, in Figure 4.6 we see the number of one-year old firms from 1994 through 2015. Notice the pronounced dip starting around 2006, and the acceleration associated with the Great Recession of 2007–2009. There has been a decent recovery beginning in 2010, but a more ominous sign is seen in Figure 4.7.

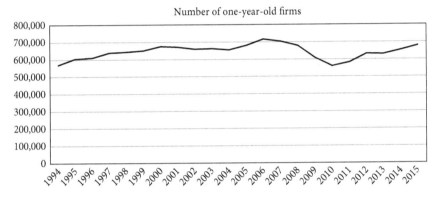

Figure 4.6. Number of One-Year-Old Firms, 1994–2015
Source: https://www.bls.gov/bdm/entrepreneurship/bdm, accessed June 15, 2017

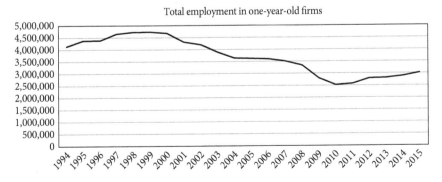

Figure 4.7. Employment in One-Year-Old Firms
Source: https://www.bls.gov/bdm/entrepreneurship/entrepreneurship.htm

In Figure 4.7, we see the total employment in one-year-old firms since 1994. An alarming drop occurred around 1999–2000 and persisted until 2010. A modest recovery began that year, but we cannot be certain that it will ever attain the levels reached between 1994 and 1999.

Perhaps a more troubling data series is shown in Figure 4.8. Here we see how many jobs have been created by the *net change in total firms* (new firms minus those that closed in each year) dating from the third quarter of 1993. These data bear a similar message to that in Figure 4.5. For the seven years prior to December 2000, there was a pronounced drop. A modest recovery then ensued, followed by a sharp drop during the Great Recession, and then another modest recovery to the level that existed prior to 2006. But there is no indication that employment will get back to the pre-1996 levels.

These data series suggest a worrying trend for total employment over the coming decades. Employment prospects in many legacy industries—manufacturing, large retailing, and construction—are falling because of shifts to global sources and automation. Will new firms, if they survive, offer employment prospects that can offset losses elsewhere in the economy? The evidence is not encouraging. As population growth continues, will work prospects remain static? The rendering of the modern household as a fox in an uncertain world of subsistence is ominous.

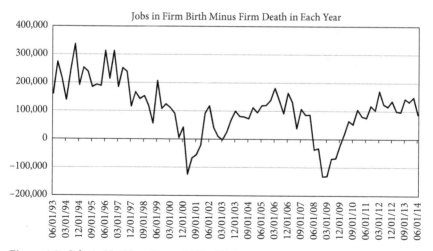

Figure 4.8. Jobs in Net New Firms, 1993–2014

Source: https://www.bls.gov/bdm/entrepreneurship/bdm.htm, accessed June 15, 2017.

II. The New Dependence and Exclusion

The foregoing discussion reminds us of the implications for households during the transition from a precapitalist agrarian economy, then to merchant capitalism, and finally to industrial capitalism. The early emergence of merchant capitalism signaled a gradual loosening of household bonds and the appearance of a somewhat liberated individual to remain tied to the land, to enter into alternative employment as a merchant capitalist, or to leave the hearth entirely and become a free laborer able to enter into satisfactory employment if it could be found. The next transition, from merchant capitalism to industrial capitalism, brought a quite dramatic shift in household autonomy. As the scale of industrial capitalism spread across Britain and then Germany—finally engulfing the rest of Europe and eventually the United States—the range of livelihood prospects narrowed. Agriculture soon encountered a new era of labor-saving technology that gradually displaced much human labor. Mechanization brought enormous productivity gains and a correlated loss of jobs. Agriculture now accounts for around 1 percent of total U.S. employment. It is similar in other Organization for Economic Cooperation and Development (OECD) countries.

Merchant capitalists were unable to fend off the inexorable scale economies and price advantages of a rapidly expanding industrialization. While the individual worker was clearly available to make important new choices about employment, in one sense the choices also narrowed considerably. The new and enlarged labor markets associated with full-scale industrialization at the end of the nineteenth century often meant that the only work to be had was associated with one of the large industrial facilities that soon dominated commerce. A worker had a choice of whether to work in textiles, furnishings, or automobiles, but there was no choice with respect to the mode of production. It was industrial, and it was grim.

The emergence of industrial capitalism seemed to prove that only in a capitalist market economy were individuals assured of the freedom to work where they wished to work, and to consume what they wished to consume. Recall that the 1917 Bolshevik Revolution in Russia and the 1949 communist revolution in China laid bare the stark differences between these two systems and the multitude of freedoms that persisted in a capitalist economy. The folk heroes of capitalism in the 1950s and 1960s—Friedrich von Hayek, Ludwig von Mises, and Milton Friedman—made sure that few could forget that a capitalist market economy was the only guarantee of individual freedom.

In a market economy, the liberated individual was not forced to consume any specific item, nor was that individual forced to rely on a particular merchant for those items that were to be purchased. Market capitalism *delivered freedom of choice*. And this also pertained to complete freedom to choose among employment options. Individuals could not be made to work in any specific job against their wishes. As above, the specter of communist regimes covering much of the world provided a certain urgency to celebration of freedoms in market capitalism.

But of course this much-prized freedom is not always what it seems. Amartya Sen (1993) challenged the abundant praise then on display. Sen asked us to consider three possible aspects of these alleged freedoms: (1) autonomy; (2) immunity; and (3) opportunity. Autonomy concerns the freedom *to choose*, immunity concerns the freedom *from encroachment* by others, while opportunity concerns the freedom *to achieve*. Sen's primary challenge was directed at claims of all-around freedom in a market economy. Sen insisted that the first freedom—autonomy (choice)—is a limited thing indeed since our freedom to choose is from a choice set that is not of our choosing. If there is only one employer in town, then being free to choose among employment options is meaningless. Or, as above, if all that is available is awful factory work, it is small consolation to be able to choose between a textile mill and a steel mill. If you lack transportation, your freedom to choose where you will buy groceries or which elementary school your child will attend is also meaningless. And of course if you live below the poverty line, your choices of what might be purchased are quite limited.

There is a larger problem with the claim for encompassing freedom in a market economy. Friedman based his claim for freedom on the idea that individuals are free to enter into—or to decline to enter into—any particular market activity. That is, every transaction is strictly voluntary. We see here shades of Bruni and Sugden discussed in Chapter 2. But of course this cannot be. If one wishes to eat, she has no choice but to participate in the market to obtain food. And since food is not free, this same individual is not free to avoid participating in yet another market transaction—the market for labor. Macpherson reminds us that real freedom means that the individual is free "not to enter into any exchange at all" (Macpherson, 1973, p. 146). As long as individuals must eat, and as long as food is not free, even a market economy is a realm of coercion.

The second freedom, immunity from encroachment by others, is also very limited in its practical effects. Those who praise immunity in market processes generally focus on freedom from encroachment by governments—regulations—on owners of firms. It is no surprise that Friedman would find this form of immunity quite compelling. He revered what he liked to call "free markets," and so the ability of firms and industrial enterprise to resist unwanted regulations would have figured high in Friedman's pantheon. On close inspection, it seems that immunity is just the other side of a coin called autonomy. A market economy simply grants to firms the presumptive opportunity to resist regulations. The horrible apartment fire in June 2017 in London's Grenfell Tower in which at least 79 people perished is now blamed on the rollback of regulations, accelerated privatization, and general austerity. There is now a discussion about whether "privatization has gone too far."[12] The issue, however, is not one of privatization versus something else. The central issue, rather, is which standards the private sector is willing to accept and how hard the private sector will fight to keep such regulations to a minimum. The Conservative government in Britain had been pleased to praise its "bonfire of regulations." Sadly, the Grenfell apartment fire was a different sort of bonfire.

Missing in this praise of immunity is any mention of whether or not employees are exposed to what Macpherson calls the *extractive powers* of employers. Occupational safety and health regulations designed to protect workers are regularly denounced by owners of capital as intruding on the operational flexibility of firms. Business groups are generally effective at advancing claims of so-called regulatory costs that imperil profits. Since every legal initiative aimed at reducing the extractive powers of firms is, *ipso facto*, a correlated liberation for workers, we see that immunity from encroachment is merely another way of praising autonomy.

We come now to the third component of freedom—opportunity. Defenders of market capitalism claim that markets provide the widest possible scope to improve one's life prospects. In a market economy there are no government officials requiring that people pursue specific careers, that they work in specific firms, or that they perform specific tasks in those firms. Individuals are free to pursue specific employment opportunities that are consistent with their goals. This freedom might appear to duplicate the idea of autonomy, but there is something more important here. Being free to choose—autonomy—concerns actions that we might take in terms of how we access the beneficial and discretionary aspects of a market economy. One of those freedoms allows us to withdraw entirely from any particular market transaction—we do not need to eat in any restaurant at all. We are not required to shop at any particular store, and a few people try very hard to avoid using most stores most of the time. It is often put as "going off the grid."

But it is important to notice an important asymmetry in our interaction with firms in a market economy. While one can make a commitment to be careful and very selective in how and when we spend our income in the market, the matter of opportunity freedom is very different when it is time to earn an income in that market economy. What if you cannot obtain specific work because you happen to be female? Or what if you happen to be African American? Slowly, such barriers have been eliminated—at least in the law, if not yet in practice. But there is a larger point. These legal innovations were motivated and justified by the need to prevent individuals being excluded from access to the means of labor by personal circumstances. That is, these unacceptable discriminatory practices were aimed at specific classes of individuals who were denied the opportunity for gainful employment because of specific traits or attributes that had nothing to do with personal qualifications.

For markets to be celebrated for assuring freedom of opportunity, it is important that one understand that nothing in the essential nature of capitalism—or market exchange—assures opportunity. Such traits have always had to be secured through great effort at the ballot box or through the courts. To say that capitalism and markets assure opportunity is to fall victim to essentialism. Research continues to suggest that when fictional job seekers submit applications with various personal traits, the differential response rates from potential employers suggest durable evidence of discrimination across several of those attributes (Rinne, 2014).

Although employment discrimination can gradually be eliminated, the labor force will still be characterized by a normal distribution of early childhood developmental circumstances, subsequent educational levels dominated by that early differential advantage, varying work experiences and aptitudes, and, ultimately, possession of the social and technical skills required in a modern economy (Bourdieu, 1990, 1998). Employers who sort or hire on the basis of these traits are not discriminatory. In a market economy it is merit and suitability for work that matters. A market economy rewards aptitude and punishes low performance. The robustness and resilience of a market economy are based on the fact that it is a meritocracy all the way down.

As noted earlier, approximately 50 percent of all new firms fail by their fifth anniversary. New restaurants close with alarming frequency. Likewise, new employees are hired, and some are unable to persist in the workplace. The presumption in a market economy is that there is a niche for all specific skills and talents. A defective restaurateur might easily apply her culinary skills to a private catering service rather than to a restaurant with its abundant staffing and billing headaches. An individual who fails to survive as a retail clerk is surely employable as an inventory and stock clerk in the same establishment. There is a job for everyone; all that is required is that they stay alert, apply themselves, and respond to the reasonable demands of a modern firm.

But there is a long-term economic issue quite unrelated to discrimination or other defects in the available labor supply. That larger issue is one of simple economics. What if one is denied access to the means of labor because those who control the means of labor—owners of capital—do not want to hire *any workers at all*? In this case, the refusal to offer work is not based on discrimination against individuals with specific traits. Rather, the refusal of capitalists to hire labor is based on quite reasonable economic calculations of their firm-specific demand for labor. No one is to blame in this circumstance: there is no discrimination, and no untoward preferences are being exercised. There simply is no demand for labor. Who could possibly believe it would be a good idea to require firms to hire workers they do not need? Isn't that what Stalin's Soviet system practiced? No one imagines that to be a good solution. It is not the obligation of private firms to offer employment to workers they do not need. For the individual firm, this idea makes perfect sense. But there is a composition problem that cannot be ignored. What if a large number of firms gradually decide to stop hiring workers?

What about firms that close their doors and move abroad where labor costs are much lower? Do such firms owe an obligation to their stranded workers? It seems odd to suggest that they do. Aren't private firms free to do whatever is required to secure their profits? At first blush, it seems that private firms could not possibly owe anything to workers they no longer wish to employ—instead showing a new affinity for Chinese or Vietnamese workers. But let us take a more general view of the process of firm creation, growth, reorganization, and ultimate demise. This is not a trivial issue as we trace the loss of manufacturing jobs over the past three to four decades. In fact, the term *Rust Belt* emerged out of precisely this phenomenon. The "New Machine Age" brings a new perspective to the world of work (Box 4.2).

Text Box 4.2 The New Machine Age

In summarizing a recent study on the effect of robotics on jobs, the National Bureau of Economic Research reports:

> Since at least the start of the Industrial Revolution, economists and policy makers have pondered how relentless technological advances might impact labor markets. John Maynard Keynes warned in 1929 of coming "technological unemployment" and Wassily Leontief predicted several decades later that "labor will become less and less important." In recent years, a range of studies has estimated that nearly half of all U.S. workers' jobs will be at risk of being automated over the next two decades, and noted that this risk extends beyond laborers to include many white-collar occupations with substantial routine components.
>
> The researchers focus on how the adoption of a specific type of automation technology—industrial robots—affects local labor markets. They use the International Federation of Robotics (IFR) definition of robots as autonomous, reprogrammable, multipurpose machines; this excludes single-purpose automated machinery and artificial intelligence technologies. By combining data from the IFR, the U.S. Bureau of the Census, and other sources, the researchers analyze the effect on labor markets of increases in industrial robot usage in 19 industries between 1990 and 2007. They measure the within-industry rate of robot adoption in countries other than the U.S., and pair that with information on the location of industrial employment across commuting zones to construct a measure of potential exposure to robots for each local labor market.
>
> The researchers find large and robust negative effects of robots on employment and wages. They estimate that one more robot per thousand workers reduces the employment-to-population ratio by between 0.18 and 0.34 percentage points, and is associated with a wage decline of between 0.25 and 0.5 percent. The effects are most pronounced on industries most exposed to robots, on workers with less than a college degree, and on routine manual, blue-collar, assembly, and other related occupations.
>
> Robots appear to have a more negative impact on the employment of men than of women.

Source: Jay Fitzgerald, The *NBER Digest*, May, 2017. Drawn from: Daron Acemoglu and Pascual Restrepo, "Robots and Jobs: Evidence from U.S. Labor Markets" (NBER Working Paper No. 23285).

Consider the life cycle of a fictional manufacturing company. In early days, say immediately after World War II, a new firm might have advertised far and wide to attract the necessary labor force. Of course, long-time residents of the immediate locale would gladly accept work, but others might have moved for the explicit purpose of gainful employment. This was certainly the history of the automobile industry in the upper Midwest. But recall that there are also a large number of ancillary manufacturing firms linked to the assembly of cars. A few young people at the local level, weighing whether to go away to college, or remain and earn what seemed like princely hourly wages, might have turned their back on college and made a lifelong commitment to one of these facilities. New livelihoods were surely created, the local economy thrived, families grew and became part of the civic fabric of the place, the company donated to local charities, and some executives perhaps became active in civic affairs.

Global competition pressed in. Factories built in 1950 became degraded and financially depreciated within 20–30 years, if not less. Machinery became outdated, if not obsolete, in less time. Buildings wore out and required expensive rehabilitation. Suburbs soon encroached on what was once a rural setting, and problems arose from noise, odors, and truck traffic. It was inevitable that one day a number of factors would undermine the social and economic logic of investing in tired and dated facilities. Eventually, the firm might be acquired, it might be closed down, or it might relocate to a new setting. The process of hiring, of expansion, and of eventual demise is repeated elsewhere. Capital is infinitely mobile, whereas labor is tied to a place. After all, it is difficult for families to be uprooted in order to follow a factory that may one day repeat this same unwanted life cycle. And if the factory moves to China it is impossible for workers to follow. Moreover, the plant is moving precisely to shed its high-cost labor in the United States.

When these life-cycle accounts are studied, we learn that a few highly paid executives might be rewarded with agreeable financial settlements, but the bulk of employees—both wage and salary labor—will be given modest severance packages and offered the very best of wishes. Under prevailing institutional arrangements, this firm has no obligation to these severed laborers, and it certainly has no obligation to the community that nurtured it—and very likely bestowed certain tax advantages on it. Capital forms no bonds to place; workers do. Is it a social problem if workers do not wish to move? Should we care, as members of the political community, if there is no local employment to absorb the newly created reserve army of unemployed?

If society does care, unemployment insurance, funded by taxpayers, will come to the rescue. Suddenly we see that taxpayer funds are implicated when firms move. Does this mean that taxpayers are paying part of the costs of labor that is stranded by the decisions of a private firm? But even this benefit will expire after a period of time. Some workers may end up unemployed, while others may be lucky and find work. Some will be eligible for Social Security and struggle to survive on that meager amount. We see that this cost-cutting decision by a private firm has dumped unwanted labor on the public purse. Taxpayers are often obligated for the future well-being of some of these now-unwanted owners of labor power. Is it fair that the firm can so cheaply abandon those who once provided its necessary labor power? To ask this question is to invite incredulity. "You cannot possibly mean, can you, that private firms should not be free to do as they wish?" Actually, that is precisely the question. Notice that the cost of moving away is artificially low because the firm does not have to fully endow its severed workforce. It seems that capital is highly mobile, while labor is less so.

The economic history of interest to us here, spanning a long period of precapitalist broad-spectrum provisioning, followed by 300 to 400 years of capitalist reliance on hired labor, is certainly one of profound improvements in general livelihood prospects for the world's inhabitants. Few adults would willingly trade places with early humans as hunter-gatherers on the vast stunning plains of Africa. Those early families may have enjoyed complete agency with respect to provisioning, but their standard of living would repel even the most dedicated contemporary recluse seeking escape from the grid (Box 4.3).

Text Box 4.3 Mobile Capital-Stranded Labor

In 1919, a Chicago butcher by the name of Oscar Meyer opened a slaughtering plant in Madison, Wisconsin, and by 1970 there were approximately 4,000 employees earning proper middle-class incomes in a city that was otherwise dominated by state government and a major research university. Here was a balanced community—town and gown and all that flowed from that blend. Oscar's wieners were famous—helped along by the iconic Wienermobile. Gradually, the slaughtering operation moved to rural Iowa, taking its abundant odors with it. Carcasses were shipped to Madison for rendering into bacon and hot dogs. One day Oscar

Meyer was purchased by Kraft Foods, and then Kraft was purchased by Heinz, thereby creating Kraft Heinz—an obscure creature of 3G Capital, which is itself an American/Brazilian investment firm associated with well-known names such as Berkshire Hathaway. It is hard to keep track of who owns whom.

This is the new world of managerial capitalism. Meanwhile, Oscar's workforce plunged drastically from 4,000 in the 1970s to 300 in the summer of 2017, when the last worker walked out into the warm evening and trudged several blocks to her middle-class home.

A spokesman for Kraft Heinz wished to "thank our employees for their hard work and commitment to the facility." Workers were committed to the facility—the commitment appears to be asymmetric.

Source: Wisconsin State Journal, August 10, 2017.

To use a contemporary expression, those now living in the metropolitan core are awash in *stuff* produced under global capitalism. This abundance of goods and services—refrigerators, cars, microwave ovens, video recorders, fancy coffee machines, computers, bounteous agricultural output, advanced medicines, and health care—has profoundly benefited millions of individuals. The pronounced increase in life expectancy is one of the most gratifying aspects of this profusion of goods and services. Around 1500, life expectancy in England was approximately 45 years; today it is just over 79 years. The average life today is both longer and more pleasant than could have been imagined in, say, the 1800s when the Industrial Revolution was underway.

The evidence is clear that, historically speaking, *living* is good. I leave to one side the vexing question of whether or not people, surrounded by all this stuff, are actually happy or happier than in former times. Whether or not they feel fulfilled and content by their materialist existence is beyond our reach.

But what about their *working* life? After all, under capitalism one cannot live and thrive unless one also works, and so there is a plausible case to be made that the conditions of work are logically prior to the conditions of living. Now, job losses are threatening, immigrants are blamed for holding down wages, and automation seems to loom on the horizon. For those who work for hourly wages, their world of necessary provisioning is a source of debilitating uncertainty. These problems are especially pronounced in the rural areas of Britain, the United States, and particular regions of western Europe. Thriving capitalism is now an urban phenomenon.

Economists typically draw a distinction between work and leisure. We consider the first to be drudgery, and therefore it is normal that individuals would find work alienating and unpleasant. On the other hand, leisure is obviously pleasurable, and so we talk of the work–leisure trade-off. But this framing can often mislead us into thinking that pleasure can only come from leisure. In fact, many people find work to be fulfilling, challenging, and a source of social contact and friendship. At least, that seems to be the common perception. Earlier we saw that "[m]an is not a bundle of appetites seeking satisfaction but a bundle of conscious energies seeking to be exerted" (Macpherson, 1973, p. 5). For the vast majority of adults, work is the place where they spend more time than practically any other *single* activity. They want it to be pleasurable, and for many it is. But that does not seem to be a universal finding.

Technology has certainly taken much of the worst drudgery out of most lines of work. But for many individuals the severe tedium and hard labor of yesterday's workplace has been replaced by frantic uncertainty. The decline of unions has eroded a wide array of protections over work conditions and compensation. The service sector, now accounting for 80 percent of U.S. employment, consists of a large proportion of part-time work with no sick leave, no vacation time, and no other benefits such as maternity or paternity leave. Many workers piece together two or more part-time jobs. Much work is in staggered shifts that can change from one day to the next. Many restaurants have two peak periods, and workers are expected to work both of them, with perhaps a break of three or four hours in between. Arranging for transportation and perhaps child care can be problematic.

In a similar vein, the "gig economy" is talked about as an exciting new opportunity for young people to move quickly from one activity to the next, depending on their interests and skills. While this work life may be ideal for those who are single and 25–30 years of age, it seems reasonable to presume that many gig workers are going to wish to settle down and start a family at some time. What do they want for a work life when they are 45–50 and have several peripatetic teenagers under their nervous and harried tutelage? It is not apparent that the gig economy works so well for such individuals. Starting afresh every several years soon loses its charm when family formation—or necessary stability—is foremost in your mind. The metaphor of the fox, always searching, is unlikely to be reassuring in middle age.

This brings us to a dilemma. We can track the historical attributes of livelihoods, and it is clear that our enhanced material abundance has contributed a great deal. One can also add in noneconomic factors such as improved life expectancy, better health care, and any number of other measures that seem interesting. But how can we measure what has happened to the world of work over a similar period? Are workers today better off than our precapitalist hunter-gatherer? What about the merchant capitalist with his or her family workshop turning out harnesses, wagons, pottery, baked goods, ale, fine dresses, and hand-made sweaters? What about the yeoman farmer feeding his family and a limited number of nonagricultural neighbors in the English midlands—or out on the plains of South Dakota? As merchant capitalists and small farmers were pushed—and pulled—into industrial capitalism in the eighteenth and nineteenth centuries, how did the quality of their working life change? And what has now transpired under financial and managerial capitalism? Obviously, finding reliable and generalizable historical measures of well-being at work is difficult. But perhaps historical trends are less important than the picture as it exists today. It seems that America is not the only economy with harried foxes; Germany is also suffering (Box 4.4).

Text Box 4.4 The New German Foxes

In West Germany, where a secure job was the norm, full-time employment served as the foundation of social integration. The classic metaphor describing this arrangement was coined by the sociologist Ulrich Beck in the 1980s: the "elevator effect." It implied that, although social inequality still existed, everyone was rising in the same social "elevator," which meant that the gap between rich and poor wouldn't widen.

Thirty years later, this society has vanished. Average real incomes declined for nearly 20 years beginning in 1993. Germany not only grew more unequal, but the standard of living for the lower strata stagnated or even fell. The lowest 40 percent of households have faced annual net income losses for around 25 years now, while the kinds of jobs that promised long-term stability dwindled.

The number of precarious jobs such as temp positions has exploded. At the height of postwar prosperity, almost 90 percent of jobs offered permanent employment with protections. By 2014, the figure had fallen to

68.3 percent. In other words, nearly one-third of all workers have inse-cure or short-term jobs. Moreover, a low-wage sector emerged employing millions of workers who can barely afford basic necessities and often need two jobs to get by.

The German middle class is shrinking and no longer functions as a co-hesive bloc. Although the upper middle class still enjoys a high level of security, the lower middle contends with a very real risk of downward mo-bility. The relatively new phenomenon of a contracting—and internally divided—middle class has set off widespread anxiety.

Source: Oliver Nachtwey, "It Doesn't Matter Who Replaces Merkel. Germany is Broken." *The New York Times,* December 7, 2018.

In this regard, a recent report from the Society for Human Resource Management offers a quite detailed assessment of the contemporary American workplace (SHRM, 2016). This particular survey covered 600 respondents drawn so as to reflect the full array of employment: 19 percent of respondents came from the retail sector, 18 percent from the professional, scientific, and technical services sector, 17 percent from manufacturing, 14 percent from finance and insurance, 8 percent from accommodation and food services, 8 percent from transportation and warehousing, 7 per-cent from administrative and support in waste management, 6 percent from health care and social assistance (and the same percentage from information as well as wholesale trade), and the remaining share from an additional 12 sectors.[13] The 600 respondents were predominantly from firms of less than 2,500 employees; 50 percent had been in their present job for less than five years; they were evenly divided among Millennials, Generation X, and Baby Boomers; they were 63 percent nonmanagerial-level workers; 44 percent had less than four years of college; and 68 percent identified as white.

The survey covered five broad categories: (1) career development; (2) com-pensation; (3) benefits; (4) relationship with management; and (5) work environment. The results are shown in Tables 4.1–4.5.

Leaving judgments of the expressed *importance* of each of these aspects aside, we see that only 27.8 of all respondents—averaging across Tables 4.1–4.5—declare themselves to be "very satisfied" with their work. It would be difficult to consider this to be a ringing endorsement of the workplace. For the 14 categories that were judged to be "very important" by 50 percent or

Table 4.1. Career Development

Career Development	Very Important	Very Satisfied
Opportunity to use skills and abilities	55%	37%
Career advancement opportunities	47%	24%
Job-specific training	42%	25%
Organization's commitment to professional development	40%	25%
Career development opportunities	39%	21%
Company-paid general training	35%	26%
Networking opportunities	31%	23%
Averages	41%	26%

Source: Society for Human Resource Management (2016).

Table 4.2. Compensation Issues

Compensation	Very Important	Very Satisfied
Compensation/pay	63%	23%
Pay competitive with local market	59%	21%
Base rate of pay	53%	23%
Opportunities for variable pay	42%	21%
Stock options	18%	16%
Averages	44%	22%

Source: Society for Human Resource Management (2016).

more of the respondents, the "very satisfied" score rose to only 31 percent of respondents. To an outsider looking in on the American workplace in 2016, it is surprising that attributes considered to be *very important* were found to be *very satisfying* to a mere 31 percent of respondents. Notice that only one attribute was found to be very satisfying to more than 40 percent of respondents—"feeling safe in the workplace." More than one-third of the responses (15 of 43) showed a score of *less than* 25 percent for being "very satisfied." These included three aspects of career development, all five of the compensation aspects, two of the benefits aspects, one of the management issues, and four questions pertaining to the work environment. The lowest score (16 percent) was recorded in the compensation cluster and concerned

Table 4.3. Benefits Issues

Benefits	Very Important	Very Satisfied
Paid time off	63%	33%
Health care/medical benefits	62%	29%
Benefits, overall	60%	27%
Ability to balance life and work	53%	31%
Defined contribution plan	48%	28%
Family-friendly benefits	35%	25%
Defined benefit pension plan	34%	23%
Wellness programs	27%	21%
Averages	46%	26%

Source: Society for Human Resource Management (2016).

Table 4.4. Management Issues

Relationship with Management	Very Important	Very Satisfied
Respectful treatment of all employees at all levels	67%	31%
Trust between employees and senior management	55%	27%
Relationship with supervisor	53%	40%
Supervisor's respect for employee's ideas	49%	37%
Management's recognition of employee job performance	48%	26%
Communication between employees and senior management	48%	25%
Autonomy and independence	46%	32%
Management communication of goals and strategies	45%	24%
Averages	49%	30%

Source: Society for Human Resource Management (2016).

the availability of stock options. This attribute was also the least important of the 43 categories. Perhaps signaling their indifference to the workplace as an important part of their life, few sought to share in its financial future.

While we cannot know what early merchant capitalists thought of their working life, it seems hard to imagine that very many of them would have shown this level of dissatisfaction. Nor does it seem reasonable to suppose

Table 4.5. The Work Environment

Work Environment	Very Important	Very Satisfied
Job security	58%	32%
Organization's financial security	53%	33%
Feeling safe in the work environment	50%	48%
The work itself	48%	34%
Overall corporate culture	44%	28%
Meaningfulness of job	43%	34%
Teamwork within unit	43%	26%
Relationships with co-workers	40%	36%
Teamwork between units	39%	21%
Contribution of work to organization's goals	39%	30%
Communication between units	36%	21%
Variety of work	35%	30%
Organization's commitment to corporate social responsibility	32%	24%
Organization's commitment to a diverse and inclusive workforce	30%	25%
Organization's commitment to a "green" workplace	21%	23%
Averages	33%	25%

Source: Society for Human Resource Management (2016).

that a nineteenth-century farmer in England or America would find work this disagreeable. After all, every household was its own boss. Isn't that the ideal we hear about even today among independent entrepreneurs—writers, wilderness guides, farmers and ranchers, house painters, skilled craftspeople, and assorted others who are free from the obligation to rent or sell their creative time to others who own capital?

We are not talking about the ease or material abundance of their lifestyle choice. Some such individuals are fabulously wealthy, while others labor in obscurity and often considerable penury. But the self-employed count themselves both fortunate and free. They have made a deal with themselves, and they live (and consume) accordingly. They generally seek little sympathy because they are the masters of their own circumstances. Such individuals are in a decisive minority.

The vast bulk of adults share a very different fate: they are at the mercy of those who own capital. Their situation is plausibly captured in the above survey. What seems to stand out in that assessment of the workplace is the absence of agency. The attributes with the lowest level of satisfaction are: (1) career development opportunities; (2) competitive pay; (3) opportunities for variable pay; (4) availability of stock options; (5) availability of wellness programs; (6) opportunities for teamwork; and (7) communication within the workplace.

III. The Problematic End Game

Capitalism is about the control of capital—its use, its deployment, and its withholding when conditions dictate. Capitalism is not, in the historical view of economics, concerned with making goods or providing services to consumers. Of course, it started out that way, with the merchant crafting useful objects and then selling them on the market. Industrialization was the logical successor to that productive activity, merely expanding and elaborating the reach and scale of what was being produced. The transition made it possible to produce more stuff per unit of time and undoubtedly goods of a higher quality. But the enterprise remained what it had always been—an engineering enterprise bringing human initiative and technical prowess to bear on the task of creating tangible value for a consumer.

But we must not lose sight of the fact that capitalism is about the use of money to make money. The merchant capitalist and the industrial capitalist were engaged in exactly the same activity. A British wagon maker from 1456 could enter a British truck factory or a German automobile factory in 2016 and instantly grasp what was going on. He would marvel at the exquisite silence and cleanliness of the factory floor. He would be left speechless at the speed with which complex tasks were carried out. Despite his shock and wonder, he would understand exactly what he was looking at, and he would therefore bring an admirer's grasp to the entire show. He might well feel a slight sense of embarrassment about how things were once done.

When our time-visitor left the factory floor and ascended to the corner office on the top floor, he would be lost. He would be confused by an obscure structure of ownership and management. He could not possibly grasp the financial aspects of this new creature. It would not be the glowing computer screens that would intrigue him. Rather, it would be his inability to understand the obscure webs of responsibility and control. He must be excused for believing that the core of the firm was the making of trucks. Eventually, he might grasp the new reality that his manufacturing firm was merely the use of capital (money) to make capital (money).[14] The engineer had been supplanted by the wrangler, who most probably was situated in a far-off corporate office suite in London, Frankfurt, Seoul, or Chicago. Stripped of the adjectives—whether merchant, industrial, financial, or managerial—that is the enduring point of capitalism. And so the adjective "financial" is actually redundant. Capitalism is about making money.

Early in the twentieth century, Thorstein Veblen distinguished between industry (making things) and business (making money). Veblen often called the business side of capitalism a mere *pecuniary* pursuit. In other words, there was industrial employment, and there was pecuniary employment (Veblen, 1904). With that in mind, pecuniary employment is the future of capitalism, and the "industry" part is a mere detail to those who make their considerable living moving capital around the world where it can be deployed to the maximum benefit of those doing the shunting. And now, with the emergence of managerial capitalism, the exacting discipline of the wrangler rules.

The obvious question becomes, what of those who own only their labor power? What does this possible end game of capitalism have to say to those who are not in a position to shunt capital around the world? What is to become of household provisioning in a world where pennies mark the difference between employment and dismissal? Is the household and the embedded family still relevant to a global economic system that is no longer defined by its relation between physical assets (embodied liquid capital) and those who apply their labor power to that stock of capital to bring forth goods and services? Of course, managerial capitalism has not eliminated ordinary labor power from economic activity. It has merely shifted the focus of managerial preoccupation. Under rather traditional industrial capitalism, those responsible for the future of the firm were focused on three central concerns: (1) the coherence and efficiency of the necessary production processes; (2) the market conditions in which it would seek to sell the results of its production processes; and (3) the necessary raw materials and other inputs that entered the firm through the "back door" as it were, before exiting through the "front door" on their way to the ultimate consumer.

With the advent of managerial capitalism, the firm now finds itself subordinated to the outside influence and control of those who provide the financial oxygen of the firm. Relentless pressure from the fiscal side of the firm—pressure for quick turnover; pressure for cost savings, however wrung from the going concern; pressure to pay competitive dividends to investors;

pressure to meet ever-more stringent accounting machinations—serves to dislodge the ordinary worker further from the traditional place of importance inside the firm. The employee of an industrial capitalist firm was part of the essential creative production (engineering) activity of that firm. With the nature of the firm now elaborated upward to reflect the central importance of highly mobile capital, the role of labor power as hands rather than brains becomes easily subordinated. With this form of demotion in the larger scheme of things, it seems unavoidable that workers will increasingly be seen not as an integral part of the going concern, but as a mere obligatory expense. Perhaps such workers will be seen as nothing more than vexing cost centers.

That idea may, in fact, already be with us. After all, workers get sick, they fail to show up for work, they may be temperamental, and they might ask for an increase in their wage or salary. They may request time off for a family holiday. When employees become cost centers, the future of remunerative work becomes more tenuous. It can be no surprise why contemporary corporations strive to undermine labor unions in those few settings where they still exist, and to squash the first sightings of such collective action where unions do not yet exist. It can often seem that workers are the least important component of the contemporary corporation embedded in a system of global managerial capitalism. The joke used to be that many American corporations were actually mere subsidiaries of the British American Tobacco Company, or perhaps of the Great Atlantic and Pacific Tea Company. Today it is often impossible to be sure who, exactly, is the owner of many corporations. This veil of anonymity seems to be a growing part of global capitalism.

One thing is clear from having arrived at this stage of capitalism. It is no longer possible to entertain visions of a Marxian world of exploitative capitalists and exploited workers. Capitalism in its present *denouement* is decidedly post-Marxist. This means that the old Marxist dichotomy of class struggle is now irrelevant. There are now few workers who are an identifiable class facing off against a small class of capitalists. The capitalists are, of course, still there. But they are a highly diffuse aggregation rather than the old captains of industry. Some of them are perhaps lovable—Warren Buffet, Bill Gates, and the benevolent Hungarian exile George Soros with his Open Society Foundations. Even the late Sam Walton escaped being villainized as a despicable capitalist, though treatment of Walmart workers was often the source of some anger. But Walmart, the largest corporation in the world in terms of total revenue (in 2016), offered goods (and some services) to the very class of people that it often treated badly in its work conditions and pay structure. If Henry Ford perfected the art of paying his workers well enough that they could afford to buy the cars they made, Sam Walton perfected the art of paying his workers just enough to make sure that they would necessarily remain loyal to his bargain-priced stores out of their inability to have the financial means to shop elsewhere. He had them where he wanted them: they needed his cheap goods more than they needed health insurance and higher wages.

The arrival of capitalism in its current form does not mean that evolutionary change in the economic system has ended. This is not Francis Fukuyama's "end of history and the last man." Rather, any further change in economic relations can only be considered as "postcapitalist." This is a most unsatisfying term because it calls attention to what the economic system will *not* be rather than what it *might* be. Notice that the history of capitalism has taken its emphasis and its name from money and the uses to which money has been put—simple and small-scale merchant production, large-scale industrial production, or the making of money by the manipulation of money. A future economic system will necessarily shift attention away from the making of money toward something entailing a dramatically different purpose, and thereby demanding a different descriptor. What sort of "ism" might it be?

Before we worry about a name, it is important to consider the salient characteristics of the next phase of economic relations. We have seen that the three early stages took their meaning and their label from the role of money—capital—in economic relations. Money was the sole organizing principle, and those participants in the system who did not control the use of money in the system were considered ancillary players in the drama. Even the merchant capitalist—at the dawn of capitalist relations—is not noticed for his exquisite skills as a craftsman fashioning perfect harnesses, durable wagons, efficient ploughs, or attractive household furniture. He was engaged in the business of managing circulating capital in the service of demands beyond his household. But his centrality to that household is seen as rather incidental to the main task at hand. His labor services, his skills, were secondary to how he used capital. His wife, or daughter, or elderly mother who might have been engaged in the fabric trades—spinning, weaving, dying—were likewise engaged in a "cottage industry." Their labor input was only mentioned because it took place in their home—their cottage—rather than in some massive factory under the authoritarian rule of steam as opposed to treadle.

And of course when industrial capitalism emerged in the early eighteenth century, the human element was pushed further into the background. Now the worker was a minor cog in the business of business, one who was most likely to be agitating for shorter hours and greater remuneration—a futile quest held hostage to Marx's reserve army of unemployed. The worker was a necessary nuisance. Thomas Malthus soon emerged as a caustic observer of current affairs, ever quick to denounce the sloth and breeding habits of the laboring family teeming with filthy infants. A short while later, Charles Dickens became famous for his chronicles of the cruelty that befell families with their children and harried mothers laboring 12 hours a day, 6 days a week. Over time, members of Parliament, hectored by reformers and various do-gooders, confronted the assured wrath of assorted industrialists for the sheer audacity to propose minimal relief for the great unwashed who, through their toil, made possible the agreeable income of the capitalists.

The scales were hard to balance. Industrial capitalists were performing such astounding miracles—improved cotton fabrics made possible by dubious colonial administration in India, sparkling new household objects much coveted by the economically comfortable, shining carriages to transport fine ladies to and from their social obligations. The Great Exhibition of London (May–October 1851) regaled all who could attend its Crystal Palace groaning under the weight of the many wonders of a new age. The emerging consumerism, achievable through the celebrated possibilities of the new industrialists, brought together the two sides of industrial capitalism— admired producers and thrilled consumers—while the laboring class rarely tasted the fruits of this new phase in modern life. Only Marx, with occasional help from Dickens, seemed to notice that all was not well.

The roots of worker action to improve their sorry lot grew deep and robust during this period and were transported to America, where they gained strong nourishment during the period of the Robber Barons. The Great Depression focused attention on the plight of the working family and the struggling farmer. But this concern was short-lived, and by the 1970s and 1980s, labor unions were under sustained attack as an impediment to efficiency in the capitalist firm—under pressure, it was claimed—to be free to hire and fire workers with alacrity. International competitiveness in a global economy demanded as much, if not more. And so the final stages of industrial capitalism—and the full flowering of financial capitalism—were characterized by accelerating indifference toward the financial circumstances of the family and the general irrelevance of the laboring household. The main story was what the business community was doing and what new gadgets and benefits it might soon bestow on a burgeoning consumerist population.

As we saw in Chapter 2, this focus on the consumer in popular culture began to be reflected in the field of economics as it developed following World War II. The essential consideration focused on making sure that the prices of consumer goods remained as low as possible. In recognition of that imperative, recall that economic theory regards individual well-being in terms of achieving a given level of consumption at the lowest possible prices. Cheaper imports from China or Vietnam, if they allow the same level of consumption at lower prices, represent increases in so-called welfare. Consumers gain when prices fall. If unionized labor causes the cost of a representative basket of consumer goods to increase over what that basket would cost in the absence of unionized workers, then consumer "welfare" is suppressed. It seems that making workers better off can represent a loss of welfare to consumers. But aren't consumers also workers? Some of them are. But an important class of consumers—the ultra-wealthy—are not.

IV. The Consequences of Possessive Individualism

The contest between firms and households has turned households into foxes—peripatetic searchers for sources of sustenance. At the same time, economic theory, focusing on the allocation of scarce income among unlimited wants, treats households as nothing but collections of consumers. Welfare at either the individual or aggregate level is measured not by how well the household is getting by. Rather, it is reckoned by a bundle of consumption items acquired at the lowest possible price. We do not say that income yields utility or welfare—consumption does that. Of course the greater one's income the greater one's consumption. The act of consuming moves the individual to a higher indifference curve and by implication to a higher utility possibility frontier.

The availability of cheap goods, which are often manufactured abroad with cheap labor, enables the individual to acquire more goods than if all goods had been made locally using more expensive labor. This centrality of consumption at ever-lower prices drives public perceptions of the accepted goal of economic policy. Political discourse is dominated by little else. It is claimed that taxes reduce the ability of people to spend "their" income on what they desire. Regulations force firms to raise prices, thereby harming consumers. Environmental regulations for clean air and water impair production at the lowest possible cost. Environmental regulations mean the loss of jobs. Unions impeded the efficiency of firms and raised the cost of goods and services provided by firms; therefore, unions harm the consumer in search of ever-lower prices.

This relentless pursuit of the lowest possible prices so that consumption can be either maintained or increased is the defining purpose of contemporary managerial capitalism. The association of freedom with this idea further shifts the argument in favor of maximum consumption. After the September 11, 2001, terrorist attacks in New York City and Washington, President George W. Bush urged individuals to go out and spend money—buy stuff, eat in restaurants, buy gasoline to visit relatives. Consume. We could not allow terrorists to deprive us of our "freedom." Consuming creates jobs.

Notice what all of this pressure on low prices does to the workplace. It encourages the shifting of jobs overseas where labor is cheap. It prevents workers from collective bargaining over wages and work conditions. It encourages automation since that will drive production costs lower than if humans were retained.

It now seems apparent that the reigning zeitgeist of possessive individualism dismisses meaningful employment as of secondary importance compared to the opportunity to consume as much as possible at the lowest possible prices. The irony is that individuals cannot possibly keep track of how much they have saved, over the course of a year, in their total consumption much augmented by the plethora of imported goods from China, Vietnam, and Bangladesh. But they certainly keep track of their earnings, and they are very much aware that their incomes have been stagnant for a number of years. While economic theory celebrates their low-cost consumption as utility enhancing, households bemoan their penurious earnings. They are voracious consumers at low prices, and yet they are unhappy with their fate in life. It seems they can never have too much stuff.

The unavoidable consequence of possessive individualism is that capitalism no longer comprises a source of hope. It has evolved into a system—an "ism"—without a compelling moral basis for its continuation. That absence of moral justification is not to be blamed on the capitalist. The money managers—the wranglers and the predatory fund bosses—are merely doing what possessive individualism has invited them to do. It seems that we all like low prices for the acquisitions we seem unable to do without. Notice that this situation is unstable.

We have seen that economic theory regards the purpose of a market economy to be the production and consumption of goods and services at the lowest possible prices. Another possible name for our current situation is the triumph of consumerism—another "ism." But consumerism and capitalism are now understood to be seriously predatory on, and destructive of, the household as a "seat of a process of living"—to use Veblen's phrasing. Capitalism has always been an engineering problem in disguise. The quest was to combine "factors of production" into goods and services by another name, and to do so at the lowest imaginable cost. Capitalism has always been a "deal funnel." Economic theory, with its model of the individual as nothing but a constrained maximizing consumer, provided the scientific gloss.

However, relentless pursuit of yet greater material abundance cannot survive as the raison d'être for any economic system. The more profound consequence that must now be grasped is that the legacy of income generation through the contentious mixing of owners of labor power with owners of the means of labor (capital) is a quaint artifact of a bygone era. Capitalism is now irrelevant because it is no longer necessary as an engineering system. This very irrelevance makes it possible to admit that it is failing at its more fundamental obligation. Capitalism is no longer a source of living. It was once a consumer's dream. It is now a worker's worst nightmare.

What "ism" is to follow? The evolutionary pathway of a postcapitalist world will bring us to a recognition that the acquisition of an income must no longer be dependent on the whims of a small group of individuals who control access to the means of labor (capital). Such individuals have held the whip hand for several hundred years, and their behavior has been amply aided by a culture of possessive individualism. In a sense, we have the "Pogo" syndrome at work: "We have met the enemy and he is us." Possessive individualism has authorized, justified, and abetted the creation of an economic system that is now understood to be comprehensively destructive of personhood.

A replacement will necessarily provide every individual an assured claim to a specific standard of living, consisting of cash (or a monthly line of renewable credit), and an associated entitlement to certain educational, housing, and medical programs. The details need not detain us for the simple reason that such a system cannot be designed de novo. As I point out in Chapter 2, we humans are unable to be sure of what we want until we start the arduous process of working out what we might be able to have. We will figure it out as we start the process of pursuing workable alternatives. It is impossible to be sure what it will look like because we have never done it before. This new dispensation—this new system—will comprise what I earlier called a constellation of *created imaginings*. They will represent imagined possibilities. Imagine that.

Because this new economic regime will be driven by the acknowledged need for a *humane* process of living, perhaps it will come to be called *humanism*.

Notes

1. Julie Cresswell, *The New York Times*, August 11, 2017.
2. Noam Scheiber, "Nissan Workers in Mississippi Reject Union Bid by UAW," *The New York Times*, August 5, 2017.
3. Patricia Cohen, "As Big Retailers Seek to Cut Their Tax Bills, Towns Bear the Brunt," *The New York Times*, January 6, 2019.
4. http://www.nytimes.com/2012/12/02/us/how-local-taxpayers-bankroll-corporations.html (accessed September 21, 2017).
5. Karen Weise, "Amazon Announces New York and Virginia as HQ2 Picks," *The New York Times*, November 13, 2018.
6. Bryce Covert, "Cities Should Stop Playing the Amazon HQ2 Bidding Game," *The New York Times*, November 13, 2018.
7. Bureau of Labor Statistics, U.S. Department of Labor, January 28, 2016.
8. *The Economist*, September 28, 2015.
9. https://www.bls.gov/emp/ep_table_201.htm, accessed June 24, 2017.
10. Lawrence Mishel, "Uber Is Not the Future of Work," *The Atlantic*, November 2015.16.
11. https://www.bls.gov/bdm/us_age_naics_00_table7.txt (accessed June 3, 2019).
12. Steven Erlanger, *The New York Times*, June 28, 2017.
13. The total exceeds 100 percent because several sectors overlap.
14. The Cambridge economist Piero Sraffa became famous for his seminal work, *The Production of Commodities by Means of Commodities* (Cambridge: Cambridge University Press, 1975).

References

Berlin, Isaiah. 1953. *The Hedgehog and the Fox*, London: Weidenfeld and Nicholson.
Bourdieu, Pierre. 1990. *The Logic of Practice*, Palo Alto, CA: Stanford University Press.
Bourdieu, Pierre. 1998. *Practical Reason*, Palo Alto, CA: Stanford University Press.
Bowra, C. M. 1940. "The Fox and the Hedgehog," *The Classical Quarterly*, 34(1/2): 26–29.
Lecomber, Richard. 1977. "The Isolation Paradox," *Quarterly Journal of Economics*, 91(3): 495–504.
Macpherson, C.B. 1973. *Democratic Theory*, Oxford: Clarendon Press.

Northrop, F.S.C. 1967. *The Logic of the Sciences and the Humanities,* New York: Meridian Books.

Rinne, Ulf. 2014. "Anonymous Job Applications and Hiring Discrimination," *IZA World of Labor*, 48, May. https://wol.iza.org/uploads/articles/454/pdfs/anonymous-job-applications-and-hiring-discrimination.one-pager.pdf?v=1

Sen, Amartya. 1993. "Markets and Freedoms: Achievements and Limitations of the Market Mechanism in Promoting Individual Freedoms," *Oxford Economic Papers* 45: 519–41.

Sivy, Michael. 2012. "The Big Winner of the Great Recession Is . . . ." *Time*, January 18. http://business.time.com/2012/01/18/the-big-winner-of-the-great-recession-is/

Veblen, Thorstein. 1904. *The Theory of the Business Enterprise*. New Brunswick, NJ: Transaction Books.

World Development Indicators. 2018. Washington, DC: World Bank.

5

The Isolated Periphery

Possessive individualism is not an affliction confined to the metropol-
itan core. Those countries at the periphery of the rich metropole are
also caught in a perverse trap of economic isolation, dysfunctional
governance, and social alienation. The household in these countries,
like their counterparts in the metropole, is precariously isolated rela-
tive to the political and economic power of international commerce.
Managerial capitalism has rendered millions of these households as
little more than the residual supplier of cheap labor. Why are these
poor countries unable to offer compelling livelihoods to their citizens?
Their colonial past is a part of the explanation, but contemporary cap-
italism continues to bear down on their economic prospects. In the
absence of meaningful work, there can be no mystery why sectarian
conflict emerges. And then we see that such conflict both encourages
the emergence of authoritarian leaders and reinforces it. In that sense,
the political climate in many countries of the isolated periphery is a
minor variant of what is now occurring in parts of western Europe,
Great Britain, and the United States.

I. Vulnerable People, Vulnerable States

The evolutionary trajectory of global capitalism has delivered a serious blow
to the economic status of most households in the metropolitan core. From
precapitalist familial arrangements, then into merchant capitalism, through
the difficulties of industrial capitalism, and on into financial and managerial capitalism, the economic fortunes of the household have waned in direct
proportion to the declining political importance of the household vis-à-vis
the capitalist firm. No clearer indication of this increasing marginalization
and political irrelevance can be found than in the steady stagnation of wages
and the constant attacks on unionized workers that began in the 1960s. If

households held any political salience in the metropolitan core, this record of real income stasis and reverence for "job creators" would be impossible to explain.

While the growing appeal of automation can be attributed to potential cost savings, automation must also be understood as one potent way to undermine the reliance on human labor inside the capitalist firm. In other words, capital in the form of machines is gradually undergoing a profound transformation from its historic role as the *means of labor*. Automation is a form of capital that *displaces labor*, and with the stark advances in computer technology, the pace of labor displacement has accelerated over the recent past. There is no evidence that this trend will slow. Cost savings from automation are but part of the calculation by firms. The aggressive embrace of automation is central to the growing irrelevance of the household to contemporary capitalism. Managerial capitalism reinforces this trend.

Our concern in this chapter is to come to a general understanding of how the evolutionary trajectory of capitalism in the metropolitan core has affected economic prospects in what I call the *isolated periphery*.

Since the end of World War II, the dominant story line concerning the global economy has been that historical disparities in per capita incomes and living standards across the globe would gradually disappear as the technology, the institutions, and the economic insights from the developed world—the metropolitan core—gradually made their way to the poorer countries in Africa, Asia, Latin America, and the Middle East. Indeed, the optimistic idea of globalization underpins this general vision. It was claimed that global trade would lift all boats. The main idea is one of *convergence*. This motivating idea can be found in the commitment in 1944 to establish the Bretton Woods organizations: the International Monetary Fund and the International Bank for Reconstruction and Development (the World Bank). A number of industrialized countries followed suit by creating their own development-assistance agencies.

Despite the very best efforts and billions of dollars, over 70 years of concerted development assistance has failed to produce convergence (Pritchett, 1997). What has gone wrong? Has capitalism given us a global economy in which the "first-mover advantage" leaves little opportunity for latecomers to share in the abundant riches now concentrated in the metropolitan core?

In pondering the persistence of problematic states in the periphery—Syria, Libya, Iraq, South Sudan, Yemen, Zimbabwe, Democratic Republic of the Congo, Uganda—it is too easy to blame corrupt leaders, religious conflicts, tribalism, or some other trait thought to be endemic to poor countries. Missing from the list of possible reasons for this disappointing state of affairs is one that is central to our work here. Perhaps there is something attributable to European colonization—and the subsequent emergence of global capitalism—that warrants consideration. Africa and the Middle East—as well as South Asia—were certainly part of European colonialism that endured in some countries until the 1960s. Perhaps we can blame the lack of convergence on the residue of colonialism?

It cannot be quite that simple, however. Stressing colonialism tends to place exclusive blame on past events, thereby lulling us into ignoring more recent circumstances that play a very important role. My proposition here is that the evolutionary pathway into managerial capitalism has made it difficult—perhaps impossible—for the vast majority of the remaining countries to break into the global capitalist system. Perhaps these countries are now so different in their economic and political architecture that it is impossible to move from their current state to something that allows a promising integration into the global economy.

Is it too late for these economies to break out of their current role as peripheral providers of a few raw materials—oil, minerals, tropical timber—and therefore emerge to play a significant role in the global economy dominated by financial and managerial imperatives? Put another way, of what possible use is a global economy driven by managerial machinations to the countries of the isolated periphery? And the obvious converse of this question is what, exactly, do the poor citizens of these rather isolated countries bring to managerial capitalism now being played out on a global scale? Is their economic fate merely to sit by and hope that some factory, in need of really cheap wage labor, will arrive? Put in stark terms, what if there is no more room at the top?

To get a sense of the disparity under discussion, consider Figures 5.1 and 5.2. We see here data for the 35 countries in the Organization for Economic Cooperation and Development (OECD) and similar data for the remaining 160 countries of the world. The OECD group—the metropolitan core—consists largely of the rich industrialized countries in the world.[1] Two comparisons are on display here: (1) total gross domestic product in 2017 U.S. dollars; and (2) per capita gross domestic product in 2017 U.S. dollars.

We see here that in 2017, the 35 OECD countries accounted for total GDP of $49,626,408,983,000 shared across a population of 1,300,865,255 individuals. The rest of the world (160 countries) had access to a total GDP of $31,057,378,454,000 shared across 6,229,494,894 individuals. In other

Gross domestic product in U.S. dollars: 2017

Figure 5.1. Total GDP: OECD and Rest of the World, U.S. Dollars, 2017
Source: World Development Indicators.

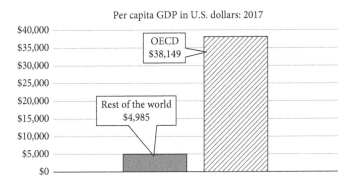

Figure 5.2. Per Capita GDP: OECD and Rest of the World, U.S. Dollars, 2017
Source: World Development Indicators.

words, in 2017 the 35 OECD countries contained 17 percent of the world's population of 7,530,360,149, and yet these individuals enjoyed 62 percent of total global GDP. The rest of the world, with 83 percent of the population in 160 countries, enjoyed just 38 percent of total GDP. If the world were perfectly egalitarian in income distribution, 17 percent of the population living in the 35 OECD countries would control 17 percent of global GDP, while 83 percent of total population living in non-OECD countries would share the remaining 83 percent of the world's GDP. But of course there is no such equality. Figure 5.2 depicts the stark disparity in per capita GDP.

The above two figures acknowledge the existence of what the development literature considers the core-periphery problem. If we think in those terms, the *core*—the metropole—consists of the OECD countries captured in Figures 5.1 and 5.2. On this view, the *periphery* encompasses those 160 countries lying beyond the metropole. Influenced by the seminal work of Raul Prebisch (1901–1986), this idea gained considerable resonance in Latin America during the period immediately following World War II (Prebisch, 1950).

Prebisch, a native of Argentina, was director of the United Nations Economic Commission for Latin America (ECLA), a position that gave him a special perspective on Latin America's growing dependence on the United States during the postwar period. Central to the idea of a core and a periphery is Prebisch's creation of what is called *dependency theory*. He saw Latin American countries—parts of the periphery—as being dependent on the United States (the core).

In the 1920s—before the Depression—Prebisch had observed the enormous wealth created in his homeland because of the export of wheat and livestock to the United Kingdom. Both countries benefited from this textbook example of the manifold virtues of trade predicated on the concept of *comparative advantage*. On the one hand, Argentina was blessed with an abundance of high-quality agricultural land and very low population levels. The United Kingdom, on the other hand, was densely populated and enjoyed ample income from its robust industrial sector, thus enabling it to import desired agricultural products from afar. Here was the perfect illustration of the theory of comparative advantage. Indeed, this was "free trade" in its purest form. We might even think of it as the simple case of emerging globalization. Argentina bought manufactured goods from the UK and exported agricultural products to the UK. Both countries benefited enormously from this happy situation.

But then the Depression hit in the early 1930s, and world demand for UK manufactures plummeted. The UK economy crashed, and with that, the demand for imported Argentine wheat and beef evaporated. The Argentine economy was stuck with wheat and livestock for which there was no market. Unlike manufactures that can be shut down—or slowed down—in response to market exigencies, wheat production is an ongoing biological process that can take 8 to 11 months to complete. Planning for the next year requires confidence in market conditions a number of months into the future. Livestock production is even more sluggish and cumbersome in a temporal sense.

Prebisch and his colleagues at the Argentine central bank watched helplessly as the price of Argentine exports plunged. The Argentine economy was exporting cheap primary products—agricultural goods and minerals—but was having to import expensive manufactured goods. It was not long until Prebisch and his colleagues at ECLA realized that, while the pure theory of free trade was elegant as a heuristic device, trade—and the idea of comparative advantage—could be harmful in practice. This experience led him to realize that Argentina had become *dependent* on the UK in a way that had not been apparent in theory. There was an added problem lurking on the sidelines—one that resonates today.

Specifically, Argentine dependence was compounded by the fact that a large number of countries around the world could produce wheat and livestock, but at that time only the UK was a manufacturing power. That is, many countries provided a market for UK manufactures, but only one country (the United Kingdom) provided a market for Argentine beef and wheat. Then, in the aftermath of World War II, with the rise of the U.S. economy, the dependency of Argentina for manufactures gradually shifted from the UK to the United States. But the United States had its own ample supply of wheat and beef production, and so Argentina lost the British market for grain and livestock but did not gain a customer for its agricultural products.

From that point forward, dependency theory would reveal itself in terms of a "core" and a "periphery." Latin America was now peripheral to the United States. In this light, it becomes possible to understand the constant tension Latin America feels toward the "big enchilada" north of the Rio Grande River. The economy of many Latin American countries was inextricably linked to that of the United States. Linkage need not be problematic; dependency is problematic. Figure 5.3 gives us a glimpse of what has become of Argentina's economy.[2] It is said that Argentina is the only country in the world that has gone backwards. In 1900, it was considered a "developed" economy, and by 2000 it had become a "developing" country.

As we turn our attention to contemporary tensions in the global economy, the problem is *not* that a large number of countries possess wheat and livestock. Rather, the problem is that they are abundantly endowed with low-cost unemployed—or underemployed—labor. These countries have little to export, and of course they cannot export their redundant workers desperate for access to the means of labor in the metropolitan core. But these countries *can* export the *products* of that cheap labor by joining with companies in the industrialized world—the core—who wish to drive down the cost of labor. The strategy, well known by now, is to outsource labor-intensive jobs— clothing manufacturing, electronics assembly—to such countries by setting up facilities in those low-cost locations.

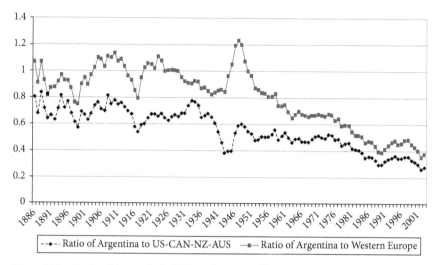

Figure 5.3. Ratio of Argentina's GDP to the GDP of Two Groups of Core Countries
Source: Campos, 2014.

In the case of U.S.-Mexico dependency theory, *maquiladoras* just south of the shared border are perfect examples of this aspect of comparative advantage. Further afield, cheap labor in China, Vietnam, and Bangladesh is eager and available to offer the same services. And, as Argentina learned the hard way in the 1930s, if labor becomes too expensive in Vietnam, there is always Cambodia and Laos to assume the role of residual provider of cheap labor. And if labor costs rise too much there, perhaps a few easily accessible countries in Africa will emerge as the next-best location.

It seems that there are many countries where labor is cheaper than in those countries now being relied upon. Under managerial capitalism, Marx's reserve army is not a domestic threat. Rather, it is now an *international resource*. Unfortunately, unlike the UK-Argentine arrangement earlier in the twentieth century, there is little consumer income in Laos or Cambodia, or in most of Africa, to be spent on items produced in the core. Moreover, it is most unlikely that these low-wage jobs in the isolated periphery will be the launching pad for economic change that will bring about a robust demand for manufactures from the metropolitan core. It is a one-way deal, with the dependent countries in the isolated periphery seriously exposed to being underbid for the only thing they can offer to the global economy—very cheap labor. Individual nations in the isolated periphery now resemble households in the metropolitan core: both are peripatetic foxes in a world of a few accomplished hedgehogs.

In other words, over the past several decades, with the emergence of the World Trade Organization and with a variety of efforts being made to stitch the world together into one large "free-trade zone," it has become increasingly apparent that the core-periphery account is not limited in scope. The North American Free Trade Agreement (NAFTA) was an effort to overcome some of the disadvantages of Latin American dependence—in this case Mexico—on the "regional core" (the United States and Canada). The results have not been altogether positive; the principles of dependence persist to this day. It is easy to find criticisms of China for its export policies vis-à-vis the United States, but a version of the perils of dependency theory is at work even here. With China's desire to escape the serial horrors of Mao Zedong's agricultural collectivization, Great Leap Forward, and Cultural Revolution, economic reforms in the 1980s were driven by the policy designed to make China rich before it grew old. And so China willingly became dependent on exports of clothing, plastics, electronics, and assorted gadgetry manufactured by cheap labor in special economic zones along the southeast coast. China needed export earnings, and it needed those earnings very quickly in order to reach a point where it could afford to turn its attention to consumer goods and services for its own population.

In recent times, as China has become richer, its citizens are now demanding access to a range of modern consumer items long denied them by the government's export orientation. As China becomes richer, its workers demand higher pay in order to purchase the goods and services they now expect. And so, as above, other countries in the region—now constituting China's periphery—are set to become the new location of export-based manufacturing that drove China's economic renaissance. Vietnam is the primary beneficiary of this phenomenon. Both China and Vietnam were—and are—dependent on the core. But it seems that Vietnam (and perhaps Laos) will soon become dependent on China.

In discussing the emergence of this core-periphery phenomenon, Jeffrey Williamson observes that in 1960, per capita incomes in Asia and Africa were slightly less than 14 percent of those in western Europe, while for Latin America, the comparable figure stood at about 41 percent. What Prebisch and the dependent theorists had first realized in the 1930s and 1940s had finally delivered what dependency theory predicted would occur. This was the salient feature of what Williamson called the "world economic order" in 1960 (Williamson, 2011). He added that

> the poor periphery exported primary products . . . , while the rich core exported manufactures; indeed 85 percent of the poor periphery's exports were either agricultural or mineral products (for sub-Saharan Africa it was 94 percent), while the figure for western Europe was only 30 percent. Trade, specialization in commodities, and poverty were closely correlated. (Williamson, 2011, p. 2)

The more interesting aspect of this new *world economic order* concerns the reasons for its emergence in the final days of the nineteenth century. That is when the "Third World" became identifiable precisely because it was falling behind the industrialized "First World." Even this terminology is quaint and judgmental. For those who wonder about the "Second World"— that consisted of the centrally planned economies of the Soviet Union and China. In other words, the world was then neatly carved into the successful countries, the unsuccessful countries, and the hopeless communist regimes missing out on the many promises of capitalism and thoroughgoing markets.

As Williamson documents, the world trade boom of roughly 1815–1913 brought important gains to what would become the Third World. During this period, prices of its primary product exports soared, while prices of what it imported from the newly industrializing economies plunged. These effects were the expected implications of rapid technical change in manufacturing that reduced production costs, and rising incomes in the new industrial economies that fueled increased interest in imports of foodstuffs and commodities (cotton, timber, and spices) from the periphery. Williamson then developed empirical support for the proposition that the great trade boom of the nineteenth century enhanced growth rates in the industrialized world by much more than those growth rates were enhanced in the poor periphery. Indeed, in a few instances, this trade boom actually harmed growth prospects in the periphery (Williamson, 2011, p. 181). Here was the origin of the great divergence in living standards that plagues us today. On this matter:

> Divergence in relative productivity levels and living standards is the dominant feature of modern economic history. In the last century, incomes in the "less developed" (or euphemistically, the "developing") countries have fallen far behind those in the "developed" countries, both

proportionately and absolutely. I estimate that from 1870 to 1990 the ratio of per capita incomes between the richest and the poorest countries increased by roughly a factor of five and that the difference in income between the richest country and all others has increased by an order of magnitude. This divergence is the result of the very different patterns in the long-run economic performance of two sets of countries. (Pritchett, 1997, p. 3)

Ironically, the 1815–1913 trade boom—a profoundly peaceful period between the end of Napoleon's assaults on the rest of Europe and the start of World War I—turned out to be a severe obstacle to the fledgling manufacturing sector in the poor periphery. The textile industry in India, a vibrant and productive enterprise, was first undermined and then destroyed by British colonialism and the associated desire to export raw cotton from India so as to undertake manufacturing of cloth in Manchester, Liverpool, and their outlying rural towns. With stiff competition in industrial activity emerging from the rapidly industrializing metropolitan core, countries in the poor periphery suffered gradual deindustrialization. At the same time, the rich countries strengthened their industrial advantage by capitalizing on the fruits of increasing returns to scale (Krugman, 1981, 1991a, 1991b). In contrast, agriculture and the export of natural resources are generally trapped by constant returns to scale—and perhaps even diminishing returns to land (Matsuyama, 1991, 1992).

In consequence, countries in the periphery retreated back to their only enduring comparative advantage: exporting primary commodities. This process was exacerbated by the growing importance of positive agglomeration externalities and economies of scale in the industrialized world. That is, agglomeration economies associated with the rise of urbanized manufactures, and the scale effects as growing demand—the result of population and income growth—served to induce ever-greater levels of output from the industrial sector in the core. We can postulate a certain momentum at work as industrialization "took off" at the beginning of the twentieth century. That momentum then pushed countries in the periphery back into a strategy of export reliance on primary products from agriculture and natural resources (Krugman and Venables, 1995).

The two regions of the emerging world economic order—the core and the periphery—were pulled in opposite directions [Hirschman, 1958; Myrdal, 1957]. In contemporary terms, we see this as the germ of endogenous growth theory (Murphy, et al. 1989). More correctly, we see here a demonstration of *endogenous comparative advantage*. The sustained growth in trade bore asymmetric impacts: it was a blessing for the new industrial economics of the core, and it spelled doom for the primary producers in the periphery. It appears that dependency is now a burden to be borne into the future. The growth of managerial capitalism seems likely to solidify and compound that burden.

The penalty to be paid by the exporting periphery was magnified by the emergence of what has come to be called the "resource curse" (Sachs and Warner, 2001). One aspect of the "curse," also called *Dutch disease*, refers to the decline in competitiveness of nonresource tradable goods and services following real exchange rate appreciation caused by the rapid infusion of new income into a country. Large inflows of foreign exchange from the export of one or two products—oil, tropical timber, minerals—cause domestic wages to rise relative to wages in other countries. This will, in turn, increase the relative cost of producing all other tradable goods, progressively narrowing the export base and increasing imports. Moreover, oil and other natural resource sectors represent attractive investments, which means that other sectors are starved for credit. We see here an insidious form of credit rationing. The promising cashew sector in Ghana is starved for credit because the country's export-based cocoa sector has such a voracious appetite for credit that bankers have become satisfied and do not seek other customers. The cocoa sector can absorb all of the available credit, and thus the increased uncertainty associated with serving new cashew clients outside of this comfortable arrangement means that lenders feel no need to extend themselves into uncharted territory.

In Iraq during the early 2000s, the Dutch disease led to non-oil tradable commodities being driven out of existence. Consumption became an increasing part of the economy, and consumer imports increased at double the pace of total imports. There simply was no demand for industrial-related imports to contribute to the revitalization of Iraq's productive capacity. Similarly, there was a progressive decrease in agricultural and manufacturing production as a share of GDP beginning in the 1980s. By 2010, these productive sectors accounted for less than 7 percent of GDP (USAID, 2012).

A second and more insidious characteristic of the resource curse is that it drives a wedge between governments and the general population. This occurs because governments receive so much of their necessary revenue from the export of natural resources that they do not need to levy taxes on their citizens. As a result, citizens who pay nothing to their government often find it difficult to hold the government accountable for its actions. The absence of taxes also makes it easier for governments to disregard the demands of their citizens. Since citizens pay little or nothing in taxes, governments can ignore them with impunity. There is no "tax-bargain."

The evidence suggests that these two aspects of the resource curse are interrelated. The tendency of the export base to narrow and import dependence to increase has been observed in many petroleum exporting countries and may arise from the absence of any efforts to pursue necessary economic reforms. This reluctance is exacerbated by the deceiving comfort of rising oil income (Auty, 1994). Since the world price of oil dropped by approximately one-half in 2014, that comfortable cushion has now disappeared. Many exporting countries are experiencing deep economic pain.

Several strategies can be used to avoid the resource curse. Norway is considered a good example of how to manage large inflows of revenue from the export of natural resources. The country has established a "Petroleum Fund of Norway"—a sovereign wealth fund—which is invested in both stocks and bonds. All earnings from the investments are reinvested in the fund. The fund is used only if the government is forced to run a deficit. Norway has a fairly high tax burden, so citizens expect and receive many public services. In other words, Norway has a robust *tax bargain*. The approach results in almost complete sterilization of oil revenues, thereby insulating the exchange rate from unwanted influences. The fund is set up to meet emergencies but primarily to benefit future generations when the oil is depleted.

In Brazil, local jurisdictions from which oil is extracted receive a royalty payment based on the amount of oil extracted from the municipality. Research shows that the oil boom has led to increases in public spending but has had little or no effect on non-oil GDP in Brazil. Research also shows that the royalty system has led to increases in corruption of public officials (Caselli and Michaels, 2009; Monteiro and Ferraz, 20010.

Chad is another useful, though negative, illustration. Despite the best efforts of the international community to see that an offshore (sterilized) fund was established—and that some of the new oil income was used to launch Chad's economic development—its fragile political process collapsed and the contracts made with the World Bank failed to stop the President from taking control of all oil revenues for current budget expenditures.

The resource curse is most pronounced in the case of oil, largely because that is where the most durable demand is felt on countries of the periphery. And, as we have seen in the case of Iraq, it is where the greatest economic value arises. There is another domain of dependence, and that figures prominently in the modern world system. This is the dependence of the industrialized world—generally the OECD countries—on imported oil.[3] Table 5.1 depicts the 10 leading oil-producing nations in 2017, only two of which are in the OECD and five of which are in the Middle East. Oil production does not easily equate to oil exports because domestic consumption may figure prominently in the oil balance of producing nations. In Table 5.2 we see the top 10 oil-consuming nations in 2015, with their respective share of total world consumption.

The resource curse must be understood as a gradual process of structural transformation in which economic activity becomes overly focused on one dominant production and export activity (sector). Canada is not in danger of suffering from the resource curse because oil production and exports are but a minor part of its economy and of its exports. But the same cannot be said for Saudi Arabia, the United Arab Emirates, Kuwait, Nigeria, Iraq, Venezuela, Kazakhstan, Russia, and Angola.

Table 5.1. Top 10 Oil Producers and Share of World Total

Country	Million barrels per day	Share of world total
United States	14.46	15%
Saudi Arabia	12.08	13%
Russia	11.18	12%
Canada	4.87	5%
Iran	4.67	5%
Iraq	4.48	5%
China	4.45	5%
United Arab Emirates	3.71	4%
Brazil	3.29	3%
Kuwait	2.93	3%
Total top 10	66.12	69%
World total	95.36	

Source: U.S. Energy Information Administration,

https://www.eia.gov/tools/faqs/faq.php?id=709&t=6, Accessed November 16, 2018.

Table 5.2. Top 10 Oil Consumers and Share of World Total

Country	Million barrels per day	Share of world total
United States	19.53	20%
China	12.02	13%
India	4.14	4%
Japan	4.12	4%
Russia	3.55	4%
Saudi Arabia	3.24	3%
Brazil	2.99	3%
South Korea	2.41	3%
Canada	2.41	3%
Germany	2.37	2%
Total top 10	56.78	60%
World total	95.36	

Source: U.S. Energy Information Administration, https://www.eia.gov/tools/faqs/faq.php?id=709&t=6, Accessed November 16, 2018.

The new country of South Sudan, born out of its liberation struggle while still part of Sudan until 2011, is suffering from the heightened exuberance of what it would be like to live with a stock of oil. When the world price of oil plummeted, South Sudan experienced the worst of two worlds. It did not have a real economy at the time of its independence, and three years of handsome oil revenue launched all manner of ill-advised government-funded activities. Paramount among them was the creation of a bloated government payroll fueled by oil earnings. With oil revenue now much below its level in 2012–2013, the economy is practically nonexistent. Government employees often go months without pay. Civil conflict has reemerged, and starvation is rampant. By mid-2017, approximately one million South Sudanese had fled to Uganda. There simply is no other economic activity to offset the negative forces of a single export activity.

This inevitable process of economic specialization reminds us of the perils of resource-dependent economies. We see the effects of unbuffered exposure to extreme price volatility in the only export available to such countries. As in South Sudan, this dramatic drop in world oil prices that began around 2014 brought severe economic grief to countries as varied as Russia, Venezuela, Nigeria, and other oil exporters. In Iraq, oil exports at the time accounted for

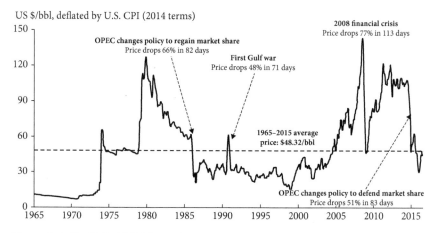

Figure 5.4. Real World Oil Prices Since 1965
Source: World Bank

over 99 percent of all export income and funded more than 90 percent of the total national budget.

Because oil exports are dominated by the Organization of the Petroleum Exporting Countries (OPEC) and a few other major exporters who are not part of OPEC (Russia, Canada, China, Mexico, Norway, and the UK), it is rather easy to associate known historical events with the price trajectory of oil (Figure 5.4). In other words, while general market conditions, notably weather and fluctuating demand, will often influence the price of agricultural products and industrial metals, oil prices are, to a certain extent, capable of manipulation by the OPEC cartel and other exporting nations who benefit from OPEC's actions.

This exposure to price volatility is not limited to oil. As we see in Figure 5.5, exporters of primary commodities have lived through over 50 years of generally declining real prices (an exception being 2005–2010) but also pronounced annual variability in those prices. The resource-dependent countries are, by definition, exceedingly reliant on an income source that is variable, unreliable, and not amenable to augmentation through technical change or innovation.

The momentary rise in oil prices between 2010 and early 2014 shown in Figure 5.5 was not matched by prices of other primary commodities in world markets. In fact, in Figure 5.6, we see that a wide variety of primary commodities have suffered severe drops since the beginning of 2011. The

Index, real (2010–100)

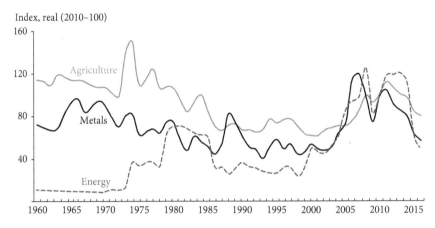

Figure 5.5. Index of Real Prices of Three Classes of Primary Commodities
Source: World Bank

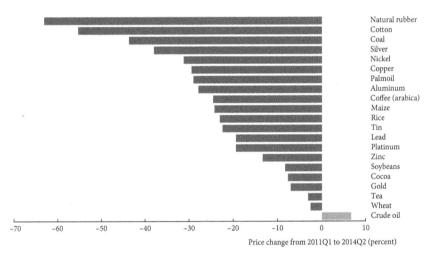

Figure 5.6. Percent Change in Real Commodity Prices, 2011–2014
Source: World Bank

evidence seems clear that national economies dependent on the export of raw commodities are exposed to severe price fluctuations that disrupt and confound not only household incomes, but general economic policy as well. Such countries are seriously dependent on global economic forces over which they have no control.

From this general picture of the economic climate in the core and the periphery, we now turn our attention to two distinct regions of the *isolated periphery*: (1) the Middle East and North Africa; and (2) sub-Saharan Africa. This detailed focus on these two contiguous regions of the periphery warrants brief justification.

First, with the exception of the Indian subcontinent and the "spice islands" (Indonesia), European colonialism had a longer and more severe presence here than in practically any other region of the world. Slaves, ivory, tropical timber, minerals, and oil were essential commodities fueling the growth of the metropolitan core during the nineteenth and twentieth centuries. Moreover, the geographic centrality of the Middle East to trade and military transport—especially since the Suez Canal was built in 1869—meant that control of the choke-point at the eastern end of the Mediterranean Sea assumed great geopolitical significance.

Coming forward in time, we clearly see that no other region presents the array of vexing sources of world disorder. The continuing dysfunction of political life in the Middle East—from ISIS to the Syrian civil war, to the stresses between Saudi Arabia and Yemen (and recently Qatar), to the continuing disarray in Iraq, to the nuclear game being played by Iran, to the Palestinian-Israeli conflict—means that very little about the modern world can be taken for granted.

These problems are, unfortunately, not limited to the immediate region. A number of European countries are, or have been, besieged by immigrants pouring out of the region seeking political asylum or economic security. North Africa, especially Libya, serves as a launching site for thousands of migrants streaming out of the Middle East and extending south and west into Africa in a treacherous voyage across the Mediterranean bound for southern Italy. Many of these African emigrants are fleeing seriously dysfunctional political and economic conditions in South Sudan, the Central African Republic, Niger, and The Gambia. Indeed, much of the recent political turmoil in the European Union can be traced to this influx. Most African countries remain stuck in economic despair. We must understand why.

II. Economic Life in the Isolated Periphery

Let us look more carefully at the two regions I call the *isolated periphery*. First we have the Middle East and North Africa, home to strong authoritarian leaders and restless and alienated Arab and Islamic populations. It is here that we see a continuing history of sectarian violence, political jockeying by contending nation-states, and failed economic systems often based on oil production. Here, the rich do not work. Ominously, most of the "working-class" population of many of these countries—those who must work—have been unable to find meaningful employment. The traditional strategy of using oil revenues to secure domestic peace has proven unsustainable.

The so-called Arab Spring of late 2010 and 2011 offers evidence of that. Indeed, the Arab Spring can be seen as a manifestation of the region's long-running dependence on supplying precious oil to the world's metropolitan core. We are addicted to their oil, and as a result our economies have become distorted by the ready availability of cheap carbon fuels that now stand implicated in the growing threat of serious climate change. At the same time, political leaders in this region are addicted to the oil revenue made possible by our perverse addiction. Here we see an illustration of the resource curse and dependency. The Middle East and North Africa recapitulate the Prebisch notion of a core and a dependent periphery—an alienated fringe economy right on the southern doorstep of Europe.

The "diaspora of death" spread by ISIS and al-Qaeda is fueling political chaos throughout several countries in the metropole. Underlying these exported threats is the continuing disarray in Iraq and Yemen, the serious civil war in Syria, and general dysfunction in Libya and Egypt. The mass exodus of refugees from this region, making the perilous Mediterranean crossing in overcrowded boats and rubber rafts, continues to encourage reactionary political movements in much of Europe. This continued migration over the past several years has threatened the European Union and has contributed to the rise of right-wing political parties in Hungary, Poland, Finland, and France. Angela Merkel's grip on power in Germany has been undermined, and she is nearing the end of her long tenure as the acknowledged champion of the European Union (EU). These pressures represent a clear and present danger to the modern world system as we know it.

The second problematic region in the periphery does not suffer from strong authoritarian leaders. Rather, sub-Saharan Africa suffers from weak leaders and generally dysfunctional political and economic systems. Here we find the vast majority of the world's poorest individuals, and their poverty has clear explanations. The legacy of colonialism bequeathed to these countries weak leaders educated and socialized to understand surplus extraction that was the hallmark of colonialism. Moreover, the increasing hegemony of managerial capitalism now threatens to leave these countries with little role to play. Many of these countries have made little, if any, income gains over the past three decades. Unlike the working class in a number of OECD countries, the citizens of these countries started with little or nothing, and so their economic stagnation continues to leave them poor and miserable. Most of them still have little or nothing. They live in countries wracked by persistent civil conflict. Many of their governments are dysfunctional. Global capitalism has largely bypassed this difficult part of the world.

Sub-Saharan Africa warrants our attention because of the enduring economic marginalization from the world economic system of the countries on this fragile continent. Their nearly one billion citizens remain mired in abject poverty and hopelessness and represent an inescapable rebuke of the optimistic notion that vibrant globalization would deliver a promising livelihood to everyone. In fact, the situation in sub-Saharan Africa seems to suggest that global capitalism has no role for these countries and their impoverished residents. Nor does global capitalism appear to have an answer for the perverse and durable desperation that envelopes the marvelous landscapes of that tragic continent. It is no longer possible to blame this situation on indigenous political dysfunction, corruption, and economic incoherence. In fact, it is possible to entertain the notion that those unpleasant traits are the result, not the cause, of the Continent's degraded economic performance.

Global capitalism emerged following World War II and flourished in the public consciousness during the Cold War precisely because it appeared to be an appealing political vision that it would deliver promising livelihoods to all citizens scattered across the globe. The triumphalism associated with Margaret Thatcher's boast that "There Is No Alternative" (the TINA doctrine) to global capitalism and free markets captures the spirit of the 1990s. Much of that idea continues to the present day, despite the 2007–2009 Great Recession.

Unfortunately, sub-Saharan Africa serves to remind us of the failure of the convergence ideology. The question worth asking is why, exactly, economic conditions have not turned out well for the one billion residents of that tragic continent. Perhaps the modern world system finds sub-Saharan Africa problematic because we do not know what to do about its durable existence as a hinterland—a periphery—to a market-oriented world that has its own economic stresses and challenges. Despite decades of economic and technical assistance, from both national and multinational donors and advisors, most countries in sub-Saharan continue to remain outside of the world economic system—except as exporters of raw materials. Their intractable poverty and despair continue to pose a challenge to the animating presumptions of the modern world system.

A. The Legacy of Colonialism

It is now well known that the modern nation-state—a creation of western Europe—emerged as a resolution of the Thirty Years' War (1618–1648) in what would become Germany, and the Peace of Westphalia in 1648 (Kissinger, 2014). The intricate institutional architecture that resulted from these changes enabled and nourished agrarian prosperity—the only economic activity at that time. It would be foolish to suppose that in the middle of the seventeenth century, political leaders understood that what came to be called *industrialism* would emerge from the agricultural countryside, and then bring about urbanization and new levels of personal income on an unprecedented scale. At that early date, the point was to stabilize the many competing principalities in the hopes of improving livelihoods. While peace did not last long, the new national architecture has largely persisted. But the idea of the modern nation-state would have difficulties arising out of the colonial experience that was the product of early European statehood. What had worked in central Europe was not so easily transportable to the difficult areas east and south of the Mediterranean.

Beginning in the earliest days of the seventeenth century, both the English and the Dutch created private chartered companies whose purpose was to explore the distant hinterland and extract various goods much in demand back home. First, the English created the East India Company in 1600, and then the Dutch East India Company (the VOC) was founded in 1602. These early private charters precipitated the spread of colonial rule throughout the smaller latitudes. In the British case, colonialism was transformed into Imperialism after the 1857 Sepoy Rebellion in the fortress at Meerut. These early colonial initiatives, most of them focused on Africa, were formalized at the Berlin Conference, which ran from late 1884 into early 1885 (Pakenham, 1991). One of the most egregious outcomes of this conference (to which, shamefully, no African leader was invited) was the granting of the Congo River basin to King Leopold II of Belgium. This was not state-based colonialism that was legitimized throughout the rest of the African continent, but rather an instance of granting this vast territory as the private fiefdom of Leopold—whose rapacious rule still shocks modern readers.

It was not long before political and military control was projected over parts of South Asia, the Arab world, and the African continent. Although some of this activity was mere political gamesmanship designed to outmaneuver a neighboring European nation, much of it was driven by a desire to control the natural resources that could be extracted and sold on world markets, or shipped to Europe for domestic use. Copper, gold, salt, diamonds, timber, and a few crops (cotton, tea, coffee, assorted spices, cacao, tobacco) were the objects of greatest interest. Slaves and ivory also figured in colonial calculations (Nunn, 2008). Oil would not appear until the early years of the twentieth century.

Colonial administrators were not interested in developing coherent governance and administrative procedures. If they did have such interests, it was so that they could control economic and political processes in order to facilitate extraction of resources and economic surplus—including taxes levied on locals. Few colonizing powers saw their defining purpose to be the creation of self-sustaining and coherent governance by and for the locals. These foreign administrators understood the meager economic potential of the vast spaces and found little reason to think of territory—conquered land—as an economic asset. But the natural and agricultural resources were a prize worth gathering in.

We see here the origins of economic dysfunction and political alienation in the region under discussion. The standard colonial model was to locate a currently oppressed social group and then to enlist the group as an ally in the task of imposed—often absentee—governance. These formerly marginalized groups were only too happy to participate in the process of revenge against their former local oppressors. They also saw the chance to change places so that they, one day, might be on top. But of course colonial administrators did not wish to establish a competing source of power, and so there was a need to create and perpetuate new social divisions and categories. In the Arab world, European colonialism replaced the Ottoman Empire dating from around 1300, until its collapse at the end of World War I. Ottoman rulers perfected the model of social atomization and alien authority: it was called divide and control. It turned out that colonial conquest was the easy part; sustained administrative control was the more difficult challenge.

With the dissolution of the Ottoman Empire in the 1920s, the Arab world was immediately victimized by a second wave of social atomization, this time at the hands of the British, the French, and the Americans. Stabilization was the overarching goal to make sure that the region did not become a staging area for Soviet influence and quest for a warm-water port. Iraq was established in 1918 by a series of strategic British moves, including the 1921 delivery of Faisal the First by ship from Jeddah to Basra to serve as Iraq's King. The previous autumn his brother Abdullah had been deposited in Amman to become King of Trans-Jordan (now Jordan). The first of these brothers was blessed—or cursed—to gain control of massive oil deposits. The other brother, just next door (in Trans-Jordan), was given a territory devoid of natural resource wealth. The Kingdom of Saudi Arabia was created in 1932, followed by Kuwait in 1961 (Meyer and Brysac, 2008).

And then, of course there was oil—lots of it. In 1933, the heir to the Crane plumbing fixture company of Chicago, Charles R. Crane, managed to acquire an oil concession from King Ibn Saud in what is now Saudi Arabia. A decade later, in 1944, the Arabian American Oil Company (Aramco) was formed to produce and distribute the prodigious flood of Middle East oil. Suddenly, stability and control in the entire region took on worldwide significance. A new brand of absentee colonialism settled in over the sands of a region that just happened to be the origin of the world's three dominant religions: Judaism, Christianity, and Islam. The outcome has been precisely what one would expect.

B. Pathways of Despair

Turning now to what colonialism and global capitalism have wrought, consider a very brief summary of a few social and economic indicators of life in the isolated periphery. For comparison's sake, similar data for the OECD core will also be included. The first indicator of interest is a trajectory of per capita Gross National Income (GNI) for three groupings of countries (Figure 5.7).[4] The lines represent the OECD, the Middle East and North Africa (MENA), and sub-Saharan Africa (SSA). We see that the promise of convergence, at least in terms of per capita incomes, has been illusory.

Profound disparities across these three groups of countries are sharply revealed in several noneconomic indicators. The first of these indicators is

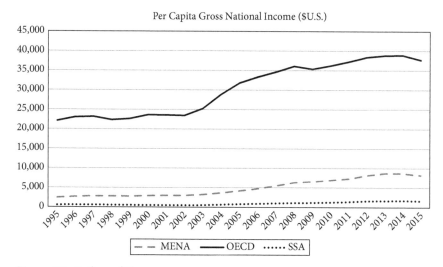

Figure 5.7. Failure of Convergence
Source: World Development Indicators, Countries in each category are listed in the Appendix.

maternal mortality (during birth) per 100,000 live births. This unfortunate event is exceedingly rare in the OECD countries, but in the Middle East and North Africa there is one maternal death for every 100,000 live births, while in sub-Saharan Africa there are 600 maternal deaths for every 100,000 live births. A related index is the mortality rate of infants under 5 years of age. Here too, we see that the Middle East, North Africa, and sub-Saharan Africa are places apart (Figure 5.8).

These comparisons accentuate the economic and social reality facing the vast majority of the world's citizens. There is no such thing as a shared prosperity, nor has the pursuit of convergence produced much in the way of meaningful progress. When reports appear celebrating the decline in global poverty over the past 20 years, it is rarely noted that the vast majority of those gains have occurred in China under the "Beijing Consensus." This warrants mention because it cannot be said that China is a democratic capitalist country. It is an authoritarian one-party state with complete government control over all aspects of economic life. Despite this, China's growth rate over the past two decades—admittedly starting from a very low level—has been greater than any other known experience. There were times when the government was seeking ways to *slow it down*. Given the constant celebrations of market capitalism, it may be a surprise to learn of such successes.

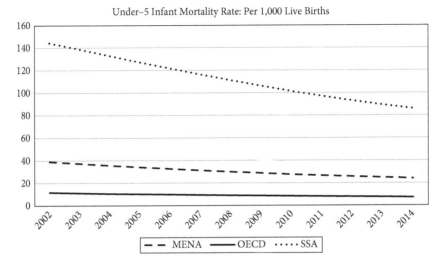

Figure 5.8. Infant Mortality
Source: World Development Indicators.

III. The Alienated Fringe: The Middle East

The common reaction when discussing the Middle East is often expressed as "What is wrong with those people?" Very often what is meant by "those people" is their religion—Islam. Such comments confuse the idea of human nature with the reality of human history. To get started in correcting the standard misconceptions requires that we grasp the important distinction between a religion and a sect. A *religion* concerns systems of beliefs, doctrines, rites, sacred texts, and various practices associated with sacred objects and the revealed meaning of human life. A *sect*, on the other hand, concerns the social organization of a community of those individuals who are affiliated with a specific religion. And so we find the familiar sects of Druze, Shi'a, Sunni, Alawite, Sufi, and Wahabi in the Islamic world. Closer to home, sects come in the form of Catholics, Methodists, Lutherans, Baptists, Presbyterians, Unitarians, and Episcopalians. The importance of sects is reinforced by pointing out that few individuals in the Western world would make the mistake of confusing a Catholic for a Lutheran or a Baptist for a Unitarian.

European colonialism in the Arab world was actually a rather late arrival. As above, the original colonialism in the region—the Ottoman Empire—was built on various layers of intermediaries who served as buffers between the general population and distant authoritarian rulers. These intermediaries, who lived among the population and who were thus accessible, were leaders of the various atomized sects. Over time, as the central control of the Ottoman Empire weakened, the former reach and authority of the central government—what we might wish to think of as the state—withered and was gradually taken over by these sectarian leaders. The historian of religion Karen Armstrong (2002) often alludes to these intermediaries as the "priestly class." All sects have them. In Christianity, they are called parsons, preachers, ministers, priests, pastors, and bishops. In Islam, they are Mullahs, Imams, and Ayatollahs.

In light of the region's long and tenacious colonial history, we can now see why these atomized and fragmented societies have weak levels of social, political, and economic integration. In addition, the so-called second tier of African countries—Sudan, Chad, Niger, Nigeria, Mali, Burkina Faso, and Senegal—have long been places of cultural and religious tension. The long-running civil war in Sudan—eventually resulting in the split into South Sudan and Sudan in 2011—is emblematic of this tension. Similarly, Northern Nigeria is struggling with the threat of Boko Haram. Indeed, the tenth parallel is cited as the fault line across northern Africa where Islam bumps up against indigenous and Christian traditions (Griswold, 2010). This ominous marker runs east from Guinea through Burkina Faso, Ghana, Togo, Benin, Nigeria, and Chad, follows the new jagged border between Sudan and South Sudan, then goes through Ethiopia, and finally reaches the Red Sea on the east coast of Somalia. Part of the program of European colonialism in the Middle East and Africa was to spread Christianity. Now there is a similar effort to spread Islam south of the Middle East and down through the African continent. These efforts gain their purpose and their successes from weak dysfunctional states—both then and now.

It is important to recognize that what is called the "Arab world"—like the "Middle East"—is an abstraction. Table 5.3 depicts the 47 largest Muslim countries in the world and also their proportion of Muslim believers. We also see the 21 countries that are considered Arabic.

Recent efforts to blame the region's problems on Islam have failed because, contrary to popular opinion, Islam is not a unifying force. Rather, Islam is a generally abstract phenomenon in the region. As above, the salient organizing principles in the Middle East are the highly tangible sects. The history of strong political leaders—first that of the Ottoman rulers and more recently that of petty authoritarians—has produced a governing

Table 5.3. Majority Muslim Countries and Whether Arabic-Speaking*

Country	Population in 2007	Percent Muslim	Arab
Indonesia	228,582,000	86	No
Pakistan	172,800,000	97	No
Bangladesh	162,221,000	89	No
Nigeria	154,279,000	50	No
Egypt	77,100,000	90	Yes
Turkey	71,517,100	99.8	No
Iran	70,495,782	98	No
Sudan	39,379,358	70	Yes
Algeria	33,769,669	99	Yes
Morocco	33,723,418	99	Yes
Afghanistan	32,738,376	99	No
Iraq	31,234,000	97	Yes
Malaysia	27,730,000	60.4	No
Saudi Arabia	27,601,038	100	Yes
Uzbekistan	27,372,000	88	No
Yemen	23,103,376	99	Yes
Syria	19,405,000	90	Yes
Kazakhstan	15,217,711	57	No
Niger	13,272,679	90	No
Burkina Faso	13,228,000	50	No
Mali	11,995,401	90	No
Senegal	11,658,000	94	No
Tunisia	10,383,577	98	Yes
Guinea	10,211,437	85	No
Somalia	9,558,666	99.9	Yes
Azerbaijan	8,676,000	93.4	No
Tajikistan	7,215,700	97	No
Sierra Leone	6,294,774	60	No
Libya	6,173,579	97	Yes
Jordan	5,568,565	95	Yes
United Arab Emirates	5,432,746	76	Yes
Kyrgyzstan	5,356,869	75	No
Turkmenistan	5,110,023	89	No
Chad	5,041,690	54	No
Lebanon	4,196,453	60	Yes
Kuwait	3,399,637	85	Yes
Albania	3,170,048	70	No

Table 5.3. Continued

Country	Population in 2007	Percent Muslim	Arab
Mauritania	3,124,000	99.9	Yes
Oman	2,577,000	93	Yes
Kosovo	2,100,000	90	No
The Gambia	1,700,000	90	No
Bahrain	1,046,814	81	Yes
Comoros	798,000	98	Yes
Qatar	744,029	77.5	Yes
Djibouti	496,374	94	Yes
Brunei	381,371	67	No
Maldives	350,000	100	No

*Note: Palestinians are Arabic-speaking people. The total Palestinian population is estimated at approximately 12 million, roughly less than half continuing to live within the boundaries of the West Bank and the Gaza Strip. In this combined area, as of 2009, Arabs constitute 49 percent of all inhabitants. The remainder, about 1.9 million live in neighboring Jordan, one and a half million between Syria and Lebanon, a quarter million in Saudi Arabia, while Chile's half a million are the largest concentration outside the Arab world.

Source: https://nosharia.wordpress.com/list-of-muslim-majority-countries-with-sectstategovernment.

climate in which the sect has become of enduring importance. The sects often organize and operate the only plausible schools, thereby assuring continuation of their centrality to local affairs. It is through the sect that the politically disenfranchised individual comes into contact with the appearance of political power and voice. The Arab sociologist Halim Barakat writes that "[t]hese sectarian affiliations are comparable to—indeed, inseparable from—tribalism or ethnicity. All . . . sub-categories of society relate in similar ways to systems of economic interdependence, political arrangements, and social movements" (Barakat, 1993, p. 125).

Barakat insists that religion, official Islam, as a spiritual, moral, and integrative force had been in a state of decline long before the emergence of radical jihadists. In fact, the Egyptian founder of radical fundamentalist Islam, Sayyid Qutb, died in 1966. His political program of the 1950s was motivated by the weakened and vulnerable position of Islam in the world. It is, after all, weakness, not strength that gives rise to radical insurgents. That lesson is relevant today. Those who cannot see a promising future have a tendency to fixate on the imagined purity of a distant past. We encounter alienation. The emergence and triumph of sectarian politics is symptomatic of what I call *social entropy*. In physics, entropy refers to dissipated thermal energy that is unavailable to do work. Entropy is the degree of disorder or randomness in the system. It would be difficult indeed to find a more fitting metaphor for the societies of interest here. Social entropy nicely captures the problem in the Middle East.

The historic creation of social entropy might seem to be an old problem that ought to be overcome with the passage of time. The cynic looking in on the Middle East, or the entire African continent, is often heard to complain, with abundant frustration, "How long are they going to blame us and our long-dead colonial ancestors for their current problems?" But of course this is the wrong question to ask. The question is impertinent because today's social and economic relations are the inescapable result of acquired patterns of interaction that cannot immediately be turned off. As Friedrich Nietzsche points out: "Rational thought is interpretation according to a scheme that we cannot throw off" (Nietzsche, 1968, p. 522). We cannot throw it off because of the customary practices and vested interests that make it valuable to hold on to the habitual scheme.

We must remember that the quest for reasons, and reason giving, operates within particular cultural traditions (Bernstein, 1983). Individuals embedded in socially entropic societies cannot change for the same reasons that we ourselves are incapable of immediately rearranging the institutional architecture of our own societies. We would have scant idea how to start. And so individual behaviors in these problematic places are deeply embedded in the attendant patterns of interaction that cannot be thrown off. The German sociologist Max Weber called them our "webs of significance." We are all the created products of our individual idiosyncratic histories—our particularistic webs.

In recent times, the term *alienation* is assumed to mean a state of being angry—as when two people are alienated. But the important connotation of alienation is one of separateness, of isolation, of being apart from something. In psychology, alienation can imply a condition of estrangement between the imagined self and the perceived objective world. Alienation concerns an individual's perception of self as it comes into contact with the world in which that self must exist and perhaps flourish. Karl Marx identified alienation as the dominant product of emerging capitalism—first observed in Britain with the full flowering of the Industrial Revolution in the eighteenth century.

Of course, in preindustrial times, there had always been lords and landowners. These individuals controlled access to capital in the form of land. In those agrarian societies, life for those who did not own or control land was, as Thomas Hobbes (1588–1679) put the matter, solitary, poor, nasty, brutish, and short. But of course those difficult times predated the Enlightenment. Then, one was born into a particular social position, and that was the end of the matter. No questions were asked, and social improvement, if any, would need to come in the imagined afterlife. The Enlightenment created the individual as a sapient discerning being. And with that, one of the early opportunities to deploy that newfound sapience was to begin to question the new reality that a few local individuals—and not some mysterious force in heaven—actually controlled the social and economic future of the huddled masses. Over time, these local worthies controlled access to capital—factories, land, and specific equipment such as steam-powered spinning machinery and looms. Without access to capital, labor is of little value. Labor needs access to capital, and capital needs labor. In this unavoidable linkage, we find the origins of alienation.

The question worth asking is, why is there so much alienation? Whether in Africa, Latin America, Europe, Asia, or North America, the single best predictor of civil unrest—turmoil, mayhem, local war, kidnappings, rape, and pillage—is the number of young men with too much time on their hands and with too little hope for a promising future. Alienation is a male problem, and in the Middle East, where the calming influence of wives and daughters is often attenuated or entirely absent, that translates into a serious social cancer. The unemployment rate among the young averages 30 percent. In a few countries—Algeria, Iraq, Mauritania, Somalia, and Sudan—unemployment of the young hovers around 45 percent.

Another look at the same problem tells us that of total unemployment in the region, the young account for over 50 percent of that share, and in Algeria, Jordan, Tunisia, Iraq, Djibouti, Somalia, Saudi Arabia, Egypt, Mauritania, and Sudan, over 70 percent of total unemployment falls on the young. Moreover, since in most of these societies women—young or old—are not expected to work, this is a male problem. Young men are unemployed and unemployable because there are no jobs to be performed. Exporting oil is capital intensive, and so there is little demand for labor in such countries. Non-oil economic activity is minimal, or restricted to service jobs; rarely is it thought to be suitable work for males.

Alienation is exacerbated because marriage in these societies is difficult—perhaps even impossible—in the absence of a job and the ability to prove to a protective and skeptical father that a young man will be able to provide for his precious daughter. Societies in which young men are closed off from any prospect of female companionship, with no alternative in sight, are not promising places. Males who cannot find work are of course supported by the extended family. But imagine what this does to an individual's self-esteem. And then with marriage and family formation impossible, the pressures of self-doubt escalate accordingly. The next stage is to find someone to blame for this situation of hopelessness and disgust. The sectarian schools, so prevalent because of the dysfunctional public school system, provide a ready answer. Many such schools are laboratories of learning and acquired victimhood. As noted, alienation is a condition between the self-perception of the individual and the perceived world out there. If the world available to the individual is one that forces apartness—apartheid in the South African narrative—then there is no hope for social cohesion. The concept of social entropy is precisely concerned with this problem.

Since the 1970s, growth of GDP in the region has been tied almost exclusively to the export of oil. On average, oil has accounted for approximately 75 percent of all exports from the region, and over that period the shares of exports from the non-oil sector have been falling. We see that oil has crowded out other productive activities. As we saw previously, this is part of the resource curse. But there are important differences. For instance, five countries—Djibouti, Jordan, Lebanon, Malta, and Morocco—have little or no oil exports. The remaining 14 countries are overwhelmingly dependent on oil income. As we saw earlier, when the world price of oil fell to approximately one-half its level in 2014, major oil exporting countries suddenly faced an uncertain future.

Other indicators are equally grim. Public spending on women's health falls below the world average—and that includes all of the world's poorest African countries. In a similar vein, the Middle East shares with sub-Saharan Africa the distinction of being home to the majority of the world's undernourished. Underlining the defective nature of economic conditions, the majority of countries must rely on imported food to meet their nutritional needs. For 15 countries, food imports account for about 25 percent of total imports. A well-known example is found in the persistent economic and political disarray in Iraq. Finding the reasons for that country's social entropy along sectarian lines requires that we address the comprehensive economic dysfunction there—a downward spiral that predates the removal of Saddam Hussein in 2003 and the subsequent chaos we now observe.

The complete lack of a functioning economy in Iraq makes these recurring struggles a necessary activity that will deliver a plausible life—or enduring misery. With the highest rate of youth unemployment—above 45 percent—among 18 Arab states in the Middle East and North Africa, the stakes could not be higher. The private sector, long stifled under Saddam's Stalinist authoritarian rule, barely exists. Livelihoods are scarce and precarious. In such an economy, most people have little to lose by chaos (they are unemployed anyway), and yet they may—if both aggressive and lucky—end up on the winning side. Iraq, as with so many countries in this vexed neighborhood, is a winner-take-all society. Those who prevail will control an enormous oil resource and access to government jobs. Those who lose—as is the regional custom—will get very little.

During Saddam Hussein's rule, Iraq's economy took dysfunction to a new extreme. Oil and gas sales accounted for about 70 percent of real GDP, for more than 90 percent of government revenues, and for more than 96 percent of export earnings. Today, long after Saddam's removal, government employment as a share of total employment runs close to 45 percent. There simply is no private sector. The general degradation of manufacturing and agriculture since 1980 means that these two key sectors account for less than 10 percent of GDP. Rankings in 2017 of the Corruption Perception Index compiled by Transparency International placed Iraq near the bottom—169th out of 180 countries.[5]

Iraq's economy remains stifled by a multitude of impediments. Electricity supply can meet only 50 to 60 percent of load requirements, which compels businesses to rely on much more expensive generators. Fuel is both scarce and expensive. Blackout periods of 9 hours per day are common—this in a country where daytime summer temperatures can exceed 40°C (104°F). GDP per employed person is less than one-half that for other countries in the region. The trend is even more ominous, with labor productivity at just 40 percent of what it was in 1990. Living standards have continued to fall. One-third of the population resides in rural areas, and 40 percent of those persons live on less than $2.00 per day. Approximately 16 percent of urban residents are classified as poor. Literacy rates for males, approximately 80–84 percent, are among the lowest in the region. In Baghdad, approximately 25 percent of the population lacks access to a water supply network. More than 30 percent of rural residents lack reliable and safe drinking water, and in some areas that percentage exceeds 50 percent. Only 30–35 percent of the population has access to a proper sewer system, and the continued destruction of the country's infrastructure has driven that number to new lows.

Ossified land markets have prevented new housing construction since the 1980s. There is a shortage of approximately 3.5–4.0 million units, and 60 percent of people live in slum conditions. Credit for a range of commercial and personal consumption items—housing and light construction—is limited, thus choking off much-needed investment and spending that would create private-sector employment. Logistics are abysmal. A large percentage of Iraq's road network is in serious disrepair. Little maintenance has been undertaken since it was built in the 1970s. Deterioration of rural roads prevents the rehabilitation of agriculture. Train derailments are frequent. Ports are silted in, and equipment is degraded.

Agrarian reforms dating from the 1960s expropriated private farmland but failed to redistribute that land to small owner/operators. As a result, there remains a montage of leases with the Ministry of Agriculture, posing a major impediment to mechanization and large efficient farming arrangements. Approximately three-fourths of Iraq's cultivatable land is leased or allocated by the government. Tenure security is nonexistent.

The Iraqi population has increased by a factor of four since the 1950s, and yet the cultivated land area has decreased. Irrigation water has declined in both quantity and quality. The government is forced to provide food subsidies—a cruel irony in the cradle of modern agriculture. At the same time, it is estimated that 80 percent of vegetables in the Baghdad market are imported from Iran, representing a profound drain on foreign exchange. Fuel for tractors and electricity for pumps is often unavailable. Having an unreliable electricity supply makes food processing and storage more costly, as well as unattractive investments.

These conditions, though extreme, point to continued economic disarray and widespread futility in the Middle East.

IV. The Notional State

> [E]cological conditions throughout most of the [African] continent do not allow high densities of people to be easily supported. More than 50 percent of Africa has inadequate rainfall; indeed, contrary to the popular imagination, only 8 percent of the continent has a tropical climate. Approximately one third of the world's arid land is in Africa. (Herbst, 2000, pp. 11–12)

Turning our attention to the African continent, we have seen that optimistic presumptions of convergence have been disappointed. The detailed figures presented earlier serve as vivid reminders of how countries in the periphery have failed to keep up with the economic and social progress of countries in the metropolitan core. With these disappointing results from so much money and international attention, the obvious question is, why have per capita incomes refused to budge? There is accumulating evidence that this situation is no longer a surprise to the experts (Bigsten, 2002; Easterly, 2001, 2006; Easterly and Levine, 1997; Herbst, 2000; Leonard and Straus, 2003; Ndulu and O'Connell, 1999; Pritchett, 1997; Rodrik, 2003; Sender, 1999; van de Walle, 2001). The accepted recipe for bringing development to the continent—the so-called Washington Consensus—is now understood to be misguided (Rodrik, 2006; World Bank, 2005). And many countries failed to meet the United Nations' Millennium Development Goals by the target year 2015. What is it that seems to defeat the best efforts of the donor community, thereby sentencing its millions of inhabitants to a continuing life of want and despair?

Several reasons have been advanced for these disappointments: (1) lack of commitment by African governments to implement and to persist in the development policies formulated for them by the international donor community; (2) unwillingness of donors to advance a consistent development scenario in the face of shifting government priorities; (3) insufficient funding by donors to accomplish the desired development agenda; and (4) chronic corruption that undermines the effectiveness of even the most coherent development prescriptions.

Missing from this list is the distinct possibility that the standard development prescriptions are based on a flawed conceptual model of the actual process of economic development in places such as these. In other words, if past and current development prescriptions and programs are based on a mistaken understanding of the reasons why many African nations seem resistant to the standard development catechism, then the blame for failed development performance—for the lack of convergence—lies not with desultory African governments, nor with endemic corruption, nor with inappropriate institutions, nor is it the fault of inadequate funding. Rather, the lack of convergence lies elsewhere.

What if development progress in Africa is elusive because of an inappropriate conceptual basis for the programs, projects, and policy prescriptions offered up as a guide to how countries ought to go about achieving development? What if the wrong medicine is on offer because the reasons for the current dysfunction have never been properly diagnosed? There is much talk of failed states, but very little analytical attention has been paid to the reasons for that alleged failure.

I suggest that the primary reason is that too many countries are *notional states* in which the "mask of citizenship" stifles the emergence of a necessary relational contract between the government and those who are governed. This lacuna then serves to undermine the development of a coherent political community whose very purpose is to negotiate and then ratify—on an ongoing basis—the institutional parameters of a shared future that will be better than the present and much better than the past. That is what occurs in the modern nation-state. However, this conversation is attenuated—often impossible—in notional states for reasons that I will explain below.

Recall the emerging economic situation in Britain and Germany between 1600 and 1900 as those countries moved from an economy of agrarian mercantilism to modern industrialization. In reflecting on that long trajectory, John Fei and Gustav Ranis call attention to the idea of "incipient nationalism."

> [I]ncreasing class mobility, tied in with the beginnings of an egalitarian spirit . . ., strengthened the forces of national trade expansion and commercialization emanating at the local level; and the emergence of the first real national consciousness in replacement of local and regional loyalties provided the necessary ideological cement for commerce. (Fei and Ranis, 1969, pp. 394–95)

This potential for incipient nationalism is absent in the vast majority of countries in Africa. This situation therefore renders development as we understand that process highly problematic. And of course as discussed previously, the majority of countries must be understood as isolated states that are economically cut off from the global economy and therefore unable to participate in that economy in a way that will produce gradual income gains. In other words, the isolated states of Africa are economically marginalized and generally irrelevant to the capitalist world system. For the most part, the metropolitan core—the OECD—has little use for these isolated states, except as a source of minerals or timber or oil. We know that this condition of dependence is not conducive to sustained economic development.

The fundamental problem facing notional states is that they lack a comprehensive institutional architecture that parameterizes economic activity. Most of these countries could be characterized as exemplars of the "free-market" dream advanced by those who imagine that markets magically appear as if they were a gift from the heavens. In contrast to much angst over "excessive regulations" that persists in certain parts of the metropolitan core, we see in the notional states of Africa precisely what happens when the institutional foundations of the economy are attenuated or entirely absent. In a tragic irony that keeps these countries, poor, there is too much of a "free" market. Anything goes, which means that transactions costs are excessive. There is imperfect information about consumption and production opportunities; it is very expensive to negotiate contracts and other forms of buying and selling at the center of a capitalist market economy; and it is exceedingly expensive to enforce contracts that have been arranged.

In many countries, the absence of a plausible system of dwelling (home or business) addresses makes it almost impossible for creditors to know how to find borrowers who fall behind in debt service. A functional credit system, which is of such great importance in a market economy, cannot function. It is often said that "the devil is in the details." Being able to locate delinquent borrowers is a profond "detail."

By way of summary, the stark social and economic transition as one travels east and south of the Mediterranean Sea is—for many experts, as well as casual observers—difficult to comprehend. The Middle East and the African continent present an elaborate tableau of surprises, contradictions, fascinations, and frustrations. Nothing is quite like it seems, and very little is as it is expected to be. The modernist urge, when contemplating these two very disparate regions, is immediately to notice defects and to offer ready-made fixes. After all, exposure to Western truths will certainly rectify the enduring religious fevers of the Middle East. Some proper technology and proper market-based policy advice will assuredly get Africa moving. The urge reaches its absurd limit when the traveler suggests that the basic problem with Nigeria is that it is not more like Norway. And the only problem with Somalia is that it is not more like Sweden. Just get them to do things the way we do them, and all will be well. And they will also be rich.

Well, not exactly. These two problematic regions tend to be embarrassments for the modern traveler because we cannot imagine how they could possibly have missed out on what seemed so obvious to us. In fact, the most vexing sentiment for many moderns is the inability to accept the Middle East and Africa on their own terms rather than on our terms. We seem unable to leave them alone. But of course they have long ceased being in charge of either their present or their future. They often resemble the merchant capitalism of eighteenth-century Britain and Germany, with contemporary flourishes thrown in to confuse the visitor. What is abundantly clear is that managerial capitalism regards them as generally irrelevant.

V. Economic Irrelevance

The idea of a *global* capitalist system is a misnomer. The rich metropolitan countries of the OECD drive and dominate an economic system that is generally irrelevant to individuals living in the alienated and isolated periphery. China contributes low-cost manufactures—and some electronics—to that system, but this contribution is the result of central planning rather than capitalist market forces. The salient point here is to ask whether or not this bifurcated global economic regime will ever change. The evidence does not authorize optimism in this regard. The alienated fringe of the Middle East and North Africa seems destined for another decade or more of civil conflict. The urban elite of the Middle East and North Africa have their comfortable life—a scaled-down version of the agreeable ostentation of the top one-percenters in the United States and Britain. Both groups of oligarchs know how to protect their ample assets and associated privileges. They too are infected with possessive individualism.

What are the long-run prospects for the notional states of Africa? There are good reasons to believe that the future will look a great deal like the recent past. The early burst of activity following independence soon dissipated as the intrusion of reality settled in across much of Africa. The development community trumpets and celebrates bursts of good news but remains silent when setbacks persist. The Millennium Development Goals, mostly unmet, have now been replaced by the Sustainable Development Goals, that will themselves be replaced after 2030 by yet another initiative whose purpose will be to—once again—focus the collective mind on this awkward region of the world. One can only hope that our continual efforts at meddling and ostensive helping do not actually make matters worse. There is no assurance of that.

Managerial capitalism—the real economy of the metropolitan core—now captures what the anthropologist Clifford Geertz had in mind by the term *involution*. The system is highly elaborated and in some sense turned back in on itself in a protective shell of layers, barriers, and codes of behavior that deflect careful inquiry and analysis. Ownership arrangements are purposely obscure. Governance is both shielded and incestuous. The old days, in which large corporations behaved as if they cared about the communities in which they were situated, are now long gone. Many corporate headquarters have moved from their original location and are now concentrated in a few large cities. Nominal bonds of community no longer exist. The pressure of greater returns to shareholders has driven local philanthropy to a fraction of what it once meant to midsize towns.

Countries in this problematic region of the world are victims of their geography and their history—and the two afflictions are intimately related. First, the region is largely devoid of compelling agroecological settings and circumstances. Two isolated stretches of promising land—along the Nile River in Egypt, and along the Tigris and Euphrates rivers in Iraq—are exceedingly favorable agricultural venues. But the harsh surrounding territory offers no opportunity for food production to break out of these narrow confines, and so this constricted space is also home to the vast majority of the population in each country. The Nile Delta of Egypt is enormously rich and productive. But it is also home to millions of individuals crowded into a number of large cities, surrounded by thousands of exceedingly small agricultural plots that have survived against urban pressure. Large-scale agriculture is impossible. Years of economic chaos in Iraq have destroyed that country's agricultural sector.

Aside from these two places and the smaller Jordan Valley, the region is largely given over to sand and nomadic herders. The bulk of the population is crowded into cities. Being urbanized, but without much of the usual diversified economic activity associated with the great cities of the OECD countries, we find an overarching fixation on the past. Weak governments encourage the primacy of family ties and clan affiliations. Trust is attenuated, and so commerce is perilous and atomized into family clusters.

A second aspect of geography bears down on the region—its location with respect to historic trade routes between Europe and the far east. In some respects, Singapore is the contemporary equivalent of the ancient Middle East; its primary political and economic virtue is its location with respect to global trade. As the seat of the Ottoman Empire and since the 1920s the political sandbox of various European powers, the Middle East has always been forced to serve the interests of others. Nowhere is this more apparent than with regard to yet another geographical feature— carbon. It is safe to say that the enormous economic boost in wealth of the industrial core after 1900 owes much to the oil resources of this region of the world.

In tracing the "great divergence" between 1870 and 1914, Williamson assigns importance to four factors: (1) a revolution in world trans- portation; (2) greater trade openness in the European industrial core; (3) the new income from the Industrial Revolution; and (4) colonialism (Williamson, 2011, p. 25). The opening of the Suez Canal on November 17, 1869, solidified the global importance of the Middle East in the burgeoning global economy. The 1870s was the beginning of a gradual shift from coal to oil for the generation of steam power in ocean shipping. As it happens, the Middle East possessed the replacement fuel for coal. And European colonialism replaced the Ottoman Empire to assure open trade routes through the Suez Canal and access to the carbon resources that would fuel that surge in global shipping.

There is one more historical fact to ponder. Beginning in 1095 with Pope Urban II's call for the Crusades, the Middle East has been at the center of religious conflict. How could it fail to be? As the seat of Judaism, Islam, and Christianity, the enduring narratives, myths, sagas, injustices, triumphs, and calamities seem to overwhelm clear understanding. Would the world be a different place if all three of these creation stories had occurred in what is now France? What if the Notre Dame Cathedral in Paris were in fact the Dome of the Rock (the Temple Mount)? Would the Middle East be problem- atic? Would we consider it the "alienated fringe"?

Meanwhile, countries in Africa, victims of the economic and political dys- function of notional states, continue to languish in general irrelevance to the emerging global capitalist order. Household incomes remain low, and civil conflict persists in places as varied as Nigeria, Ivory Coast, Niger, Mali, the Democratic Republic of the Congo, Zimbabwe, South Sudan, Sudan, and Uganda. It is a mistake to view corruption and civil conflict as separate is- sues. Both activities signal weak and dysfunctional governance, which then undermines coherent economic activity, leading to despair and alienation. Individuals decide to take matters into their own hands. These actions then feed back into the problems of economic incoherence, stripping economic rents out of the agricultural sector operating at considerable distances from the final market. With rents suppressed, the net profitability of these commodities is undermined.

With suppressed incomes, investment is postponed or forsaken entirely, yields fall, net returns suffer, and farmers are caught in a cycle of falling productivity, reduced critical mass of tradable production, and perhaps even higher costs to arrange shipments. Tree crops such as shea and cashew become vulnerable to clearance for cotton or other crops. Vegetable production reverts back to desert. We see that notional states are also threatened, in the long run, with further environmental destruction.

Unfortunately, there are good reasons to suppose that the future of this problematic periphery will not look very much different from the desultory circumstances that continue to relegate the periphery to a large number of vulnerable people mired in vulnerable states.

Appendix

The countries included in sub-Saharan Africa are Angola, Benin, Botswana, Burkina Faso, Burundi, Cameroon, Cape Verde, Central African Republic, Chad, Comoros, Congo (Democratic Republic), Congo (Republic), Cote d'Ivoire, Equatorial Guinea, Eritrea, Ethiopia, Gabon, The Gambia, Ghana, Guinea, Guinea-Bissau, Kenya, Lesotho, Liberia, Madagascar, Malawi, Mali, Mauritania, Mauritius, Mayotte, Mozambique, Namibia, Niger, Nigeria, Rwanda, Sao Tome and Principe, Senegal, Seychelles, Sierra Leone, Somalia, South Africa, South Sudan, Sudan, Swaziland, Tanzania, Togo, Uganda, Zambia, Zimbabwe.

The countries included in the Middle East and North Africa are Algeria, Bahrain, Djibouti, Egypt, Iran, Iraq, Israel, Jordan, Kuwait, Lebanon, Libya, Malta, Morocco, Oman, Qatar, Saudi Arabia, Syrian Arab Republic, Tunisia, United Arab Emirates, West Bank and Gaza, Yemen.

The countries listed in the Organization for Economic Cooperation and Development are Australia, Austria, Belgium, Canada, Chile, Czech Republic, Denmark, Estonia, Finland, France, Germany, Greece, Hungary, Iceland, Ireland, Israel, Italy, Japan, Korea (Republic), Latvia, Luxembourg, Mexico, Netherlands, New Zealand, Norway, Poland, Portugal, Slovak Republic, Slovenia, Spain, Sweden, Switzerland, Turkey, the United Kingdom, the United States.

Notes

1. See the Appendix.
2. Data based on the authors' (Campos, 2014) calculations using GDP per capita data from Maddison (2007). Western Europe includes Austria, Belgium, Denmark, Finland, France, Germany, Italy, The Netherlands, Norway, Sweden, Switzerland, and the United Kingdom. US-CAN-NZ-AUS is Australia, Canada, New Zealand, and the United States.
3. Notice that there are only three OECD countries (Canada, the United States, and Mexico) with significant oil reserves.
4. See the Appendix for countries in each of these groupings.
5. https://www.transparency.org/country/IRQ

References

Armstrong, Karen. 2002. *Islam: A Short History*, New York: Random House.

Auty, R. M. 1994. "Industrial Policy Reform in Six Large Newly Industrializing Countries: The Resource Curse Thesis," *World Development*, 22: 11–26.

Barakat, Halim. 1993. *The Arab World: Society, Culture, and State*, Berkeley: University of California Press.

Bernstein, Richard. 1983. *Beyond Objectivism and Relativism: Science, Hermeneutic, and Praxis*, Philadelphia: University of Pennsylvania Press.

Bigsten, Arne. 2002. "Can Africa Catch Up?" *World Economics*, 3(2): 17–33.

Caselli, Francesco, and Guy Michaels. 2009. Do Oil Windfalls Improve Living Standards? Evidence from Brazil, CEP Working Paper No. 960, December.

Commons, John R. 1968. *Legal Foundations of Capitalism*, Madison: University of Wisconsin Press.

Easterly, William. 2001. *The Elusive Quest for Growth*, Cambridge, MA: MIT Press.

Easterly, William. 2006. *The White Man's Burden: Why the West's Efforts to Aid the Rest Have Done So Much Ill and So Little Good*, New York: Penguin Press.

Easterly, William, and Ross Levine. 1997. "Africa's Growth Tragedy," *Quarterly Journal of Economics* 112(4): 1203–50.

Fei, John C., and Gustav Ranis. 1969. *Development of the Labor Surplus Economy*, New Haven, CT: Yale University Press.

Griswold, Eliza. 2010. *The Tenth Parallel*, New York: Farrar, Straus, and Giroux.

Herbst, Jeffrey. 2000. *States and Power in Africa*, Princeton, NJ: Princeton University Press.

Hirschman, Albert O. 1958. *The Strategy of Economic Development*, New Haven, CT: Yale University Press.

Kissinger, Henry. 2014. *World Order*, New York: Penguin.

Krugman, Paul. 1981. "Trade, Accumulation, and Uneven Development," *Journal of Development Economics*, 8: 14961.

Krugman, Paul. 1991a. "Increasing Returns and Economic Geography," *Journal of Political Economy*, 99: 483–99.

Krugman, Paul. 1991b. *Geography and Trade*, Cambridge, MA: MIT Press.

Krugman, Paul, and Anthony Venables. 1995. "Globalization and the Inequality of Nations," *Quarterly Journal of Economics*, 110: 857–80.

Leonard, David K., and Scott Straus. 2003. *Africa's Stalled Development: International Causes and Cures*, Boulder, CO: Lynne Rienner.

Maddison, Angus. 2007. *Contours of the World Economy, 1-2030 AD*, Oxford: Oxford University Press.

Matsuyama, K. 1991. "Increasing Returns, Industrialization, and Indeterminacy of Equilibrium," *Quarterly Journal of Economics*, 106: 617–50.

Matsuyama, K. 1992. "Agricultural Productivity, Comparative Advantage, and Economic Growth," *Journal of Economic Theory*, 58(2): 317–34.

Meyer, Karl E., and Shareen Blair Brysac. 2008. *Kingmakers: The Invention of the Modern Middle East*, New York: W. W. Norton.

Monteiro, Joana, and Claudia Ferraz. 2010. "Does Oil Make Leaders Unaccountable? Evidence from Brazil's Offshore Oil Boom," unpublished, PUC-Rio.

Murphy, K., A. Shleifer, and R. Vishny. 1989. "Industrialization and the Big Push," *Journal of Political Economy*, 97: 1003–26.

Myrdal, Gunnar. 1957. *Economic Theory and Under-Developed Regions*, London: Duckworth.

Ndulu, Benno J., and Stephen A. O'Connell. 1999. "Governance and Growth in sub-Saharan Africa," *Journal of Economic Perspectives*, 13(3):41– 66.

Nietzsche, Friedrich. 1968. *The Will to Power*, London: Vintage.

Nunn, Nathan. 2008. "The Long-Term Effects of Africa's Slave Trade, *Quarterly Journal of Economics*, 123(1): 139–76.

Pakenham, Thomas. 1991. *The Scramble for Africa*, New York: Random House.

Prebisch, Raul. 1950. The Economic Development of Latin America and Its Principal Problems, United Nations Department of Economic Affairs (reprinted in *Economic Bulletin for Latin America*, 1962, Vol. 7, pp. 1–22).

Pritchett, Lant. 1997. "Divergence, Big Time," *Journal of Economic Perspectives*, 11(3): 3–17.

Rodrik, Dani (ed.). 2003. *In Search of Prosperity: Analytic Narratives on Economic Growth*, Princeton, NJ: Princeton University Press.

Rodrik, Dani. 2006. "Goodbye Washington Consensus, Hello Washington Confusion? A Review of the World Bank's Economic Growth in the 1990s: Learning from a Decade of Reform," *Journal of Economic Literature*, 44(December): 973–87.

Sachs, Jeffrey, and A. M. Warner. 2001. "The Curse of Natural Resources," *European Economic Review*, 45: 827–38.

Sender, John. 1999. "Africa's Economic Performance: Limitations of the Current Consensus," *Journal of Economic Perspectives*, 13(3): 89–114.

USAID. 2012, March. *Assessment of Current and Anticipated Economic Priorities in Iraq*, USAID-Tijara Provincial Economic Growth Program, Final Draft Report. Washington, DC.

van de Walle, Nicolas. 2001. *African Economies and the Politics of Permanent Crisis, 1979–1999*, Cambridge: Cambridge University Press.

Williamson, Jeffrey G. 2011. *Trade and Poverty: When the Third World Fell Behind*, Cambridge, MA: MIT Press.

World Bank. 2005. *Economic Growth in the 1990s: Learning from a Decade of Reform*, Washington, DC: World Bank.

PART III
RECOVERING HOPE

*Promising livelihoods will require an escape
from the ravages of managerial capitalism.*

*This necessary process will revitalize
the revered idea of personhood.*

~~~~~~~~~~~~~~

The burden will fall on those of us who care.

6

Escaping Possessive Individualism

*Contemporary economics stands implicated in the triumph of posses-
sive individualism. In viewing the individual as nothing but a utility-
maximizing consumer, economic theory offers apologetics for the
self-interested tendencies that now imperil personhood. Managerial
capitalism reifies the acquisitive urges embedded in contemporary economics. As the defects of managerial capitalism become apparent,
escape seems impossible to imagine. This mental barrier persists because economics is not an evolutionary science. An economy is always
in the process of becoming, and yet economic theory denies this "becoming" to consumers whose tastes and preferences are assumed to be
unchanging—and none of our business. The escape requires an evolutionary economics that recognizes the individual as constantly engaged in a process of experiencing life and necessarily adapting to it.
In that dynamic process, individuals are also crafting their own future.
An evolutionary economics can help light the way as societies seek escape from the grip of possessive individualism.*

I. The Task Before Us

[T]he economic life process [is] still in great measure awaiting theoretical formulation. The active material in which the economic process goes on is the human material of the . . . community. For the
purpose of economic science the process of cumulative change that
is to be accounted for is the sequence of change in the methods of
doing things,—the methods of dealing with the material means of
life. (Veblen, 1898 [1990], pp. 70–71)

In 1898, when Thorstein Veblen wrote these words—in an article entitled
"Why Is Economics Not an Evolutionary Science?"—he was lamenting the

fact that economics was not an evolutionary science. The abiding problem now, over a century later, is that economics is still without a plausible theory of evolutionary change. Societies and their economic architecture—their institutional arrangements—are necessarily evolving systems of living and provisioning. However, economic theory is trapped by models of the individual as a mere consumer in a relentless quest for greater utility. We lack a coherent way to think about the persistent and necessary task of creating a more compelling future in reaction to our lived experiences from the immediate past, mindful of the discontents of the present.

Economics as currently crafted forces economists to abdicate our civic obligations by handing off the difficult quest for new economic policies to legislators, judges, and bureaucrats. We insist that they ought to do what is efficient, and we may offer suggestions along the way. But we fail to offer these individuals a conceptual roadmap—a "theory"—that will help them to create compelling solutions to present problems. It is not enough to advise them on the implications of various tax-reform programs, or the most cost-effective job training programs, or to point out the implications of existing inequalities. Economics can do better than that. Doing so will require an admission that our models fail to fit the world out there (Box 6.1).

Text Box 6.1 Two Different Worlds

Alan Blinder, a distinguished Princeton economist, recently discussed the fraught political economy of free trade. His observation about the acceptance of trade captured a fundamental point under discussion here. He writes:

"As important as the lack of public understanding and the perverse political incentives are, the single biggest reason why economists can't sell free trade may be philosophical: the worldview that underpins the discipline of economics differs dramatically from the worldview of most people.

Economists see the central goals of an economic system as producing goods and services at the lowest possible cost and then distributing them to the people who want them. Every elementary economics textbook describes those goals, touts how well free markets accomplish them, and then notes some problem areas in which markets don't get it quite right (pollution, for example). Economists' focus is squarely on the well-being of consumers. The well-being of producers is secondary—if it enters the picture at all. In the economists' vision, firms exist to serve the ultimate goal of consumer welfare. Work is something people do to earn the income they need to support their consumption. It is not an end in itself, nor a direct source of satisfaction or self-worth. The interests of producers, including the value people get from their jobs, count for little or nothing in standard economic calculus. In fact, work is scored as a negative—something people dislike and do only to support their consumption.

But what if economists have this wrong? What if people care as much (or more) about their role as producers—about their jobs—as they do about the goods and services they consume? That would mean economists have been barking up the wrong tree for more than two centuries. Maybe the public sees the central goal of an economic system as providing well-paid jobs, not producing cheap goods. If so, the standard case for free trade evaporates. The argument for trade would then have to be based on the idea—also found in Ricardo—that comparative advantage moves people into jobs where they are more productive and therefore earn more. That seems a harder sell and, in any case, is not the pitch economists have been making for centuries.

The producer perspective seems to dominate public opinion. A 2016 Bloomberg poll, for example, asked Americans whether they would pay a little more for domestically produced merchandise. Even with no direct mention of saving jobs, the results were lopsided: 82 percent of respondents said they were willing to pay a little more; only 13 percent wanted the lowest prices. A Quinnipiac poll that same year posed a similar question, asking respondents whether they supported renegotiating trade deals, even if that meant paying higher prices. Again, neither jobs nor imports were mentioned directly. But again, public opinion was overwhelmingly protectionist: 64 percent were willing to pay more for U.S.-made products; only 28 percent weren't.

Talk is cheap, of course. Maybe consumers would not be willing to shell out more to buy domestic rather than foreign goods. After all, they frequent Walmart and other big retailers where imports line the shelves. But even if the attitudes that show up in polling don't have much effect on how people shop, those attitudes may still resonate with politicians"

Source: Alan Blinder. 2019. "The Free-Trade Paradox," *Foreign Affairs*, January/February, pp. 126–27.

An evolutionary economics must start from the idea that the purpose of economic theory is to provide guidance to societies as they struggle with the enduring problem of how to organize themselves for their material provisioning. This means that the standard microeconomic approach of allocating scarce resources to achieve some prespecified goal or objective is impertinent. It is impertinent because the essence of crafting necessary public policy is the realization that currently accepted goals and objectives— and the means of achieving those ends—are now lacking in widely shared support. They are no longer wanted. A new institutional architecture is sought that will bring about a modified suite of goals and objectives, and a new way of achieving those ends.

It is clear that the concept of efficiency, of constrained maximization, can play no role in evolutionary economics. Efficiency is not and cannot possibly be a design criterion. The only approach to meaningful institutional change is to: (1) focus on careful diagnosis of problematic settings and circumstances; (2) entertain new ideas that seem most promising in solving a particular problem; (3) embrace the most reasonable of those possibilities; and (4) then undertake ex post monitoring and assessment as the new policies are allowed to run their course. This is what the philosopher John Dewey characterized as "putting our values on trial." That is, if some new idea seems superior to the status quo arrangements, let us see if the claims for it are actually warranted. Dewey was a committed empiricist; let us experience alternatives to see if they work.

In other words, a new presumed ideal—a new set of goals and objectives, and plausibly associated institutional arrangements—must be allowed to run its course and thereby to "settle down." Has individual and aggregate behavior been altered by this institutional change? If so, are the observed changes for the better? That is, has the earlier dissatisfaction that provided the reasons for the institutional change been rectified? The test here is certainly not to determine if so-called efficiency has been attained. Efficiency is impertinent and unknowable. The only thing that matters is whether or not the new institutional configuration—and the new behaviors it brings forth—is deemed better (not more efficient) than the *status quo ante*. If so, then the new institutional architecture is accepted as preferable to the prior setup. On the other hand, if the realized outcomes are no better, or if they are deemed to be worse than under the *status quo ante* institutional setup, then more adjustment is called for. This is how economies and societies become.

Economic circumstances and technical possibilities are always undergoing profound change. Retail stores are devastated by the new e-commerce. Workers have enormous computing power at their fingertips. An evolutionary economics requires the ability to explain institutional change because it is the institutional architecture that determines what is a cost, what is a benefit, and what accounts for the constellation of incentives that push individuals in particular directions. We need a structure of if–**then** propositions that can explain why institutional change gets animated, debated, and eventually adopted.

I now turn to the essential components of an evolutionary economics.

II. Human Systems as Purposeful Evolutionary Constructs

[T]he canonical ideas of orthodox microeconomic theory obscure essential features of the processes of economic change. The insistence on strict "maximization" in orthodox models makes it awkward to deal with the fact that, in coping with exogenous change and in trying out new techniques and policies, firms have but limited bases for judging what will work best; they may even have difficulty establishing the range of plausible alternatives to be considered. . . .Over time the least satisfactory of the responses . . . may tend to be eliminated and the better of the responses may tend to be used more widely, but . . . these selection forces take time to work through. Since orthodox microeconomic theory is based on the ideas that firms maximize and that the industry . . . is in equilibrium . . . models built according to the orthodox blueprints miss completely or deal awkwardly with these features of economic change. (Nelson and Winter, 1982, pp. 399–400)

This quote from two economists who have devoted most of their distinguished careers to the development of an evolutionary economics serves to highlight the nature of the challenge. The Nelson–Winter account is cast in terms of the profound difficulty in modeling how firms respond to changing market conditions. Of equal salience for our purposes is the issue of what households are to do under similar dynamic conditions. It is not only firms that are faced with the need to adjust and adapt to new circumstances. Indeed, households under managerial capitalism are more vulnerable than firms. If firms are ruined by economic circumstances, we are quick to acknowledge that "capitalism eats its children." In the demise of certain firms, new firms will rise—phoenix-like—from the ashes. Notice how little attention is paid to households that are degraded or destroyed under the rule of a competitive market economy. They must fend for themselves. Many households in rural America and in the north of England are the degraded remnants of this on-going process of creative destruction.

Moreover, dealing with a changing institutional environment is not a problem confined to owners and managers of commercial firms. All of us— whether legislators, judges, members of city councils, or simply participants in the daily decisions inside of a household—are confronted by shifting circumstances to which we must adapt. This means that we must situate the quest for an evolutionary economics in the *thought process* that engages individuals as we work our way through the exigencies of an ever-changing world. I start here because the individual is, in Veblen's terms, the "seat of a process of living."

To motivate the discussion, it seems useful to offer a brief reminder of evolutionary change in biological systems. Such systems and their constituent parts change over time through a process that rewards deviation from the norm. Variability is the source of serendipitous fitness in an environment that is itself undergoing continual change. Being in the majority has short-term advantages and long-term disadvantages. Change is the inevitable constant in the continual reconstitution of living organisms and their embeddedness in their specific ecological settings and circumstances. Change is a constant companion of variation.

Human systems are also buffeted by exogenous events that challenge fitness. Here, the resultant is not drawn from or limited to some random process that rewards deviance from the existing blueprint by mere accident. Rather, the difference is found in the technology of these two different systems. In natural systems, the pertinent *social technology* is the genetic architecture that explains (is the reason for) observed variation in the members (the species) of the particular community under study. Notice that this genetic architecture is not under the control of individual members who are themselves the embodiment of a specific genetic constitution. No individual member of a natural community can be held accountable for evolutionary change in that community; each is but the passive carrier of a specific architecture.

It is the genetic and phenotypic attributes that comprise the essential replicators of the members of the system projected into the future. Individual members of a biological community are in the majority—or they are at the tails—by virtue of the genetic and phenotypic composition of all other members of the same community. Their general fitness is therefore a resultant, and their specific fitness is a function of which particular stochastic events in the ongoing life of the community impinge on its members. Drought punishes and rewards rather differently from an early frost, or the appearance of some specific threat to the community in general, and more correctly to some (but not all) of its constituent parts. Those members of a particular genotype (and phenotype) in the community that manifest the right variation will survive, while others, being less fit to the evolving settings and circumstances, will perish. The survivors comprise the gene pool for the next generation, and therefore a particular community is continuously reconstituted under a new and evolving biological architecture.

In contrast to biological systems, which are properly understood in terms of *function*, human systems must be understood in terms of *purpose*. Human systems evolve in some purposeful way. We must not assume that there is, or could be, a clear and direct mapping between a single a priori purpose and the evolutionary trajectory of the constructed institutional architecture that constitutes human systems. But it *would* be correct to understand the general parameters of the evolutionary trajectory of human systems as being the result of conscious thought and action dedicated to a continual reconstitution of the institutional underpinnings of the economy and the polity. That is public policy at work.

An evolutionary theory of economic change or an economic theory that is evolutionary requires three components.

First, if we are to understand human systems in evolutionary terms, we must find some *source of animation* in virtue of which the system's substantive organizing principles—its institutional architecture—come to be seen as ill-suited to the nascent perception of likely circumstances in the future. We may consider this first condition as the gradual accumulation of plausible reasons to question the *status quo* institutional setup. In essence, the prevailing organizing principles—approaches and policies—are found to be unpopular or defective. Notice that this situation is analogous to the lack of fitness of the majority of organisms in biological systems.

Second, there must be a *source of adjustment* or revision in the *status quo* institutional setup. Think of this as the specific reasons to alter the *status quo* institutional setup in particular ways. In this second consideration, we encounter the process whereby human communities become involved in the serious matter of reconstituting their own institutional setup that, from the earlier process of animation, is now acknowledged to be in need of revision. We may usefully regard this as a diagnostic activity in which focused collective effort is mobilized to seek an understanding as to why, exactly, the current institutional setup is no longer adequate—and therefore what might be done to rectify the situation in the interest of correcting the perceived problems. The introduction of such solutions representing institutional (policy) changes is precisely the essence of evolutionary economic change. Such institutional change then redefines how the society alters the way it organizes itself to improve its necessary provisioning.

Finally, there must be a stopping rule in the process of institutional *adjustment*. We may think of this as the culmination of the working out of reasons to adopt a specific institutional arrangement over one or more of its plausible alternatives. In essence, the participants in the process of institutional adjustment finally agree that some particular variation seems like the best thing to do at this time. The agreement is an implicit ratification of (1) the need to change; (2) the specifics of the best change to be made; and (3) the need to let the change get started so that the results can be observed and evaluated. The stopping rule in an evolutionary system must provide sufficient reasons to act in particular ways, and then to allow the new institutional setup to give rise to new patterns of interaction and new outcomes.

The analogue here is to the replication function in biological systems. If, upon observation and assessment, the specific institutional change represents a clear and desired improvement, then that specific institutional arrangement will be transmitted to future generations. After all, the institutional arrangements that now define the economy—with a defective old-age pension scheme, poor day-care options, unwanted unemployment—are the transmitted institutional architecture from the volitional actions of prior legislatures, courts, city councils, and administrative agencies. When those earlier institutional arrangements were adopted, it was presumed that they would be adequate. However, in the fullness of time, that was an incorrect prediction. Human societies adopt, act, learn, and then react. As we will see, this is what John Dewey meant by *trying* and *undergoing*. Societies are, we must keep in mind, organic evolutionary going concerns. The economy moves forward.

Obviously, there is no assurance that other conditions will remain the same into the future, and so it would be a mistake to presume that the specific problem is fixed forever. The problem is only "fixed" for as long as all of the other conditions defining this particular realm of the economy remain reasonably similar over time. When the *ceteris paribus* conditions no longer hold, the ideal institutional adaptation from the past may well need once again to be modified.

With this introduction, we can now turn to an elaboration of the three aspects of an evolutionary human system: animation, adjustment, and adaptation.

III. First: A Theory of Animation in Human Systems

[T] action of thought is excited by the irritation of doubt, and ceases when belief is attained; so that the production of belief is the sole function of thought. (Peirce 1957, p. 36)

The starting point in the evolution of human system is one of *animation*. That is, individual members of the going concern that we call the nation-state come to the realization that to continue with the *status quo ante* institutional setup seems likely to result in particular outcomes that are no longer compelling. This realization may originate in the public at large, or it could emerge from within particular highly regarded organizations. Perhaps the National Cancer Society launches a campaign to alert us to the dangers of smoking—the end result being institutional change that restricts smoking in public places. Perhaps the Centers for Disease Control and Prevention calls attention to the serious public health implications of obesity—the end result being institutional change concerning the nature of foods and beverages available in the nation's schools. Perhaps the Occupational Safety and Health Administration calls attention to the increased prevalence of serious hearing impairment among certain industrial workers—the end result being institutional change requiring that protective devices be worn in the industrial workplace. Perhaps education experts call our attention to the fact that many elementary school children cannot read at grade level— the end result being institutional change requiring an adjustment in educational practices.

Notice the role of surprise in moving us to question the desirability of the *status quo ante* institutional setup. We are surprised to learn about the health implications of cigarettes. Only recently, cigarettes were symbols of glamour and success. We are surprised to realize that school lunches are a plausible contributing factor to childhood obesity. We are surprised that industrial workers appear to suffer hearing loss. Once we learn of these surprises, doubt sets in. Why is this happening? The essential animating ideas in the evolution of human systems are *surprise and doubt*. Because these circumstances are unexpected, we are surprised by them. It is their quite unexpected properties that give rise to doubt. Things are not supposed to be this way. Doubt and surprise challenge the fitness of the specific institutional architecture that stands as the plausible explanation for these outcomes. Perhaps these particular institutional arrangements are no longer suited (fit) for the tasks they were originally designed to perform.

We come to grips with doubt and surprise through a diagnostic process called *abduction* (Peirce, 1934). An abductive syllogism is of the form:

> The surprising fact C, is observed:
> But if A were true, C would be a matter of course,
> Hence, there is reason to suspect A is true.

Abduction starts with a surprise (C) that calls our attention to particular outcomes that are noticed precisely because they are unwanted. If they were real surprises and yet regarded as desirable, no further thought would be devoted to them. For instance, if school children were suddenly found to be reading far above their grade level, we might well be surprised, but we would be unlikely to deem that a serious problem worthy of corrective action. On the contrary, glowing praise would be lavished on teachers, school administrators, parents, and the children themselves, and then we would get on with life, pleased that teachers and school administrators had figured out how to bring about that happy outcome.

However, surprise, coupled with an assessment of the desirability of that unexpected outcome, motivates diagnostic attention. And when it is time for diagnosis, we wish to know what, exactly, are the reasons for this unwanted state of affairs? In the above syllogism, those reasons stand as the assumptions (A) of our diagnostic undertaking. They are assumptions because, if they are found to be true, then they offer a quite plausible explanation for the observed outcomes. After all, if the assumptions are indeed found to be implicated, then the outcome C would *not* be a surprise but would be quite expected.

The purpose of investigating—diagnosing—the fitness of prevailing institutional arrangements is to see if we can come to an understanding as to the reasons for the unpleasant surprise. We want to explain those unwanted outcomes so that we might then be able to rectify them. If you are an engineer seeking to explain the unexpected destruction of a spacecraft upon reentering the earth's atmosphere, then abduction is your avenue to explanation. The essential purpose of abduction is the production of belief about specific events that have been recognized as both surprising and unwelcome.

When we can identify reasons for actions or outcomes we have acquired a plausible basis for making predictions about, and for advancing explanations of, those actions or outcomes. When individuals or collections of individuals face the need to choose (to act), abduction is the process we deploy to get a grip on the reason for the new surprise—that surprise (and its reasons) constituting the necessary precursor to choice and action. Diagnostic thought is deployed for the sole purpose of fixing belief. And a belief is that— and only that—upon which we are prepared to act.

IV. Second: A Theory of Adjustment in Human Systems

[A]n evolutionary economics must be a theory of a process of cultural growth as determined by the economic interest, a theory of a cumulative sequence of economic institutions stated in terms of the process itself. (Veblen, 1898 [1990], p. 77)

I have mentioned the process of selection in biological systems, and have suggested that the analogue in human systems consists in a process of adjustment. But how do individuals go about the process of adjustment— alteration—in those institutional arrangements that define our collective existence? Getting a grip on that process of collective choice requires that we first understand the process of individual choice. And this will require a rather profound change in how we model human choice and action.

John Davis has offered an important reconsideration of the individual, and his work warrants careful attention (Davis, 2003, 2008). For now we must consider the concept of situatedness of the individual in what Max Weber calls our "webs of significance" (Geertz, 1973), and what Jurgen Habermas calls our "lifeworld" (Habermas, 2001). The central idea here is that the individual is both situated in—and largely constituted by—the settings and circumstances that make up the idiosyncratic personal history of each of us. Notice that this idea of the individual stands in stark contrast to the standard line in economics that all of us—everywhere—are uniform utilitarian calculators. It is claimed that with our preferences quite intact and unchanging, we rationally calculate before we act.

Notice that alterations in the institutional setup of an economy require three things: (1) an explanation of—the reasons for—the new perception of inadequacy; (2) the mobilization of one or more policy prescriptions that seem to offer improved outcomes in the future; and (3) plausible predictions that if one or another of the policy prescriptions is adopted, the situation can reasonably be expected to improve in specific ways. This aspect of institutional change—the source of adjustment—can be understood as analogous to the process of selection in biological systems. But notice that adjustment in human systems is active and purposeful, while selection in natural systems is passive and accidental.

As we consider the need for adjustment, our individual comprehension of the settings and circumstances within which we are situated must be understood as our individually constituted impressions of the world around us. And since we come to the task of apprehending our surroundings as previously constituted individuals, we inevitably construct quite different reports concerning what is out there in the world. Pragmatism teaches us that there is no single true and reliable report to be sent back by earnest observers who venture out into some singular reality—for the simple reason that there is no singular reality. Each of us apprehends different aspects of the particular settings and circumstances within which we are situated. These comprehended aspects comprise our individualized impressions of those settings and circumstances. These impressions constitute the raw material for understanding our situatedness. When we redescribe these impressions to ourselves (and to others), these accounts constitute our expressions concerning the world around us (Bromley, 2006). This idea is congruous with Antonio Damasio's *autobiographical self* (Damasio, 1999). These expressions constitute the mental stage on which we live our individual lives.

However, when we are confronted with surprise and doubt, the habituated mind becomes unsettled—irritated—and we seek an understanding of this novel situation. This is Peircean doubt of such irritation to the habituated mind. Only when we understand it will we abductively construct plausible inferences about the reasons for the new surprise, about the need to act, and about the most plausible actions to take in the light of the abductive belief just formulated (Bromley, 2006).

Recall the previous reference to G.L.S. Shackle's concept of created imaginings (Shackle, 1961). Expressions are accounts we tell ourselves (and others) about our present situatedness. Created imaginings are accounts we tell ourselves (and others) about possible future outcomes—and our possible future situatedness among those outcomes. It is here that we formulate the reasons that will come to provide the grounds for choosing among the array of plausible created imaginings. Individual choice and action is a contest—a struggle—between expressions and imaginings. We act when we find a feasible created imagining that satisfies expectations about our situated outcomes in the future. And we also act when we reject all created imaginings (perhaps because they seem infeasible) and stick with our current action trajectory. To do nothing is to do something (Bromley, 2015).

With this reformulated theory of individual action, let us now consider how groups of individuals charged with the task of promulgating institutional change—judges, legislators, members of city councils—come to decide what ought to be done. The obvious problem is one of contending expressions. After all, each of us formulates and holds individualized expressions of the world around us. As Charles Sanders Peirce (1839–1914) insisted, the meaning of an object to us is nothing but the sum of its perceived effects on us (Peirce, 1934).

The obvious difficulty in joint action is that everyone else is doing the same thing. This means that there is not a single stage (expression) upon which our disparate created imaginings are to be projected. Instead, there are as many stages as there are participants in the group whose task it is to ascertain but a single course of action for the future. Collective action forces all participants to agree on the many aspects (effects) of expressions and imaginings.

The purpose of institutional change is precisely that a legislature or a court is called upon to advance new institutional arrangements whose very purpose is to solve a particular problem—day-care facilities, food safety, old-age pension schemes, etc. This means that legislatures or courts must reconcile a multitude of contending imaginings about the future held by their individual members. Notice that the issue here is not one of discovering, a priori, the right created imagining. Indeed, the very notion of prescriptive certitude about the right created imagining is misplaced. Rather, the task in an evolutionary model of economic change is to focus on the various reasons for the disparate imaginings. Progress is to be found in reasoned debate—the asking for and giving of reasons (Brandom 1994, 2000). An evolutionary economics requires that individuals must do the hard analytical work of figuring out what at the moment seems better to do.

Public policy is nothing but thinking about, weighing, and ultimately choosing among alternative institutional setups that will give rise to alternative imagined and plausible futures. Institutional change redefines realms of individual action. When the process of sifting and winnowing through the various created imaginings reaches the point that several of them have come to dominate the others, the third essential component of an evolutionary economics comes into play. This final stage is the actual process whereby the working rules—the institutions—of the economy are modified for the explicit purpose of implementing one of these dominating created imaginings. We may properly consider this emergent and now reigning imagining as the reason for the new institutional arrangements. That is, the *emergent created imagining is the outcome in the future for the sake of which the new institutional arrangements must be implemented now*. This dominant imagining comprises the sufficient reason for the new institutions. It explains the institutional change.

This process is repeated ad infinitum in a democratic society. Recall that public policy—institutional innovation—is nothing but collective action in restraint, liberation, and expansion of individual action. And the essence of public policy is that of redefining economic settings and circumstances. Public policy necessarily advances the economic and social agenda of some individuals, and it impedes the economic and social agenda of others. Individuals will strive to have their interests represented in that process, but there can be no doubt that public policy is precisely concerned with such reallocations of relative advantage in the economy.

V. Third: A Theory of Adaptation in Human Systems

[O]ne may say that truth is a matter of collective judgment and that it is stabilized by the collective actions which use it as a standard for judging other claims. (Shapin, 1994, p. 6)

As above, collective choice—public policy—is a process of reconciling contending expressions and imaginings. This is an essential activity leading to the formulation of what seems best, in the eyes of the individual (or of the group), to do. Individuals and groups work out what seems best by working out what seems possible as they work their way toward what they will come to realize seems best. The process entails not only working out the best means but also the best ends.

The issue now concerns whether or not correct and rational decisions can be said to emerge. In other words, the problem now becomes one of judging the decisions reached. An evolutionary economics requires that acknowledgment of the correct decision occurs *after* a consensus has been reached regarding what seems best to do (Bromley, 2006). Notice that the cause of (the reason for) the correct decision is not some external truth rule (a correct decision protocol) but rather the arduous yet democratic working out of—the diligent searching for—what seems the better thing to do in the current situation. Once that better thing has been worked out, the emergent choice *becomes the correct choice by virtue of having been worked out and agreed to.* After all, would it not be surprising to discover that an individual (or a group) decided to do something that had been identified as clearly *not* the best (or the better) thing to do at the time? As Peirce insisted:

> The opinion which is fated to be ultimately agreed to by all who investigate, is what we mean by the truth, and the object represented in this opinion is the real. That is the way that I would explain reality. (1934, p. 405)

Arrival at a consensus about what is better (best) to do is always predicated upon a clear but evolving notion of the purposes of the future—an outcome in the future for the sake of which action must be taken today. In philosophy, this is called *final cause.* Purpose is central here, and settled belief about both purpose and how to get there represent the essence of correct thoughts and belief about the appropriate action to be taken. Adaptation to new institutional arrangements therefore encompasses a gradual process in which the political community comes to identify with the created imagining that emerged as the reason for the institutional change that occurred in the adjustment phase. Legislators will argue about their reasons for making specific adjustments—new legislation—but when the dust has settled and a new institutional architecture becomes the law of the land, the citizenry will settle down as it adapts to the new setup. Those who had been accustomed to smoking where they wished must now figure out how to respond to the new dispensation. School administrators will realize that they must figure out new meal plans for their schools. Factory owners and their workers will adapt to new rules about wearing protective equipment on the shop floor. As we will see, Dewey says that the very process of *trying* changes us; we are always *undergoing*.

Notice that adaptation need not imply that the problem has been fixed once and for all. Perhaps the imagined solution to a problem is not quite right because the original problem was not correctly diagnosed. Or, if the diagnosis was correct, perhaps the institutional change introduced to fix the problem was not quite right. The matter will be revisited and a new solution will be advanced. As above, the economy becomes.

VI. Toward an Evolutionary Economics

I have offered the general outlines of a theory of an evolutionary economics. To summarize that theory, we must account for three conditions that are present in natural systems. First, the theory must account for *reasons* why "fitness" is challenged. Second, the theory must account for the emergence of *an adjustment process* that leads to new expected outcomes. Finally, the theory must account for *adaptation* in individual behaviors as the new institutional arrangements are allowed to run their course—get a chance to perform—so that the predicted expected values of the hoped-for (desired) outcomes can be compared to what actually materializes in the fullness of time.

Notice that the new institutional arrangements are the *reason* for new outcomes. Veblen regarded *cumulative causation* as the cumulative cultural momentum from the past. John R. Commons (1862–1945) referred to the relation between new "working rules" and specific economic outcomes as instances of *institutional causation* (Ramstad, 1990, p. 77). Both of these approaches to an evolutionary economics recognize that rules of the economy—its institutions—are the *reasons* for particular actions. That is, institutions (rules) are the output—the operational blueprint—of authoritative agents of the political community who possess the collectively sanctioned capacity to formulate and implement specific rules with a particular purpose in mind. These can be regarded as *institutional transactions*. This purpose—this volition of the authoritative agents—is a cause of the behaviors its hoped-for attainment elicits from the citizens of the going concern.

We now see that the fundamental economic problem is not that of re-source allocation emerging out of Adam Smith's alleged harmony of interests. Rather, the primary economic problem is how to create and then constantly to reconstitute order in the face of new surprises in the going concern. It is clear that out of material scarcity comes conflict. But it is also clear that out of material scarcity comes mutual dependence. And so out of conflict and mutual dependence emerges the need for order. A nation's institutional architecture provides that order and changes in that institutional architecture move the economy along some volitionally constructed evolutionary pathway. This institutional adjustment, and this purposeful adaptation, is what Commons meant by *artificial selection*. It is artificial precisely because there is no natural trajectory for human systems. All trajectories are the volitional result of conscious choices by authoritative agents.

It is necessary to acknowledge that the process of institutional adjustment and adaptation in human systems is highly prefigured. That is, the shared conception of a workable solution to a problem facing the individual (or the legislature) is quite inseparable from the customary practices to which the individual mind has become accustomed. In practical terms, this means that the purposes and expectations toward which problem-solving thought is directed are simply instances of what Commons called "institutional causation." It is extremely difficult for individuals to imagine solutions to problems that are not already bound up in—prefigured by—the very circumstances giving rise to the problem that is now in need of correction. Truly imaginative thinkers—innovative conceptualizers—are in short supply. More profoundly, all sustainable social reengineering—institutional change—must be continuous with the past. Coherent change is found in reform, not revolution. Societies that cannot bend will break.

Another implication flows from this—one that is more profound for economists. Specifically, because choice and action are shaped by the working rules of custom and law, and because market processes are but a reflection of volitionally created working rules, it is logically impossible for an individual—or a group of individuals—to oppose new rules concerning individual behavior simply on the grounds that these new rules are coercive in their imposition on the exercise of alleged free will. From an economic point of view, it is therefore illogical to regard new rules (new institutions) as somehow subversive of economic efficiency. The only pertinent question for the economist becomes one of whose will—whose interests and volition—is to govern the creation and modification of new rules, and for what purposes?

The primary challenge in policy reform—institutional change—is to recognize that public policies in an economy are not mere disembodied rules derived from abstract principles of economic efficiency or political expediency. Public policies are the collective codification of evolving principles of socially approved behavior. A policy (a rule) requiring children to remain in school until a certain age is not just an arbitrary exercise of state power over children and their parents. Public policies evolve over time as societies collectively reflect on changing views about child labor and the importance of education. Pollution-control policies are yet another illustration of changing social beliefs. At one time, rivers were for transportation and the disposal of human and industrial waste. Gradually, the social purpose of rivers underwent change, and with those evolving ideas about what rivers are for, new policies were adopted to change how humans ought to interact with rivers.

The institutional architecture of well-functioning nation-states is therefore a reflection of underlying customs and norms that are anchored in the past, and yet are gradually changing to embody new scarcities, new technological opportunities and threats, new attitudes about how society ought to be organized, and new priorities that now seem urgent. Returning to the example of pollution, we note that the custom of depositing human and industrial waste in nearby rivers emerged from the belief that this is precisely what rivers are for. With this belief in hand, it was obvious enough that a new rule (a new pollution policy) to prevent pollution would not be the sensible (rational) thing to do. We see that a new policy on pollution of rivers would be quite impossible until widely shared beliefs about the *purpose of rivers* had undergone a profound shift.

In this case, the process of policy reform was not really about whether pollution was good or bad (or right or wrong). The social discussion—the political debate—concerned the socially desired purpose of rivers. As long as rivers carry away pollutants at no obvious cost to society, and until opponents could create a new vision concerning the purpose of rivers, it would be foolish (economically irrational) to insist that pollution be stopped. Once it was documented that pollution killed fish and other living creatures, and that pollution made rivers unsafe for swimming, rivers acquired a new purpose. Only then was it possible to introduce new policies to prohibit pollution.

We see that policy reforms must always be anchored on—situated in—the emergence of new beliefs about what now seems the better thing to do. But how do new beliefs arise and work their way into policy discussions? How, exactly, does institutional change get going? For that we need John Dewey.

VII. Engaging Dewey's Arc

The nature of experience can be understood only by noting that it includes an active and a passive element peculiarly combined. On the active hand, experience is trying—a meaning which is made explicit in the connected term experiment. On the passive, it is undergoing. When we experience something we act upon it, we do something with it; then we suffer or undergo the consequences. We do something to the thing and then it does something to us in return; such is the peculiar combination. The connection of these two phases of experience measures the fruitfulness or value of the experience. Mere activity does not constitute experience. It is dispersive, centrifugal, dissipating. Experience as trying involves change, but change is meaningless transition unless it is consciously connected with the return wave of consequences which flow from it. When an activity is continued into the undergoing of consequences, when the change made by action is reflected back into a change made in us, the mere flux is loaded with significance. We learn something. (Dewey, 1916, p. 139)

This quote contains the profound observation that will now elaborate the previous theoretical development of an evolutionary economics. In the latter part of that quote, we see the core ideas of what I shall refer to as "Dewey's Arc." This idea stands as Dewey's core psychological contribution to economics and public policy. Dewey regarded the continuity of life as an ongoing process of putting our values on trial.

The idea of Dewey's Arc appears in an 1896 paper in which, at the young age of 37, he wrote what many experts believe to be his most significant contribution to psychology (Dewey, 1896). In that paper, Dewey challenged the dominant notion concerning the classic stimulus-response model of human action—the *reflex arc*. A child, singed by a candle flame, quickly withdraws her hand. Dewey noticed a disjunction in this model—the stimulus (heat) was separable from the response (withdrawal). We see here the standard confusion over cause and effect. Dewey deconstructed the classic reflex arc model by insisting that what is at work here is a circular process rather than a linear one. This means that the effect cannot so easily be disentangled from the cause. Surely the child had been warned of the relation under discussion. Why then was the proposition tested?

Dewey was not satisfied to tie it to the foolishness of children. Adults too often defy similar linear models. Something more is at work. What about the role of the light of the candle as an attractant to the child? Did the light signify something desired? Light is quite mysterious after all. And a flame is even more beguiling. The real beginning here, received by the body, is called seeing. It is *the looking that matters*, not the light that is then seen. The seeing and reaching are part of a coordination problem and cannot be considered distinct. Reaching and seeing—or seeing and reaching—help each other out. The hand and the eye are part of the same internal act of sapience. Seeing is not just for seeing; seeing is for reaching. Dewey showed that the traditional reflex arc model was defective because it presumed that

> sensory stimulus and motor responses are distinct psychical existences, while in reality they are always within a "coordination" and derive their significance purely from the part played in maintaining or reconstituting the coordination. (Dewey, 1896, p. 360)

Dewey's reinterpretation of the reflex arc model is central to the understanding of an evolutionary economics. It is important because it gives us a psychological heuristic to develop a model of institutional change.

We saw in the above quote from Dewey that when a particular activity is *continued into the undergoing of consequences* a change that we have made *is reflected back into a change made on us*. Notice what Dewey implies by this flux. Humans make choices and undertake actions that, when followed through, require that we undergo consequences. *But those consequences are reflected back in the form of changes made on us.* Those changes do not simply bounce off of us—they become part of us. We *learn* something and we are therefore changed. Unlike the simple reflex arc, in which a child withdraws her hand and then moves on wiser but unchanged, the child is changed in a number of ways—not just in her aversion to a flame. She becomes a different person by experiencing the unpleasant consequences of her seeing.

We may now bring Dewey's psychological insights to the task of creating an evolutionary theory of economics. Our journey cannot start unless we are clear about the precise constituents of an economy that will be the subject of evolutionary interest. That is, what aspects of the economy will undergo the initial change? It cannot possibly be prices (or costs) since those changes arise from within an existing institutional structure. Momentary scarcity and abundance explain those changes. We need to focus attention on the *structural parameters* of the economy rather than on the *variables* in that economy.

The rear sprocket of a bicycle is mechanically linked (by a chain) to the front sprocket. One does not explain the turning of the rear sprocket by appeal to the empirical claim that the front sprocket is turning. The turning of one is the required turning of the other; they are a single entity within the structure of which they are a part. One would only seek an explanation if the rear sprocket failed to turn when the front one did. Notice that the link between the two sprockets is pertinent to explanation in the latter case, but not in the former. Notice also that we can explain the turning of the rear sprocket only if we are prepared to look beyond the structure that ties the two events together—that embeds the one in the other. That is, an explanation allowing us to escape the trap of mechanical entailment can only be found if we look for an exogenous source (the application of force to the front sprocket) of the turning of the rear sprocket.

This is precisely the same reason why conventional economics does not and cannot have an explanation for individual choice. Individual choice is endogenous in economic models, and by being endogenous it no longer qualifies as *choice*. Its endogeneity strips it of any capacity to differ from that which its very structural dependence preordains for it. This is not choice but mere mechanism. The rear sprocket has no choice but to turn as the front sprocket dictates. The endogenization project of Douglass North and the new institutional economists is correctly understood as an effort to reduce institutional change to nothing but mechanical determinism. Melvin Reder has commented on this doomed endeavor.

> Associated with the assumption of stable preferences, but logically distinct, is the "thrust for endogenization." A leading manifestation of this tendency is Stigler's attempt to explain—and constrain—the behaviour of political decision makers, but this is not the only one. . . . Successfully to endogenize a new variable is to enhance the explanatory power of economics. . . . However, it must be noted that where variables are made "endogenous," they can no longer serve as objects of social choice. . . . To the extent that variables are endogenized—choice is explained—"society's" freedom of choice is seen as illusory. Freedom appears to consist not in power of choice, but (*pace* Hegel) in recognition of necessity. This is not a likely conclusion for followers of Adam Smith, and surely not one they desire, but one

from which they can be saved only by failure of this direction of research. (Reder 1982, pp. 34–35)

We see that the gain in explanatory power for economics comes at the cost of producing plausible explanations of institutional change. Such explanations should, I suggest, be an abiding goal of the social sciences. But such explanatory coherence can only be secured if the quest for endogenization fails—as it must. An economy is a set of *ordered relations* among atomistic individuals. The *order* in those relations is provided by the institutional architecture—the working rules—of the society in which the individual is born and soon comes to regard as normal. It is here that we find the relevant parameters of an economy that are the focus of interest in an evolutionary theory.

Here we drive on the right side of the road, here we do not smoke in airplanes, here December 25th is a national holiday, here there are few government subsidies for child-care facilities, here the federal minimum wage for "covered nonexempt employees" is $7.25 per hour—and it has not increased over the past eight years, here it can cost up to $240,000 to obtain a four-year undergraduate degree at some colleges or universities, here new mothers are lucky to receive several weeks of sick leave when delivered of their baby, here we do not celebrate the Queen's birthday, here we do celebrate a large meal of gratitude on the fourth Thursday of November. Notice that some of these working rules are mere customs, others are the result of decisions by firms or organizations in the economy (managerial transactions), while still others are legal parameters established by legislative or judicial decree (rationing transactions). Regardless of their origin, these working rules define "how we do things here."

We now come to a graphical depiction of Dewey's Arc. For this we need to recognize three distinct realms of human action. I call these realms (1) people doing; (2) people deciding; and (3) people believing.

A. People Doing

It is now possible to understand the economy so described as a realm of human action that is parameterized by thousands of rules—both customary and legal—that determine what economists call choice sets. These choice sets reveal the domain of possible and prohibited actions. Commons referred to choice sets as defining *authorized transactions* (Bromley, 2016). When augmented by an individual's budget constraint, such choice sets define feasible (available) actions for the individual. They are often called "budget sets." We have before us a realm of human action—we may usefully think of it as *people doing*. They are doing what they can do, and what must be done, parameterized by the institutional architecture that liberates and constrains. In the terminology of Jurgen Habermas, they are in their lifeworld. To Max Weber, they are enmeshed in their particularistic webs of significance. They do what they do because that is what they have come to be socialized to do. As Veblen put the matter:

> The economic life history of the individual is a cumulative process of ad-aptation of means to ends that cumulatively change as the process goes on, both the agent and his environment being at any point the outcome of the past process. His methods of life to-day are enforced upon him by his habits of life carried over from yesterday and by the circumstances left as the me-chanical residue of the life of yesterday. (Veblen, 1898, pp. pp. 74–75)

The obvious question arises: what is the provenance of this institutional ar-chitecture that parameterizes such durable choice sets? Who, exactly, was au-thorized to define the structure of working rules that now seem to enmesh the individual in a well-defined world—all the while imagining that her every action is an instantiation of her presumed free will? What, exactly, is this ubiquitous and pervasive realm of rules? This realm of rules comprises the institutional foundations of an economy. Institutions are the rules whereby going concerns (families, clans, villages, firms, nation-states) discover what may and may not—must and must not—be done. Institutions regularize and channel individual action and interaction.

We have seen that institutions define and specify opportunity sets—fields of action—for members of a going concern. Institutions are the means whereby the collective control of individual action is specified. This brings us into direct contact with the socially constructed norms, working rules, and entitlements that shape and influence individual fields of action. Clarity is found by regarding institutions as both liberation and restraint of individual and group action.

Some economists, for instance, Douglass North (1990), consider institutions to be "humanly devised constraints." However, it is odd to re-gard the prohibition of child labor as nothing but a constraint on business firms. Are not children liberated by such a rule? How is it possible to regard a ban on DDT as only a constraint? Are not those who care for bald eagles (and other animals) plausibly devastated by that chemical compound liberated by the prohibition of its use? How is it possible to regard urban growth boundaries only as a *constraint* on the relentless march of houses and dubious strip malls into green space at the urban fringe? Are not those who treasure rural amenities liberated by such restrictions? We see that, in each case, new institutions simply modify choice sets—fields of action—for atomistic maximizing individuals.

A clear understanding of institutions requires that we see them as both liberating and restraining individuals. In fact, the proper way to regard institutions is that they define choice sets—fields of action—for members of a going concern (family, clan, village, firm, nation-state). With a proper focus on institutions as constitutive of social and economic relations rather than as simply constraints on those relations, we can begin to bring useful analytical attention to bear on these essential aspects of an economic system. This new perspective draws attention to institutions as the structural parameters in an economy rather than as mere constraints on some prior and allegedly natural entity called the market. There is, after all, no such thing as *the market*. Recall the meatloaf problem. There are, instead, arenas of exchange that are the product of prior human creation. Any market is a social construct, and changes in the parameters of that construct—new institutional arrangements—are also human creations.

If we start by recognizing that institutions define fields of action for individuals (and groups) in society, then there is hope of explaining their existence at any particular time. And there is hope, too, that we might build explanatory models to understand the forces that cause institutions to change. Understanding this central realm of rules requires that we grasp three fundamental aspects of human thought and action: (1) ethics; (2) economizing; and (3) jurisprudence. *Ethics* deals with the rules of conduct arising from the inevitable conflict of interests, necessitated by scarcity, and enforced by the moral sanctions of collective opinion. *Economizing* deals with the rules of conduct arising from the inevitable conflict of interests, necessitated by scarcity, and enforced by the collective accounting sanctions of profit or loss. *Jurisprudence* deals with the rules of conduct arising from the inevitable conflict of interests, necessitated by scarcity, and enforced by the organized sanctions of collective (and state sponsored) violence (Commons 1931).

Institutions represent the application of ethics and jurisprudence to the ubiquitous economizing behavior that defines our daily life. More specifically, existing economic institutions represent the ethical judgments of those who, in the past, were in a position to determine which institutional arrangements were adopted. We see that current institutions are a mirror on—a reflection of—prior scarcities, prior purposes, prior values, prior economic agendas, and prior political processes. Once those institutions are in place, individuals and groups engage in economizing behaviors that hold economic (and noneconomic) implications for themselves and for others.

B. People Deciding

We see that an economic system is defined by—parameterized by— collectively ascertained and articulated rules and entitlement regimes. This leads us to the obvious questions of whence this apparatus arises and how (and why) it persists? The quick answer is that economic institutions arise from the prior choices and actions of the authority system in the society under consideration. As we saw earlier, the well-functioning state is the political domain over which there is a continual reassessment of existing institutional arrangements, such reassessment being motivated by an emerging sense that current institutional arrangements are not well suited to new settings and circumstances. That is, current behaviors, parameterized by prevailing institutional arrangements, no longer seem to conduce to agreeable outcomes. Institutional change now seems necessary. These visions and priorities drive the law-making process, and it should be no surprise that when new visions and priorities begin to emerge, new institutions will become the subject of great interest.

As above, institutions are manifestations of collective action in restraint, liberation, and expansion of individual action. When I say *collective* action, I mean that new institutions (*not* norms and conventions, but new working rules and new entitlement regimes) are products of the processes and structures of *governments*. That is, institutions are given form and content (and enforcement) by the agents of the state. The concept of *collective* action used here differs in important ways from traditional usage. We know that legislatures and courts are the law-giving bodies in democratic societies. What is less well understood is that the legislative activity of democratic societies is the essence of collective action. This law making is collective precisely because democratic societies create legislative bodies for no other reason than to craft (and re-craft) the institutional foundations of the going concern we call the nation-state. We can consider these institutional arrangements as collective-consumption goods because their use by one or more individuals does not diminish their capacity to do work for others. Sometimes they are called public goods, though the adjective *public* is often confusing. It is better to refer to them as collective-consumption goods. They are nonrivalrous in consumption, and, once they are made available for one person, they are available for all persons (they are nonexcludable).

Members of well-functioning nation-states agree—explicitly or tacitly—to abide by the rules promulgated by their law-giving entities. This does not imply unanimous agreement in principle with all of the undertakings of law-giving bodies, but it does imply general acquiescence in behavior of members of the entity governed by the relevant law-giving body. We may say that law-giving is the essence of collective action in redefinition of individual action. In constitutional democracies, the judicial branch will have a role to play in assuring that the results of law giving are consistent with guiding constitutional principles. And of course the judicial branch is essential to arbitration between individuals (or groups) in a society. Even the actions of the judicial branch, including the decrees of a *single* judge, are the essence of *collective* action. Such judicial decrees are collective because, in virtue of her sanctified role (official position) in that society, a judge speaks both *to* and *for* all members of the polity.

Given this definition of collective action in democratic societies, we see that the state, through its organizations and processes, is necessarily *a party to every transaction*. I say necessarily because it is the state—the political community—that decides which transactions shall be allowed. Hallucinogenic drugs, child labor, slavery, and extortion are classes of transactions that are not allowed in most societies. That is, members of the nation-state have previously asserted, through their law-giving entities, that these particular transactions shall not be permitted. They are not *authorized transactions*. Once particular transactions have been deemed by the collective to be acceptable, there remains the problem of state ratification of contracts and other aspects of transactions. After all, if contract disputes arise, where do the aggrieved parties go but to the nation's courts? Nation-states cannot avoid being a party to every transaction. By agreeing to be a party to every transaction, the state agrees that it always stands ready to consider the interests of all citizens. By agreeing to be the enforcement agent for private transactions, the state is declaring that it cares about the well-being of individuals who choose to enter into contracts. And the state is signaling that it recognizes the high social and economic costs to arise from contracts broken on a whim.

By being a party to all transactions, the state defines important aspects of the individual, and the state liberates and expands the powers of the individual. Official categories define who we are and what we may do. The terms *husband* and *wife* are legal concepts, and so the state sets the minimum age (even the gender) for which individuals may acquire those appellations. The age of majority must be collectively determined, and this is often contentious. The terms *worker* and *supervisor* carry legal entailments and open up varying ranges of *command and obedience* between the parties in managerial transactions. The idea of owner carries with it a wide range of opportunities in the firm—for owners are central to all contracts over the necessary factors of production. And the owner is the residual claimant on all profits and the residual risk bearer in the case of negative profits. We see that an individual's *legal personality* is determined by collective action in the legislative and judicial branches of government.

We should also understand the nation-state as a domain of redistribution of advantage, opportunity, and therefore of income and wealth. It is within the boundary of the nation-state that debates over particular institutional arrangements occur. What shall be the new minimum wage? Should the social security system be changed, and if so, how? How shall health insurance be organized and financed? Shall there be paid maternity leave, and if so, how many days with full pay shall be allowed? Shall there be paternity leave? If so, how will it differ from maternity leave? These conversations serve to define the realm of activity we recognize as the nation-state. After all, the citizens of Sweden would be unlikely to have a serious and legally binding conversation about the above topics with the citizens of Australia.

And so we finish this second domain—the realm of rules to live by—with the understanding that here is the domain in which the working rules of a society are debated and finally settled. This is the place where disputes go to die—at the hand of either the legislative branch or the judicial branch. In a rural village in India, it is the Panchayat. In a First Nation village in northern Canada, it is the council of elders. This is where law givers both reside and decide. This is where the *order* of a social system is *ordained*. Here is where authoritative agents announce "And so it shall be—until further consideration."

C. People Believing

The final realm to explore may be the most difficult to capture. We come to the idea. Ideas comprise our beliefs about the settings and circumstances of our everyday existence. The difficulty here is that our ideas are so familiar to us that we often fail to grasp what they do for us and what we do to them. In an important sense, ideas are our *theory of the case*, and humans tend to be highly resistant to altering what we believe and thus what we claim to know. But believing and knowing are two distinct aspects of living. As we have seen, Peirce talked of life-taking habits, and Veblen talked of the habituated mind. Dewey said that we do not take or acquire habits. Rather, we *are* our habits.

Ideas are either of the *framing* or the *instrumental variety*. Framing ideas reveal to us how we imagine the world to be. Instrumental ideas reveal to us a causal structure that informs how we will interact with that framed world. In a sense, the framing ideas are structural—"this is how the world is and how it works." Instrumental ideas are behavioral norms—"if I do X in the world as I imagine it to be, it is reasonable to believe that Y will occur."

Notice the absence of any allusion to rationality or rational choice. It is important to grasp the idea that the term *reasonable* is a perfectly suitable substitute for the term *rational*. Much jurisprudential activity is centered on what the *reasonable* person would do in specific circumstances. Trials by jury seek to enlist reasonable individuals into the rendering of justice. The reason we reason is to create reasons for solutions to vexing problems that we—and others—will come to regard as reasonable.

As we saw in Chapter 5, "Rational thought is interpretation according to a scheme that we cannot throw off" (Nietzsche, 1968, p. 522). We cannot throw it off because of the customary practices and vested interests that make it valuable to hold on to the habitual scheme. We must remember that the quest for reasons and reason giving operates within particular cultural traditions (Bernstein, 1983).

Actually, we have already explored the realm of ideas in the earlier discussion of the working rules of society—the institutional arrangements. Those rules are the eventual result of a long process of working out what it seems reasonable to believe about a particular situation. In this process of working out our ideas about a novel situation, we each draw on our individual and shared ideas that then provide the mental stage upon which our life is played out. Ideas provide us with credible causal relations, whether or not those relations are, in fact, true. Truth is beside the point.

Humans learned a long time ago how to survive in a world in which our existence was structured on the basis of quite untrue ideas—a universe centered on the earth rather than the sun, witchcraft, ghosts, creation stories concerning the origin of the earth and our existence thereon, the purpose of the moon, and the irresistible glamor of cigarettes. Ideas emerged, seemed useful, and were embraced. We stuck with them until they no longer seemed plausible or useful, at which point they were soon abandoned for new ideas. But those new ideas—beliefs—took a great deal of time and effort to emerge as a reasonable replacement for the beliefs now considered worthy of abandonment. Once the transition to new beliefs—new ideas—has been finalized, humans look back in amusement, perhaps disgust, at what we once believed to be true. Few people now find cigarette smoking to be glamorous. Few people now believe that the earth is flat, that it is the center of the universe, or that it was created 6,000 years ago in a mere six days. Ideas evolve. Beliefs are abandoned. Knowledge turned out to be wrong. We move on. Beliefs come and go, but living is a constant obligation.

It is precisely here, in the evolution of ideas, that Dewey's Arc is most useful. I earlier mentioned the durability of what it is we claim to know. As Ludwig Wittgenstein (1889–1951) insisted: "We can only know what it makes sense to doubt" (Grayling, 1988, p. 94). This seems troubling. How can knowledge be subject to doubt? We encounter the common assumption of an allegedly inevitable progression from ignorance, through believing, and then finally arriving at knowing. In other words, to "know" something seems to represent the final step in the acquisition of certitude—knowing is thought to be more secure than mere believing. In a debate over climate change, *believing* that carbon taxes are the preferred policy instrument is a weaker position than *knowing* that carbon taxes are the ideal solution. Few people are interested in what others believe, but there is abiding interest in what they know. But the difference is nothing at all. It is a mere linguistic trick.

For an evolutionary economics—that activity in which the institutional architecture of a functioning state is altered for instrumental reasons—it is normal for people on both sides to make stronger claims than they are justifiably capable of defending. We rarely see claims about believing, yet there is an abundance of claims about knowing. Habituation encourages a certain laziness of thought and action; it is easier to know something than it is to undertake change in the face of some inconvenient problem. Consider Wittgenstein's famous argument with G. E. Moore over Moore's claim that he knew he had two hands because he could see (and count) them. Wittgenstein objected to this claim of knowing on the grounds that to observe something is not the same as knowing something. In Moore's case, since it was impossible for him to reach any other conclusion about the number of his hands, it was wrong for him to use the word "know." The impossibility of being wrong about the number of hands undermined Moore's claim that he knew that he had two of them. He only *saw* that he had two hands. Knowing, Wittgenstein insisted, required more than mere observation. Real knowing starts with doubt, and in Moore's case, it was silly to suppose that inquiry as to the number of his hands began with doubt. Everyone could see two of them.

Notice the difference between observing and informed diagnostics—alone by which understanding can emerge. Only if it makes good sense to investigate something, motivated by doubt and surprise, will we be able to come to know or understand it. And once careful investigations of a matter by a scientific community have been carried out, and there emerges a general consensus, it will no longer be reasonable to doubt what they have produced. In other words, to really know something we must first hold it in doubt. That doubt then becomes the necessary animation for careful study by those individuals qualified to undertake such inquiry. Once they have investigated the matter thoroughly, it is then justified for that community to claim to understand (to know something of) the topic of interest.

In practical terms, when members of a scientific discipline, after much study, arrive at settled belief about a particular matter, they are often called upon to offer public statements on specific matters of interest to the rest of us—smoking is a plausible cause of lung cancer, chlorinated fluorocarbons are plausible causes of the depletion of atmospheric ozone, surface temperatures of the earth do seem to be on an upward trajectory. When a discipline speaks with one voice on such matters, the rest of us, not experts, will generally regard their statements as warranted. That warrant comes from the fact that a specific epistemic community has investigated a particular matter, and now that community seems to have arrived at settled belief. The matter is no longer in doubt. We will usually regard these announcements as constituting warranted assertions. Dewey considered such claims to have warranted assertability (Dewey 1939).

However, it is not enough that a scientific community has reached agreement on some vexing matter. The citizenry is the real audience for those warranted assertions. After all, it is the views of ordinary citizens that provide the basis for political action—the crafting of new institutional arrangements. This is where the realm of ideas gains its salience for an evolutionary economics. The term *valuable belief* can be applied to a warranted belief that can be justified to an audience of attentive sapient agents actively contemplating a particular action (Bromley, 2006). In other words, a valuable belief is one that will put individuals in a receptive mental state such that they are now prepared to act on that belief. It is now a good idea—they are now disposed to act. As Peirce put the matter:

> Belief does not make us act at once, but puts us into such a condition that we shall behave in a certain way, when the occasion arises. Doubt has not the least effect of this sort, but stimulates us to action until it is destroyed. (Peirce 1957, p. 11)

It is here that the realm of ideas brings pressure to bear on the realm of rules. But for that to be the case, there must be some new pressure that is brought to bear on the rather widespread pattern of settled beliefs in that realm of ideas. What is this animating force? It is none other than Dewey's Arc. Recall Dewey's claim that the undergoing of consequences of particular actions is reflected back on individuals—we are changed by that flux. We are changed because we learn something. And when we learn something, it is clear that our ideas—our settled beliefs—are now different from what they once were. We are now a different being, and when our ideas change we expect that the working rules of the society in which we are embedded—working rules (institutions) derived from prior (different) beliefs—will also undergo change.

Acceptance of the warranted belief that smoking is implicated in lung cancer—a new idea—leads to a change in the working rules, so that smoking in public places is gradually eliminated. Individual behavior thereby changes. New ideas (beliefs) bring about new rules (institutions) that bring about new behaviors. People believing new things results in people deciding in new ways, which then leads to people doing things in new ways. Once we are doing new things—or doing old things in new ways—we are no longer who we once were. We are now newly constituted individuals. The economy is always in the process of becoming, and so are we. All things, and all individuals, undergo evolutionary change.

The dynamic nature of an economy is revealed when we realize that the ongoing business of a nation-state is a process of "cycling through" the three realms depicted in Figure 6.1. New beliefs—animated by unwanted outcomes in, or emanating from, the left box via Dewey's Arc—are gradually

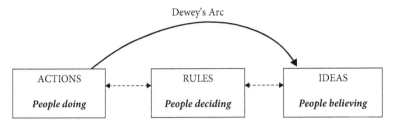

Figure 6.1. Realms of Ideas, Rules, and Actions

worked out until a "better idea" emerges (right box). Once that better idea—the new (valuable) belief—has been accepted, the policy process is launched and after much debate, new institutional arrangements (rules) will emerge (middle box) to redefine the fields of action for individuals in the left box (*people doing*).

The economy becomes by a continual process of re-creating the institutional arrangements (middle box) that redefine fields of action for individuals in the left box. New beliefs inform and rationalize new rules that liberate and restrain individual behaviors. Those new behaviors produce outcomes that will be judged good or bad, and those assessments will then signal to the realm of beliefs that things are now fixed—or that yet further institutional manipulation is called for. The economy becomes, and we become along with that Deweyan *undergoing*.

VIII. Why Political Systems Fail

The above illustration concerning the realms of *ideas, rules,* and *actions* gives empirical substance to Dewey's Arc, and it helps us to understand how economies undergo institutional change in response to new problems, new opportunities, new technical possibilities, and new relative scarcities. Nowhere do we find reference to efficiency, to Pareto Optimality, to the virtue of markets, or to welfare (or utility). The process of living is the daily need to confront new problems as they arise. A British Prime Minister, on being asked about the most difficult aspect of his job, is said to have responded: "Events my boy, events."

An evolutionary economics must be predicated on this reality that events drive political and economic systems forward. Humans have limited ability to *control* events, but we are infinitely clever in *responding* to events.

Well-functioning nation-states learn how to dissipate concentrated advantage and reroute self-interest into social useful directions. Figure 6.1 offers a new way to think about how economies undergo their own idiosyncratic becoming—or lack thereof. Indeed, the diagram helps us to understand how economies gradually fail to serve their citizens. When the dynamic adjustments implicit in Figure 6.1 fail to emerge, we can begin to see how *world disorder* can gradually arise. Ranging from the frustrated households of many OECD countries, to the ignored and impoverished households in the notional states of the isolated periphery, the necessary processes of institutional change—animation, adjustment, adaptation—are blocked or fail to work well. Notice in the diagram that if problems arise in the left box—where households are struggling to flourish—yet there is no mechanism for feedback reaching the right box—the realm of ideas—political problems are sure to arise.

Here it seems that Dewey's Arc, the necessary feedback loop, is missing or atrophied. This is what he called the return wave of consequences that flow from the process of *trying* (people doing). As we try new things, in an effort to solve new problems, we experience an *undergoing,* and we are therefore changed by that fact. When we are thus changed, we will necessarily see the world and our place in that world differently. And having come to this revelation, we will quite naturally produce new understandings and new ideas.

But we see in the diagram that if there is no "receptor" in the right box to receive the results of the undergoing in the left box, a dynamic system can begin to fail. New ideas will be forestalled or defeated because calls for change will be dismissed as the whining of a few malcontents. In a mature meritocracy, the range of voices controlling the realm of ideas can become restricted. In a system of managerial capitalism, where economic inequality becomes exceedingly pronounced, money further distorts or silences necessary discourse in the realm of ideas. Before long, it is too easy for this realm of surprise, diagnosis, discourse, and debate to fall under the control of those well served by the *status quo ante* institutional setup (rules in the middle box).

Much has been made of the importance of urban elites and rural resentments that drove the Brexit vote in Britain. Similarly, the American election of 2016 reflects severe sclerosis in the realm of ideas. Rural residents were sure that the urban elites were not listening and that they did not care to listen. When the realm of ideas becomes the exclusive domain of a few well-served interest groups, danger is assured.

Coherent political systems require a steady flow of novel ideas, new rules, and modified behaviors to keep the ship of state stable and seaworthy. When the feedback channel—Dewey's Arc—does not work, problems arise. Perhaps it is now possible to understand the otherwise inexplicable political fracturing and social discord in much of the United States and western Europe. Democracies work well when a rising tide is lifting all boats because, as Macpherson pointed out in the early days of possessive individualism, everyone was held together by a common understanding of improving livelihoods. However, when that process of becoming begins to privilege some but not all citizens, the loose and fragile concordance of democratic market capitalism begins to fray. The threads of community become worn and weakened.

This conversation pertains to the metropolitan core where the overriding concern can be thought of as sclerosis within the necessarily dynamic operation of governance depicted in Figure 6.1. The same heuristic can be helpful in understanding the notional states of the isolated periphery. In such places, with minimal governance, it would be reasonable to suggest that these three realms—of ideas, of rules, and of people doing—must be modified in profound ways. Most directly, the left box—people doing—must be understood as the only pertinent realm in the economy. This is where millions of vulnerable individuals in the Middle East and Africa spend their desultory lives, dealing with problems that should not persist. But those problem endure because there is no feedback via Dewey's Arc. There is no feedback because there is no realm of ideas to receive that feedback. There is no place where the problems of "people doing"—what Dewey called *undergoing*—are considered, debated, and resolved. Moreover, the link from the realm of ideas to the realm of rules is largely missing or perhaps atrophied because there is no interest in developing that link, and there is no process to translate new ideas into new rules (new policies).

The King of Jordan can easily change Prime Ministers every 12–18 months, and he regularly does so, but nothing changes because nothing can change. The political-economic landscape of Jordan—as with so many places—is built to last. It is not built to change. As the Arab world learned in late 2010 and early 2011, societies that do not bend are easy to break.

And with few ideas and fewer rules, the economy of many poor countries languishes in its defective governance, unable to respond to urgent problems as they arise. If such problems are not addressed and rectified, the resulting flawed functioning gradually takes on the air of normalcy—and before long its very ubiquity serves to render it no longer problematic. In the current vernacular, *it is what it is.* Too many people will consider it fate or God's will, and with that designation, such problems cease to be problems. After all, a problem is something that ought to be fixed. If there is no capacity to fix problems, they become redefined as "the way things are." Despair thrives where institutional change is impossible.

References

Bernstein, Richard. 1983. *Beyond Objectivism and Relativism: Science, Hermeneutic, and Praxis*, Philadelphia: University of Pennsylvania Press.

Brandom, Robert B. 1994. *Making It Explicit: Reasoning, Representing, and Discursive Commitment*, Cambridge, MA: Harvard University Press.

Brandom, Robert B. 2000. *Articulating Reasons*, Cambridge, MA: Harvard University Press.

Bromley, Daniel W. 2006. *Sufficient Reason: Volitional Pragmatism and the Meaning of Economic Institutions*, Princeton, NJ: Princeton University Press.

Bromley, Daniel W. 2015. "Volitional Pragmatism," *The Pluralist*, 10(1): 6–22.

Bromley, Daniel W. 2016. "Institutional Economics, *Journal of Economic Issues*, 50(2): 309–25.

Commons, John R. 1931. "Institutional Economics," *American Economic Review*, 21: 648–57.

Damasio, Antonio. 1999. *The Feeling of What Happens*, New York: Harcourt Brace.

Davis, John B. 2003. *The Theory of the Individual in Economics: Identity and Value*, London: Routledge.

Davis, John B. 2008. "Sraffa, Wittgenstein, and Neoclassical Economics," *Cambridge Journal of Economics*, 12(1): 29–36.

Dewey, John. 1896. "The Reflex Arc Concept in Psychology," *Psychological Review*, 3: 357–70.

Dewey, John. 1916. *Democracy and Education*, New York: Macmillan.

Dewey, John. 1939. *The Theory of Valuation*, Chicago: University of Chicago Press.

Geertz, Clifford. 1973. *The Interpretation of Cultures*, New York: Basic Books.

Grayling, A.C. 1988. *Wittgenstein*, Oxford: Oxford University Press.

Habermas, Jürgen. 2001. *Moral Consciousness and Communicative Action*, Cambridge, MA: MIT Press.

Nelson, Richard R., and Sidney G. Winter. 1982. *An Evolutionary Theory of Economic Change*, Cambridge, MA: Harvard University Press.

Nietzsche, Friedrich. 1968. *The Will to Power*, London: Vintage.

North, Douglass C. 1990. *Institutions, Institutional Change and Economic Performance*, Cambridge: Cambridge University Press.

Peirce, Charles Sanders. 1934. *Collected Papers*, Vol 5, Cambridge, MA: Harvard University Press.

Peirce, Charles Sanders. (ed. by Vincent Tomas). 1957. *Essays in the Philosophy of Science*, New York: The Liberal Arts Press.

Ramstad, Yngve. 1990. "The Institutionalism of John R. Commons: Theoretical Foundations of a Volitional Economics," in Warren Samuels (ed.), *Research in the History of Economic Thought and Methodology*, Boston: JAI Press.

Reder, Melvin W. 1982. "Chicago Economics: Permanence and Change," *Journal of Economic Literature*, 35: 1–38.

Shackle, G.L.S. 1961. *Decision, Order, and Time in Human Affairs*, Cambridge: Cambridge University Press.

Shapin, Steven. 1994. *A Social History of Truth*, Chicago: University of Chicago Press.

Veblen, Thorstein. 1898 (1990, July). "Why Is Economics not an Evolutionary Science?" *Quarterly Journal of Economics*, 12(4): 373–97. Reprinted in Thorstein Veblen, *The Place of Science in Modern Civilization*, New Brunswick, NJ: Transaction Publishers.

7

Reimagining the Private Firm

Escape from possessive individualism will require that the terms of engagement between households and firms be rebalanced. The household's relationship with the firm is that of utility-maximizing consumers interested in low prices. Rarely is the firm seen as the essential component in the economic well-being of households. And when it is seen in this light, contestation over wages and work conditions arises. Two profound revolutions emerged when owners of capital revealed indifference to the well-being of households. The postrevolutionary regimes in China and the Soviet Union then tried to situate that obligation on the government. We know how that turned out. A better solution—economically and politically—is to bring capitalist firms into a joint obligation with the government in this essential task. The persistence of union-busting, desultory pay and fringe benefits, layoffs, plant closings, automation, and outsourced jobs to foreign countries ought to remind politicians—and capitalists—that radical solutions are always available if hope is too long delayed. The previous chapter spelled out a theory of institutional change. We now concentrate on the difficult realm of ideas—the right-hand box in Figure 6.1. For here lurks the greatest barrier to necessary institutional change—defective imagination.

I. The Presumption of Autonomy

Two examples offer insights into the problematic autonomy of private firms. There are many examples from which to choose, but these two offer clear lessons for reimagining the private firm. The first example concerns a widespread practice of treating employees with disregard, and the second concerns treating a particular group of customers with disrespect. The first example reveals antisocial behavior by stealth, whereas the second reveals blatant discrimination. Both instances illustrate antisocial behavior made possible by the defective understanding of actual autonomy of the private firm. The first behavior is apparently in the process of being corrected—the guilty firms were embarrassed by public exposure. The second harm, now corrected, required the force of law. The lesson here is that when public shaming is inadequate to reimagine the private firm, institutional change will be necessary. This legal transition is always contested because owners of capital presume they are protected by their flawed self-serving grasp of property rights.

A. Trapped Labor

It has recently come to light that a large number of fast-food chains—Burger King, Carl's Jr., Pizza Hut, and McDonald's among them—have contract clauses that prohibit franchisees from hiring workers who now work for a different franchise within the same corporation. This practice is also found in several large retail chains and a number of other national companies. Why are there restrictions on labor mobility? Economic theory tells us that labor mobility offers the promise of higher wages and salaries. Perhaps that is why these corporations seek to prevent labor mobility. It is common to hear of workers losing their jobs for a variety of reasons—automation, closings, and mergers with other firms. It is not often we learn that some workers are trapped in their current job. It appears that some firms imagine that they own their workers.

It is standard practice for employees with highly specialized knowledge of privileged firm-specific information to be required to sign noncompete contracts that prevent their being hired by competitors until after a certain period of time. The delay is intended to erode the value of their specialized knowledge, thereby making such individuals less valuable to a competitor. These restrictive clauses enjoy both ethical and legal justification.

But why are unskilled workers in fast-food restaurants—the vast majority of whom work for the minimum wage—bound by "noncompete" clauses? What special skills do they possess that would advantage the hiring firm or harm the firm they might leave? Actually, there is more to the story. Unlike such clauses for highly paid corporate executives with specialized knowledge, these noncompete clauses are *not* agreed to by the affected employees. In fact, it seems they are unaware of such constraints. The restrictive clauses are contained in obscure parts of the contract that franchisees sign with corporate headquarters. The purpose of such restrictions would seem to be to preclude franchisees competing against each other for workers. Such no-hire rules are in place for approximately 70,000 restaurants—more than a quarter of all fast-food outlets in the country. It is estimated that more than 4 million individuals are now working in fast-food outlets—an increase of 28 percent since 2010. Average wages are said to be about $300 per week before taxes, an amount that is one-third of what the average worker in the private sector earns.[1]

Do restrictions on labor mobility among franchises lead to wage stagnation? Are such noncompete contracts warranted to protect trade secrets? It is hard to see that a franchisee for Burger King has a trade secret that must be shielded from another Burger King franchisee five blocks away—and perhaps closer to the residence of an employee who seeks to switch places of employment. What is the purpose of such clauses? Perhaps it is to suppress possible wage increases that are often the reason why workers switch jobs. After all, if a particular franchisee needs to hire additional workers, attracting employees from a similar firm would save on training costs and would therefore seem to warrant a slight increase in pay. Apparently, franchisees do not want their employees looking around for a better deal. Mobility in the labor market is celebrated because it matches the best workers with the most promising employment. However, it seems that fast-food restaurants have little interest in economic theory and the alleged benefits of vibrant labor markets. The obvious question is whether or not such noncompete contracts are ethical? Or is ethics the correct way to frame this problem?[2]

B. Forbidden Customers

A restaurant owner in Atlanta, Georgia, closed his popular Pickrick Restaurant in 1964 rather than serve African Americans who wished to eat there. The owner had a reputation for brandishing an axe handle to make sure that only whites would enter his restaurant. The Civil Rights Act of 1964 altered his flawed understanding of the autonomy of the private firm. Lester Maddox closed his restaurant and then, in defiance, constructed a nearby monument to "private property rights." This was a waste of his time and money.

Why should ownership of a restaurant lead one to suppose that he is free to chase off customers he prefers not to serve? We see here an instance of the conflation between the ownership of land and related assets, and the profusion of rights talk so dominant in a society defined by possessive individualism.

The defective presumptions of autonomy on display by Lester Maddox, and the stealthy prohibition of desired labor mobility by employees of thousands of restaurants and retail establishments, reveal to us that owners of capital fail to understand that the private firm is a contingent social construct. To be blunt, the capitalist firm exists *not* to serve its owner(s) but the society that has granted it a license to operate. This alarming reality may require elaboration.

II. The Contingent Private Firm

> Only those economic advantages are rights which have the law back of them . . . whether it is a property right is really the question to be answered. (Justice R. Jackson, Willow River Power Co. 324 US 499, 502 [1945])

The prevalence of rights talk and a culture of possessive individualism infects each of us in our pursuit of exactly what we wish to have at the lowest possible prices. More importantly, possessive individualism infects owners of the capitalist firm. It is somehow imagined that ownership of land and related assets carries with it rather complete autonomy as to firm behavior. This defective presumption is on display in many environmental disputes when an owner will declare, with certitude, that "this is my land and I can do as I wish." Such claims are soon found to be silly. Ownership and control are social constructs. We must explore why that is the case.

We start with the simple case. There was a surge of interest in business ethics in early 2000, much of it spurred by the many outrages associated with the Enron debacle. Business schools came under pressure to introduce courses in business ethics. The phrase "moral managers" soon emerged. The idea seemed to be that future business employees needed a college course in ethics in order to introduce improved behavior inside firms. The issue in play is whether the quest for improved business ethics is the responsibility of firms, or must it be situated outside of the firm where the collective sentiment of the nation-state can be brought to bear? In other words, is it best *to induce* managers and employees to become exemplary moral agents, or must morality be *forced on* firms by means of institutional change?

John Boatright's 1999 presidential address to the Society for Business Ethics challenged the emerging view that it was essential to introduce ethics into the thought processes of managers so that they would behave morally (Boatright, 1999). In resisting this urge, Boatright argued that the "Moral Manager Model" rests on the flawed assumptions that: (1) the business organization is the fundamental unit of analysis for business ethics; and (2) a business organization is directed by its top executives. To make the manager (or the firm) the focus of business ethics defies both the logic of bureaucracy and the logic of the marketplace. The logic of bureaucracy is that firms contain a large number of individuals and that it is therefore impossible to make sure that all of these semiautonomous decision makers acts morally. The logic of the market insists that firms must survive in competitive markets, and thus asking them to act morally in the face of this competition is to expect the impossible.

Boatright's claim was that markets must be made moral through adherence to community norms—not those that recent college graduates might bring into the firm. He writes:

> The Moral Manager Model places the responsibility on the leaders of business organizations and seeks to influence their discretionary decision-making authority. The model I propose—let's call it the Moral Market Model—would place responsibility on all of us to improve the business system. That is, to create more efficient markets and more effective regulation. (Boatright, 1999, p. 586)

Boatright's argument against the "moral manager" was reinforced by Joseph Heath (2006). The ethical operation of a nation's firms must be specified by the political community and cannot be left to the discretion of firms competing against each other. As someone once observed: "moral fiber is strongest when not threatened by the sharp blade of self-interest."

We are left, therefore, with the need to confront the contingent nature of the private firm. In both examples we have given—trapped labor and a racist owner—the "moral manager" was revealed to be unreliable. In the case of trapped labor, public shaming seems to have been decisive: the practice was apparently abandoned in response to a campaign exposing the guilty firms to public ridicule. However, two questions arise. First, why did these corporate behemoths adopt such restrictive clauses in the first place? And why did they suppose it would be a good idea to prohibit the mobility of labor among their various restaurants and stores? Actually, we know why they thought it would be a good idea. It would hold down labor costs, it would make franchises more valuable, and such practices would thereby redound to the advantage of the corporation and its franchise partners. What did such practices do for the earnings of their employees? We know the answer to that question.

Second, why did these firms so quickly abandon the practice on the basis of nothing more substantive than public shaming? The answer here is equally obvious, but it warrants brief mention. Participating firms knew that the practice was socially and politically offensive and hoped that it might remain unpublicized. That must be why they did not reveal it to their employees but buried it deep in the arcane legal language binding franchisees to the corporate structure. When finally exposed, the corporations understood that to fight it would invite more political outrage. Shaming was quick and effective.

So much for the "moral manager" model of corporate social responsibility. But notice that a number of individuals will look in on this practice and defend it on the grounds that the "business of business is business." They will assert that the corporation's first obligation is to its shareholders. Milton Friedman's odd capitalist manifesto—*Capitalism and Freedom*—was clear in this regard:

> In (a free economy) there is one and only one social responsibility of business—to use its resources and engage in activities designed to increase its profits so long as it stays within the rules of the game.... It is the responsibility of the rest of us to establish a framework of law such that an individual in pursuing his own interest is . . . led by an invisible hand to promote an end which was no part of his intention. (Friedman, 2002, p. 133)

And therein lies the naïve paralyzing proviso: "it is the responsibility of the rest of us to establish a framework of law" that will force the profit-maximizing firm to do what it has no intention of doing in the absence of legal coercion. The private firm under managerial capitalism has little interest in subjecting itself to a set of intentions that it has no interest in attending to. We have seen how nineteenth-century British capitalists were able to defeat a number of labor reforms over an extended period of time. When Parliament was finally persuaded to adopt those changes, the capitalists succeeded in preventing funds for monitoring such reforms. History tells us that the capitalist firm will not subject itself to urgent social norms without a protracted and expensive fight. It is their money against an impecunious working class and the meager public purse. And if the public purse is severely limited through associated efforts to keep taxes low and regulatory oversight limited and ineffective, it is no contest.

It would seem that the private firm, if it is to attend to the larger public good, must be coerced into a new legal structure that it will resist with all of its substantial economic and political clout. The necessary reimagining of the private firm comes down to a legal contest between the owners of capital and the rest of society. Let us explore how that contest might evolve.

The earlier theory of institutional change and the discussion of Dewey's Arc introduced us to the concept of animation and to the realm of beliefs (ideas) that hold the germ of innovation in how the economy is constituted.

The most obvious innovation—the novel idea—is to grasp the *contingent nature* of the private firm. Firms are contingent precisely because the state—the political community—must decide to what extent the public interest is served by the grant of a limited degree of autonomy to certain kinds of nonhousehold going concerns. Recall from above that there is nothing natural about the purpose, structure, and activity of firms. Only households are natural entities. Firms are artificial contrivances that enjoy a contingent and revocable grant of autonomy over circumstance and conditions inside of the firm. This contingent grant of autonomy also extends to the products and services that firms hope to sell beyond their legal boundary. Firms may not undertake the production of poppy seeds for the derivation of opium. In other words, firms may only advance claims to *socially sanctioned rights*, and they must adhere to *socially sanctioned obligations*. Firms may not engage in *unauthorized transactions*. It is a primary role of the political community to determine the boundary between authorized and unauthorized transactions (Bromley, 2016; Commons, 1968).

This recognition of contingency means that firms are the obliged and encumbered creations of the political community—the nation-state. There is no such thing as an autonomous firm, and thus there is no such thing as a "private" company (firm). The alleged boundary of the firm is highly permeable. The legal boundary of the firm merely defines the arena of temporary and conditional command and obedience inside the firm, as distinct from the arena of market forces beyond that boundary. The boundary of the firm is also where products or services meet potential buyers, and where sellers of labor power meet potential buyers of labor power. The political community—the state—retains the authority to penetrate that boundary at will. And the state does indeed penetrate that boundary when circumstances indicate it is warranted.

There is a range of activities for which the making of money is deemed—at any particular moment—to be unacceptable. And there is a range of practices inside firms, and at the boundary of firms, that are deemed—at any particular moment—to be acceptable. The qualifier *at any particular moment* is necessary to remind us that the precise definition of acceptable activities and practices is dynamic; what was acceptable behavior inside firms in the nineteenth century is not acceptable in the twenty-first century. The political community keeps a close eye on what transpires inside of firms. It does this because of the special contingent liberties granted to the single place in society where wealth creation is the sole animating purpose.

It may seem alarming to learn that there is no such thing as a "private" firm. I need to justify that claim.

III. Taking Kant Seriously

The fundamental Kantian contribution here is to establish the surprising idea that what an individual owns depends on what *others* say that person owns and *not* on what the individual (the owner) claims to own. We see that the issue under discussion is the precise *idea of ownership*—and ownership is nothing but an idea. Ownership is a concept by postulation (Northrop, 1967). Lester Maddox had the idea—he thought—that his ownership of the restaurant (a "business") included the right to control who his customers might be. Instead, he learned that ownership of his firm entailed certain duties toward others. More recently, certain businesspeople—photographers and bakers—have been repeating the Maddox mistake. They seem to imagine that their ownership of a firm entitles them to refuse to serve gay couples. They will learn otherwise.[3] Customers are free to choose firms, but firms are not free to choose their customers. Signs admonishing customers as to proper dress are obviously appropriate. One's appearance (clothing) is a choice to be made; one's ethnic or racial makeup is not. More importantly, dress standards are an important aspect of the nature of the experience for other customers.

This brings us to the Kantian idea of *intelligible possession* as distinct from *empirical possession*. Intelligible possession requires the application of pure reason, while empirical possession entails only physical control (Williams, 1977).

> A person has intelligible possession of something when, and only when, everyone else, or in the case of a promise, some specified individual, has an obligation not to affect it without his consent. Intelligible possession of an external object is the right to control the object through controlling other persons' wills by obligating them with regard to the object. (Mulholland, 1990, p. 241)

It seems that we have dueling ideas: John Locke versus Immanuel Kant. Locke's doctrine of property and freedom was congenial to a new nation keen to have yeoman farmers tame the frontier. The appropriation doctrine—really, Locke's labor theory of property—permitted European immigrants to mix a little labor with the land and then claim that this justified confiscating most of North America from the Native Americans who were here first. Private properly may not necessarily constitute theft, as Pierre-Joseph Proudhon (1809–1865) insisted, but a good deal of theft has certainly ended up as private property.

Lockean ideology remains strong in a land of ubiquitous rights talk. As we saw with Lester Maddox, such ideology pervades the discussion of property rights and the alleged sanctity of firms. Kant takes us to the heart of the matter when he notices that rights are not tangible empirical realities (*possessio phenomenon*) but rather are **noumena** (*possessio noumenon*). Those things that cannot be apprehended by the senses but are knowable only by reason constitute **noumena**. Kant motivates his inquiry on rights by asking what conditions are necessary in order that an individual might be able to make internal something that is, by its very nature, external. The key idea here is one of belonging—of belonging to. Something external to an individual—a parcel of land, a firm—is made internal by the mental trick of understanding the idea of belonging to. And how is it decided that something external *belongs to* an individual?

The individual may well declare that some particular object or situation belongs to her. But this declaration stands as a contestable claim against all others to whom the object or situation might otherwise belong. Such claims are asserted by those who wish to make the point that the speaker is the rightful (justified) possessor and controller (owner?) of the thing under discussion. Something external has now, by mere proclamation, become internal to the speaker.

In the present context, where the degree of managerial discretion inside of firms is under review, a commercial enterprise (a firm) is mentally transformed into an object that is possessed and controlled by a single party—the owner. But Kant noticed something important in this mental transformation. He recognized that such claims of ownership and control represent negations of the interests of others within the same community. Lester Maddox's assertions about property rights negated the interests of potential customers. The noncompete contract clauses of fast-food restaurants negated the interests of employees seeking a higher rate of pay.

We now see that unless others to whom the owner directs her assertion of absolute control are willing to respect those claims, the situation is unstable. Kant noticed that it is only from the consent of all others in the political jurisdiction—the nation-state—that an individual can gain complete autonomy from shared social norms. After all, if the external thing—Lester Maddox's restaurant—can belong to anyone within the community, what mental trick is necessary and sufficient to grant to any particular member of that community complete autonomy to use that firm as an instrument of his or her personal wishes? Why should others willingly accept binding duties on nothing more compelling than the self-serving assertions of those temporarily in possession of something of potential value to others? And the mere fact that Lester Maddox paid for the going concern is irrelevant.

Kant pointed out that such assertions are nothing but the affirmation of empirical possession. And by being based on mere possession (*possessio phenomenon*), they confuse physical control with something much more profound. That more profound circumstance is intelligible possession (*possessio noumenon*). We see intelligible possession at work when a community of sentient beings reaches agreement that indeed it is both right (moral) and good (prudential) that someone among them should be able to control the lives of others. Lacking that agreement, there can be no grant of control. The political community grants me *possessio noumenon*—I cannot take it and exercise it for myself.

John Locke gave us a basis for justified acquisition and holding of private property, but he clearly failed to offer guidance on what to do when that holding conflicted with other obligations. Kant clarified the defective Lockean vision of justified holding—acquisition running into the future.

Contemporary Lockeans have a ready answer to this question: let the aggrieved parties buy it from those who have justly acquired it (or who have previously purchased it). If African Americans wish to eat in the Pickrick Restaurant, let them buy it from Lester Maddox. The Lockean escape will obviously not work in practice.

We see that private property cannot be presumed to induce behavior that is either moral or prudential. Kant provided the idea that the community itself must determine whether private property is held and used in a socially acceptable manner. The dividing line is determined through reason emerging from a civil society. It is the community itself that must set the standards by which the range of autonomy to private property is to be judged. But what is this thing called reason—alone by which the empirical content of ownership might be realized?

IV. Taking Peirce Abductively

We saw earlier, in Chapter 6, that Charles Sanders Peirce insisted that reasoning, the search for new belief, required a diagnostic approach whereby novel hypotheses might be brought on to the stage. We learned that abduction is a class of inference that yields explanatory hypotheses for observed phenomena or possible explanations of them. Most of us believe that deduction and induction exhaust our ways of understanding. This is not a true belief. Abductive belief starts with a particular observed phenomenon and then invokes specific axioms, assumptions, and applicability postulates to produce explanatory propositions (testable hypotheses) about that phenomenon. In the quest for clarity about the meaning of property rights, these propositions might then come to constitute the core of a theory of the nature and content of property rights.

Abduction is not confined to particular cases, though it can tell us something about those cases. Rather, abduction seeks, just as with deduction, a general theory of the case—property rights—under scrutiny. Aristotle called this way of knowing *diagnosis,* and it is indeed the very process engaged in by those whose task it is to diagnose empirical phenomena—physicians faced with a distressed patient, automobile mechanics contemplating an engine that will not start, and pathologists who perform autopsies (Ducasse, 1925). One can work backwards as far as necessary to pin down the family of probable explanations. In economic matters, it is necessary to go very far back.

Indeed, we cannot explain economic phenomena until we encounter one or more noneconomic hypotheses. To quote Joseph Schumpeter:

> [W]hen we succeed in finding a definite causal relation between two phenomena, our problem is solved if the one which plays the "causal" role is non-economic. We have then accomplished what we, as economists, are capable of in the case in question and we must give place to other disciplines. If, on the other hand, the causal factor is itself economic in nature, we must continue our explanatory efforts until we ground upon a non-economic bottom. (Schumpeter, 1961, pp. 4–5)

In addition, it is often helpful to go forward to see if we can offer insights concerning other events that are plausibly implied by the realized role of the hypotheses (assumptions). When we do this, we are exploring the full entailments of our hypotheses. In other words, we can gain a purchase on the exact empirical content of property rights by deploying abduction. There is a rich empirical record concerning this problematic issue, and abduction invites us to consult the evidence.

In the United States, the exact content of what is called "property rights" is worked out at the federal level under the "takings clause" of the Fifth Amendment to the U.S. Constitution. At the state and local level, the Fourteenth Amendment is applicable. The basic idea of the Fifth Amendment is that what is called "private property" may not be taken for public use without the payment of just compensation. In simple terms, if the Pickrick Restaurant were needed ("taken") for the construction of a new road, Mr. Maddox would receive fair market-based compensation. But if a regulation, notably the Civil Rights Act of 1964, reaches into the Pickrick Restaurant, thereby requiring Mr. Maddox to serve customers he would rather not, then the regulation has not taken from him anything he ever had. His ownership of the firm did not entitle him to discriminate, and the Civil Rights Act of 1964 confirmed that inability.

Returning to the dispute as framed by the Supreme Court, the deductivist will want to ask the following question: "does this particular Supreme Court respect (protect)—or fail to respect (protect)—property rights?" The deductivist will then invoke hypotheses (assumptions) that will render a tentative answer to that question. Or the deductivist will ask a somewhat subtler question: "what is the position of this particular Supreme Court with respect to property rights?" Notice that both of these questions start with a prior idea of the nature of some "thing"—in this case "property rights." The earnest investigator then seeks to answer her own question by reading carefully, and by parsing, particular legal decisions and linguistic niceties in footnotes. There is a certain ancient mystical quality to it. The query seeks to find or discover the empirical content of an a priori abstraction called a property right.

The abductivist finds this quest pointless. The question is flawed because it presumes the prior and definitive notion of what property rights *are*. Yet that is the very idea requiring a clarifying explanation. As we saw above, Justice Jackson reminded us that "whether it is a property right is really the question to be answered." In other words, property rights do not exist, lying around out there waiting to be discovered. Property rights are *created* as courts struggle with conflicts advanced by contending parties, each claiming to have a right with respect to what is called property. A right is not a phenomenon waiting to be discovered. Rather, a right is a *noumena* awaiting as the need arises. A "right" is the essence of contingency.

Starting with this understanding, the abductive (diagnostic) approach will observe a series of Supreme Court decisions that, on their face, appear to hold quite different implications for the concept (the a priori idea) of property rights. Rather than finding these diverse cases perplexing, the earnest diagnostician would embrace their very confounding reality as the starting point for working out a theory of property rights. That is, these cases and their findings are the reality that begs for a theory—an explanation. And there is an explanation for these seeming disparate decisions by the Supreme Court. Notice that this query will not clarify the meaning of property rights in the general case. But we are not interested in the general case. We are interested in why Lester Maddox could not use a claim of property rights to exclude African Americans from his restaurant. We do not care about property rights in Rio de Janeiro or Berlin. We care about property rights in America.

It seems that the only way to understand the practice—the actualization—of property rights is to realize that this term (property right) is the *benediction applied to those settings and circumstances that, when the dust of consideration by various levels of jurisprudence has finally settled, are found worthy of protection by the state* (Bromley, 1993, 1997]. Notice that the term *property right* is not something known a priori or axiomatically—something whose essence is clear to us by intuition or introspection before the specifics of a particular legal struggle is joined. Rather, the empirical content of property rights is arrived at—*created*—in the process of resolving mutually exclusive rights claims that come before the nation's courts. That is, property rights are not a priori essences that exist and await mere application in a particular legal scuffle. Rather, property rights are *created* in the process of resolving disputes originating in conflicting rights claims brought before the courts.

This means that the American judicial system does not seek to locate where the a priori property right lies. Rather, the courts offer a necessary forum before which, from time to time, conflicting and mutually exclusive rights claims will be brought. When the more compelling rights claim has been determined, the courts will issue a decree to that effect. We see that *property rights are made, not found*. And those rights are made in a civil society by a process of jurisprudence motivated and justified by the pressing need to arrive at clarity in a problematic dispute. Civil peace requires as much. *Noumena* is the instrument.

This idea follows necessarily from the meaning of a right. To have a right means that you have been granted the ability to compel the coercive power of the state to come to your assistance against the contrary claims of others. Rights entitle an individual to enlist the wondrous powers of the state as your very special ally. The granting of a right by the state (and the courts are but the final arbiters of state action) does not imply passive support by the state. Rather, that grant bestows active assistance for those to whom the state has granted that status of a right. That is, the state stands ready to be enlisted in the cause of those to whom it has granted rights. We say that rights *expand the capacities* of the individual by indicating what one *can do with the aid of the collective power* (Bromley, 1989, 2006; Commons, 1968; Macpherson, 1973). Lester Maddox learned that he did not have quite the extent of property rights he thought he had. The private business is subject to a wide array of conditions. The state refused to recognize his interests. Maddox's inability to exclude certain customers was matched by the expanded capacities enjoyed by African Americans to eat in restaurants of their choosing.

We see that to have *civil rights* means that the state will come to your aid if, for instance, you wish to eat in a particular restaurant or enroll in a particular university. Federal marshals, under a binding decree from the courts, stand ready to assist you in those desired acts, regardless of their personal views about the legitimacy (justifiability) of your demands. You have rights and the state is your ally, the reality of which is the necessary condition for you to be said to have rights. Notice that the state only grants rights to parties and circumstances that it wishes to embrace in the future. Others—owners of restaurants unhappy about your desire for a meal there, governors intent on keeping you out of particular universities—have duties to comply with the wishes of the state on pain of police action (itself possibly coerced by the courts and, if necessary, federal marshals, as at the University of Mississippi in 1962).

We are reminded that this thing called "property" is *not* an object such as land or a building where meals are served. Rather, the concept of property is that of a *value*. When one buys a piece of land (in the vernacular, a "piece of property"), one acquires not just some physical object. The most important acquisition is the recognized control over a benefit stream arising from that setting and circumstance that runs into the future. That is why one spends money (one benefit stream) in order to acquire a different benefit stream arising from the fact of ownership. Notice that the magnitude of that new benefit stream is a function of the legal parameters associated with it: can one build a tall office tower on it, or a mere bungalow? Is it now covered by water six months out of the year, and if so, will local ordinances allow it to be drained for some "higher" (that is, a more remunerative) use? The price paid to acquire that new benefit stream is simply the expected discounted present value of all future net income appropriable from owning the thing. This is why property is the value, not the object (Bromley, 1991; Macpherson 1973, 1978). These two concepts—property and right—are put together to arrive at the understanding that this pertains to the grant of authority by the state to a person now called an *owner*. That authority promises that the state is a willing participant in the imposition of binding duties on all those in the class of individuals called *nonowner*.

The implications of this for the presumptive autonomy of the private firm is obvious. John R. Commons insisted that the Supreme Court constituted the quintessential "volitional theorist" in American history. In his book *The Legal Foundations of Capitalism* (1968), Commons sought to develop a theory of the evolution of institutional arrangements—of which property rights are of a fundamental kind—by studying how disputes and conflicts got "worked out." Commons insisted that Adam Smith got it wrong when he sought to work out a general theory of economic life predicated on harmony and mutual benefit from exchange. To Commons, the very essence of the human condition is one of conflicts over scarcity, and those scarcities are not mediated by mutually beneficial bargaining but rather by negotiations and struggle. Ultimately, those struggles, many of which start out at a local level or in a national legislature, stand a good chance of ending up in the courts. And indeed a fraction of those disputes will find their way to the Supreme Court.

Commons insisted that in the American system of judicial oversight, all legislation is a mere recommendation to the Supreme Court.[4] He further noted that it was at the Supreme Court that "disputes go to die." That is, the Supreme Court must pick a winning side; Commons used the phrase "to pick a value." In essence, the decisions of the Court must look to the future and decide which possible future it seems better to endorse. All struggles are, in fact, about the future. The Supreme Court must create a future it finds compelling and must then decide the cases before it in light of that future. Commons knew that the Court does not act on principles—legal doctrine. It decides cases in terms of what, at the moment, seem to be the more compelling reasons. In doing so, the Court "picks values."

Commons called this *reasonable valuing*. This is an important economic insight because courts settle disputes by issuing findings (decrees) that—had those findings been the law and thus in effect—the disputants would not have been in doubt about their legal position and their dispute would not have required litigation. In this way, the Court serves the valuable purpose of reducing economic uncertainty and enhancing the workings of the economy.

A coherent theory of the evolution of property rights—and the domain of choice open to private firms—requires that we understand property rights as part of the process of emergent created imaginings (Shackle, 1961). The Supreme Court considers and imagines possible futures, and it then figures out which of the claimants before it has the more compelling claim in light of those imagined futures. The economic implications are clear. Because the law is concerned precisely with defining property rights (and so endowments), the very foundation upon which economists might be inclined to discuss "efficiency" is elusive. If we understand new regulations to be concerned with the creation of new institutional arrangements—laws—that modify choice domains for atomistic agents in response to the existence of unwanted social costs in the absence of those regulations, then regulations modify production possibilities frontiers and utility possibilities frontiers in a way that makes all such changes Pareto noncomparable (Boadway and Bruce, 1984).

A full *general equilibrium approach* is required. Recall that the institutional arrangements of an economy—the working rules—are always undergoing refinement. This institutional change is motivated by circumstances and conditions that cannot be understood and explained by a model that regards a new law as either contributing to economic efficiency or simply redistributing income. Our understanding of the reimagined firm will be enhanced only with a more careful consideration of the reasons for institutional change. Regulatory activities in a market economy are best comprehended as instances in which collective action results in new institutional arrangements whose explicit purpose is to alter existing choice domains of individuals and groups. New regulations arise to address the existence and incidence of unwanted social costs in the economy. Indeed, we might best think of regulations as redefining the parameters of the market; yesterday's regulations become fully integrated into, and define, today's market. We see the necessity of a general equilibrium analysis. The economy is always in the process of becoming. Meatloaf comes in many varieties.

V. Contested Moral Choices

The appeal of a market economy is that one can enter and leave any particular market with perfect ease; there are no obligations. Engaging the market is entirely volitional—unless one needs to eat. Since eating is essential to survival, living in a market society leaves one with no choices to make. In other words, rather than thoroughgoing freedom in a market economy, the need to eat gives rise to coercive pressure to participate in the market for the fictitious asset called labor. Refusal by firms to hire those who need work in order that they might eat gives rise to coercive pressure against the will to live. Who can believe that a capitalist market economy is free of coercion?

The two essential going concerns of capitalism are households and firms. The question we must now confront is whether or not these two necessary components stand on equal moral footing. Of course the most *natural* human organization—the family—is taken for granted. Neither the family nor the evolving household requires explanation or justification. The household is self-justifying by its very nature. The same grace cannot be granted to those social entities called firms—companies, corporations, businesses, joint-stock companies, sole proprietorships, or cooperatives. Each specialized form of those entities and many others not listed require social justification. They must, from time to time, explain and justify their legitimacy to us. In other words, these various artificial going concerns—these legal contrivances—obtain their legitimacy by our periodic and collective grant of usefulness.

All such contrivances are examples of a *public trust*. In plain terms, there is no such thing as a private firm, nor is there, in the economic realm, anything to which the adjective "private" might properly be applied. A private firm is a contradiction in terms. The mere fact that virtually all such contrivances must be licensed, authorized, sanctioned, inspected, monitored, and taxed accordingly makes clear that these contrivances are artificial. While they are owned by individuals in various legal arrangements, all firms exist and function by the grace of the political entity we call the nation-state.

This claim may be novel, but it cannot be controversial. We know well that all such artificial contrivances are imbued with extraordinary political urgency and sanctity. In some political circles, there is nothing quite as revered as the private firm. Firms (and their owners) are job creators, firms are the engines of prosperity, and firms are the fount of redeeming social habits such as thrift, efficiency, accountability, and fiscal probity. Actually, the notion that the private firm is a paragon of efficiency is open to serious doubt (Nelson, 1981. Often, we will hear politicians act as if they consider it unpatriotic—ungrateful—to expect firms to pay taxes. Doing so might well jeopardize their central role as the savior of a capitalist market economy. Are there good reasons for this stark asymmetry between the shared reverence for private firms and a general indifference toward the household?

Perhaps the answer is to be found in their raison d'être—their purpose. The private firm, regardless of its idiosyncratic role in a market economy, is a known and standard entity. Of course, some are limited liability corporations, some are joint partnerships, and some are sole proprietorships. But they have a single thing in common: all of them are organized to provide a marketable good or a service, and they are driven by the same imperative. They must survive in an often-ruthless competitive environment. Like an athletic team, there is a known and quantifiable measure of their success. If they thrive, they are good. If they grow and expand, perhaps acquiring other firms, they are exceptional and worthy of fame and social approval. This cannot be a surprise.

A market economy is a hypercompetitive setting, and survival requires extraordinary diligence, agility, and acumen. Only the very best win in a meritocracy, and private firms offer each of us an opportunity to admire and marvel at their financial success. Amazon, Apple, Starbucks, and Google are wonders to behold. Corporate leaders write smart-sounding books for airport bookstores, they appear on television shows, they set philanthropic examples, and they often grace the local society pages. They are *dramatis personae* and represent suitable replacements for public intellectuals who seem to have gone out of fashion. Personal status in a capitalist society is measured by the size of one's income. If that is often hard to discern, then homes, cars, ostentatious jewelry and clothing, and other possessions offer a readily accessible proxy. Veblenian conspicuous consumption comes to mind. The firm is publicly accessible to us, and we marvel at its successes. What does the New York Stock Exchange and the Nasdaq Index have to say about them today? We are bombarded by these indices of their prowess—or their stumbles.

Firms, unlike households, must be noticed and contended with. Firms need to be accommodated in a market society. And since firms hold the key to the ability of households to earn an income and acquire the necessities to survive, firms are in actuality at the very center of the existence and flourishing of households. Consumers need firms, and firms need consumers. The ability of households to affect firms is only one-way—they affect firms by negation. They can withhold their custom from firms, and they can withhold their labor power from firms. But aside from trying to harm firms by spreading malicious rumors about them, members of households have little ability to exert or impose harm on firms.

In contrast, firms have the capacity to inflict considerable harm on households. Firms can refuse to hire members of households when asked to do so. Firms can fire members of households. Firms can make extraordinary work demands on members of households. It will be said that of course firms should not have to hire workers they do not need or workers who are not qualified. Of course firms should be able to dismiss incompetent or unworthy workers. Of course firms should be able to tell workers what they must do during work hours. And obviously firms must be able to monitor the clothing and general appearance of those individuals they employ. Under ideal circumstances, each of these objections is obviously true. By adopting advanced technology, the number of workers that a firm needs will certainly diminish in the fullness of time. However, is this new technology being adopted because it is cheaper than hired labor? Or is it being adopted to liberate firms from their dependence on households and their incessant labor needs?

The standard answer is to encourage such workers to find other lines of work. This churning of the labor force is thought to be good. Of course replacement jobs might offer slightly lower pay, but the economy will move nicely along on its new lower-cost path. This will be thought good since displaced workers entering the labor market might actually reduce existing wages a little and allow the economy to become even *more* "efficient." And if there is an influx of new workers into the economy—perhaps because of immigration or because universities are suddenly more expensive and out of reach for high school graduates who decide to enter the workforce—then overall wages may be pushed down slightly and profits will be further enhanced. As long as costs are driven down, prices in a market economy will fall and consumers will benefit. That is how economic welfare is measured. If the cost-saving measure is not due to mere technical change, then perhaps the firm will realize that automation is not possible or is too expensive. But it may be possible to take the production process to a country where labor costs are really low. In such cases, the impact on domestic households is profound.

The above scenarios, presented in their extreme form, are precisely concerned with the fraught interplay of households and firms. Notice who is the active agent: it is firms adopting labor-saving technology, putting downward pressure on wages, fighting off unions, perhaps even moving abroad. Members of households—those who are currently employed and those who would like to be employed—are passive observers and recipients of profound changes that affect their livelihood prospects. Members of households are not asked if they are in favor of labor-saving technology. They are not asked how they feel about downward pressure on wages, and they certainly are not asked how they feel about their employer shuttering its plant and moving to China, Mexico, Thailand, or the Philippines. And of course the standard response is that it is entirely within the rights of firms to do these things and whatever else is necessary for them to survive. Capitalism may eat its children, but households quake at the feast.

Therein lies the fundamental challenge to capitalism—how to reconcile the inevitable tension between the livelihood imperatives of individuals in households, and the survival imperatives of the owners of the artificial contrivances known as firms. This is a problematic point because the reigning *zeitgeist* is to celebrate the revered freedom for firms to behave as they see fit in the name of efficiency and low prices for consumers. In return, members of households—who gain what is called "welfare" by the abundance of goods and services at low prices—must adapt as best they can. We assure those individuals that they will be better off in the long run by the relentless downward pressure on prices and that this will enable them to consume what they wish at ever-lower prices—unless of course they do not have an income from the sale of their labor power to firms. Consumers in households gain when prices fall. Workers in those same households lose when wages fall. No wonder foxes are nervous, always looking over their shoulder.

I have referred to firms and households as "moral agents" because they are realms of choice and action that hold profound implications for others beyond the boundary of the firm or household. Referring to them as moral agents does not imply that they act morally. It simply means that they are the locus of choices with moral implications. A member of a household who abuses the family pet—or a child—is making a moral choice. An employee who steals pencils or notepads from her employer is making a moral choice. An employer who rejects a qualified job applicant because of the applicant's race is making a moral choice. A corporation that establishes a tax haven in the Cayman Islands to hide net income is making a moral choice. Both of these core components of capitalism—firms and households—have the capacity to make choices with moral implications for others. But there is not perfect symmetry. The scope for actions of firms to visit harm on households far exceeds the scope for households to visit harm on firms (except by withholding their purchases). Indeed, the entire history of labor policy has been devoted to efforts to limit the scope of harm to households by actions of the capitalist firm.

When workers first sought improved work conditions and higher pay, owners of firms fought them on the grounds that it would harm their net income. And of course that was true. The political fight, therefore, turned on balancing the interests of net income to the artificial contrivance of a firm as against the income of households whose members were employed by those firms. The discourse about this moral choice was often bizarre, however normal it might have appeared to those deeply socialized into the cultural mores of capitalism. There was concern that if firms were required to make the workplace safer, or offer shorter working hours, or increase pay, the firm might not be able to survive.

Firms in this battle were rarely seeking relief on the grounds of sympathy for their plight. To pursue that avenue would have put them on the same tack as that employed by workers and their allies. There was always a much more powerful weapon to be deployed: if those changes were required, the firm would simply close, and then individuals working there would really suffer. Notice that households lack the option of simply closing and depriving firms of their labor power. Short strikes are a temporary expedient but lose their effectiveness in the presence of a reserve army of workers willing to assume unpleasant work in exchange for a paycheck—no matter how meager. We are back to the special political legitimacy of firms in a capitalist culture in their enduring struggle for advantage over those who provide labor power to those firms. It is an uneven playing field.

The evidence is now clear that the capitalist firm cannot be relied upon to assure the economic future of households. As managerial capitalism progresses, two aspects of this assertion will become even more apparent. The first dimension can be thought of as behavioral; the second is structural.

At the behavioral level, opposition to unions, pressure to keep wages low, and affinity for labor-displacing technology are now familiar features of the world of work. Added to this behavioral aspect, we see extreme disparity between compensation received by officers of large companies and that received by their employees. Recent data for 2018 reveal just how extreme this disparity has become.[5] In other words, the capitalist firm is making a conscious choice to privilege its officers and owners of capital (shareholders) over workers. Left to its own devices, the capitalist firm has revealed where its values lie—and workers do not figure in that consideration.

These defects can be rectified by several means: (1) a federal minimum wage; (2) tax reform to capture the majority of ostentatious compensation gifted by self-dealing incestuous boards of directors; and (3) endowed employment programs in which workers—after several years—become vested in a company. If they are disemployed because of automation, mergers/acquisitions, or closings, they would receive some modest level of compensation until reaching retirement age. These, and perhaps other, behavioral changes would clarify the notion that indeed the private firm is a public trust and that it therefore carries social obligations. The business of business may be business, but the social legitimacy of any business is contingent.

We come to the second challenge to managerial capitalism—the structural problem. To focus the mind on this vexing issue, I here reproduce Figure 4.4 showing U.S. manufacturing employment plotted against an index of manufacturing output over the period 1985–2016.

As pointed out in Chapter 4, this startling picture attests to the profound "efficiencies" realized by American manufacturing since 1985. We are impressed with the continued rise in manufacturing output at the same time that manufacturing employment has plummeted, especially since around 1997. Worker productivity in manufacturing has accelerated at a remarkable pace. Technical change in manufacturing, but especially automation, has profoundly transformed the historic tedium of the industrial factory. A single worker can now produce so much more than was dreamed of as recently as, say, the early 1990s.

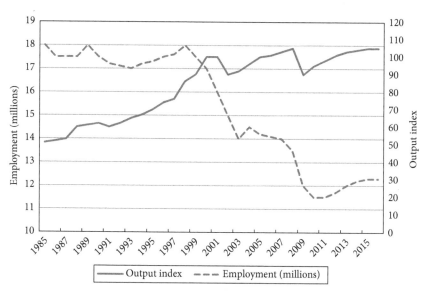

Figure 7.1. U.S. Manufacturing Employment and Index of Manufacturing Output: 1985–2016

Source: Thomson Data Stream: Business Insider, chart-2016-12.

In contemplating Figure 7.1, one might inquire about the 6 million "missing" workers made redundant by this startling evidence of "labor-saving" technical change. We will be assured that we should not worry: many of them probably retired, another large share likely found other lines of work, and a few probably enjoyed the remainder of their lives on unemployment insurance and Social Security. The specifics of Figure 7.1 are not important. I offer it only to suggest that the dashed line in the figure serves as a metaphor of the coming crisis of capitalism. The future is not one of abused and degraded workers of early industrial capitalism. The future is one of too little work. Or, to put it more elegantly, the supply of opportunities for work will fall seriously short of the demand for work. And to put that assertion in even starker terms, how are households going to acquire the means of life—food and shelter—in a world where work is gradually disappearing under the onslaught of automation?

Experts who ponder these issues seem to suggest that within a generation, approximately one-half of the American workforce *could be* rendered unwanted because of automation. We need not worry if the "real" figure is 32 percent, or 21 percent, or even 54 percent. The need for deliberation is upon us.

The 300-year arrangement of household income predicated on the mixing of labor with capital is now coming to an end. The era of "capital hiring labor"—capitalism—is coming to be seen as quaint and unsustainable. As above, current workers disemployed by the sort of technical change on display in Figure 7.1 could be covered by an endowment contract to protect them until they reach retirement age. But what of those millions who may not be able to find any work at all? We must look at the dashed line in Figure 7.1 as a portent of the disappearing world of work under managerial capitalism.

The question I raised at the outset of our journey was straightforward: is capitalism a spent force?

It is, but not because it will be overthrown by a class of angry workers as Marx would have it. Capitalism is a spent force because its defining purpose can no longer be fulfilled. Capitalism was always able to justify itself because it was a simple and intuitive bargain. One group of citizens would mobilize capital and offer another group of citizens an opportunity to mix their labor with that capital (machines). Both groups would thereby gain. Workers benefited from the ingenuity and entrepreneurial abilities of those called owners, and owners benefited from the diligent hard work of the workers. Of course, the allocation of those gains across the two groups was always contested—and remains so today.

However, the future of capitalism cannot resemble its past. The making of objects, and indeed many aspects of the "service" sector, now reveal themselves unable to abide the historic "wage bargain." A growing share of household incomes will, in the future, necessarily come from elsewhere. Household incomes will become a basic *right*. I shall let others worry about design specifics.

VI. The Coming Reckoning

Invoking Dewey's Arc reminds us that old notions of the private firm have given rise to practices—*people doing*—that fail to fit the world as it now is. The idea that owners of private firms are free to pick their customers seems quaint to us now. But of course prior to the 1960s that was standard practice in large swaths of the United States. Restaurants refused to serve particular individuals, and hotels refused them accommodation. Private clubs were tenacious holdouts in this regard, but those barriers are under constant assault—and they too will fall. I have deployed Dewey's Arc in an epistemological sense, but interestingly, it is a mirror of what we call the Arc of History. It is a cliché to note that our obligation to history is to learn from it so that we do not repeat earlier mistakes and errors. I prefer to suggest that our sole obligation to history is to rewrite it. By rewriting it, I do not mean simply going back to correct minor mistakes. I mean our obligation is to look again and to find circumstances that were there all along, but were missed because those who were writing history were not sensitive enough to look for them. Seeing is not believing. Rather, believing is seeing—and with the aid of our modern sensitivities we can take a fresh look at history. This second glance will help us to alter our beliefs, our rules to live by, and so our patterns of interaction. As we do that, and as the wheel of time continues its slow turn, we will see that indeed we are writing a new history as we are crafting our future.

Reimagining the private firm seems an impossible task. The political and economic momentum behind this creature called managerial capitalism is formidable in the extreme. However, any sapient adult who is aware of the depth and breadth of economic and political frustration thick on the ground in the so-called red counties of the United States would be a fool to ignore the incipient revolt. Donald Trump did not produce the anger he exploits for political gain. He is merely a noxious messenger. The authoritarian nationalist poseurs coming to power in parts of Europe, thriving on the distant scent of Fascism, are not innocents in search of a political message. Frustrated Brexit voters in the United Kingdom may be confused about what is to come with liberation from the hated Brussels Bureaucrats, but they are very clear about what angers them. In this ancient seat of capitalism, the reigning economic system ignores them, offers them scant respect, smiles at their bucolic sentimentality, and infuriates them into a suicidal withdrawal from the European Union.

These odd behaviors—disparaged by the urban elites of Europe and the United States—are a *crie de coeur* raised against an economic system that is a meretricious trauma of possessive individualism. The private sector has abdicated any obligation for the economic well-being of the household. The culture of possessive individualism robs the political system of the will, the mental acuity, and the financial means to rectify the threatening imbalance between firms and households. The reimagining of the private firm—acknowledged as a public trust—now begins.

Notes

1. Rachel Abrams, "Why Aren't Paychecks Growing? A Burger-Joint Clause Offers a Clue," *The New York Times*, September 27, 2017.
2. In early July 2018, the chief legal officers of 10 states sent inquiries to a number of fast-food corporations seeking clarification of such noncompete (or no-poaching) clauses in their franchise contracts. Allegedly, McDonald's had already removed such clauses in 2017. https://www.nytimes.com/2018/07/09/business/no-poach-fast-food-wages.html (July 10, 2018). Less than two weeks later, seven major restaurant chains agreed to eliminate the clause from franchise contracts affecting approximately 70,000 restaurants in the United States, employing more than 25 percent of fast-food workers https://www.nytimes.com/2018/07/12/business/fast-food-wages-no-poach-deal.html (July 12, 2018).
3. At this time (2019), the U.S. Supreme Court appears to allow such religious-based discrimination, but that recent litigation was driven by a technical point and it seems highly unlikely that future courts will allow discrimination on the basis of so-called religious conviction.
4. This view, expressed in the foundational 1803 case *Marbury v. Madison*, stands today as the definitive manifesto of what is called "judicial oversight."
5. https://www.nytimes.com/interactive/2019/business/highest-paid-ceos-2018.html?searchResultPosition=12.

References

Boadway, Robin, and Neil Bruce. 1984. *Welfare Economics*, Oxford: Blackwell.

Boatright, John R. 1999. "Does Business Ethics Rest on a Mistake?," *Business Ethics Quarterly*, 9(4): 583–91.

Bromley, Daniel W. 1989. *Economic Interests and Institutions: The Conceptual Foundations of Public Policy,* Oxford: Blackwell.

Bromley, Daniel W. 1991. *Environment and Economy: Property Rights and Public Policy*, Oxford: Blackwell.

Bromley, Daniel W. 1993. "Regulatory Takings: Coherent Concept or Logical Contradiction," *Vermont Law Review*, 17(3): 647–82.

Bromley, Daniel W. 1997. "Constitutional Political Economy: Property Claims in a Dynamic World," *Contemporary Economic Policy*, 15(4): 43–54.

Bromley, Daniel W. 2006. *Sufficient Reason: Volitional Pragmatism and the Meaning of Economic Institutions*, Princeton, NJ: Princeton University Press.

Bromley, Daniel W. 2016. "Institutional Economics," *Journal of Economic Issues*, 50(2): 309–25.

Commons, John R. 1968. *Legal Foundations of Capitalism* Madison: University of Wisconsin Press.

Ducasse, C. J. 1925. "Explanation, Mechanism, and Teleology," *Journal of Philosophy*, 22: 150–55.

Friedman, Milton. 2002. *Capitalism and Freedom*, Chicago: University of Chicago Press.

Heath, Joseph. 2006. "Business Ethics Without Stakeholders," *Business Ethics Quarterly*, 16(4): 533–57.

Macpherson, C. B. 1973. *Democratic Theory*, Oxford: Clarendon Press.

Macpherson, C. B. 1978. *Property: Mainstream and Critical Positions*, Toronto: University of Toronto Press.

Mulholland, Leslie A. 1990. *Kant's System of Rights*, New York: Columbia University Press.

Nelson, Richard R. 1981. "Assessing Private Enterprise: The Exegesis of Tangled Doctrine," *Bell Journal of Economics*, 12: 93–111.

Northrop, F.S.C. 1967. *The Logic of the Sciences and the Humanities*, New York: Meridian Books.

Schumpeter, J. 1961. *The Theory of Economic Development*, New York: Oxford University Press.

Shackle, G.L.S. 1961. *Decision, Order, and Time in Human Affairs*, Cambridge: Cambridge University Press.

Williams, Howard. 1977. "Kant's Concept of Property," *Philosophical Quarterly*, 27: 32–40.

8

Reimagining the Individual

Beginning in the 1980s, inequality of incomes in the metropolitan core began to increase. This great divergence was most pronounced in the Anglophone world—Great Britain, the United States, Canada, Australia, and New Zealand. This divergence suggests that there is nothing inherent—structurally determinative—in capitalism as it operates in the rich metropole that brings about this unwelcome trend. Rather, income inequality is willful—intended. Ironically, that inequality is enabled by the prevalence of possessive individualism that reveals the acquisitive individualist to be the source of his or her own unwanted economic marginalization. The individualist's embrace of a livelihood strategy based on the celebration of rights and the illusion of freedom—being free to choose—has placed him or her at the mercy of the capitalist firm equally committed to possessive individualism. The capitalist firm may well be transformed into a public trust. However, this will not be sufficient. Improved livelihoods will also require that the possessive individual be reimagined.

I. We Have Met the Enemy

The necessary reimagining—reconstituting the legal status of the private firm—is not something to be advocated out of political indignation or economic resentment. Undertaking the difficult work of re-creating the separate realm of the capitalist firm can only be justified if we are first clear about the purpose to be served thereby. Being clear about that desired purpose requires that we also be clear about the diagnosis that underlies the theory of the case. In plain terms, is the capitalist firm as it is currently constituted—and politically defended—the singular explanation for our current economic and political despair? Of course not.

Where then are we to look for the necessary explanation? I propose that we look at ourselves—in a deep and reflective quest for understanding our own unpleasant circumstances. We, who have become thoroughly modern under the twin conceits of possessive individualism, stand as the reason for the much-regretted results that now stalk the beleaguered household.

I earlier suggested that economics now comprises our civic religion; the individual is nothing but a utility-maximizing consumer. This consumer will denounce China for its predatory trade policies and for its poaching of manufacturing jobs, while filling up an imported mini-van with abundant clothing, toys, and assorted plastics from—yes, China. The search for the best bargains drives the relentless consumer forward. It will be claimed that this behavior is made necessary because of inadequate pay. That is not a good reason. It is, in fact, an excuse. A more honest reason is the enduring culturally prized urge toward persistent low-cost acquisitiveness.

It must be noticed that the urge to acquire yet more possessions crowds out disposable income that might otherwise support activities that bring people together. Perhaps new taxes would buttress the funding of public schools so that underpaid teachers need not spend their own meager income to purchase pencils, paper, books, and—yes, sometimes food—for their students. Perhaps new sources of funding for improved urban transportation systems would allow people to escape the isolation of long commutes in their Japanese cars. Perhaps new taxes would improve technical education programs so that alienated and disenfranchised rural (or urban) youth might gain access to meaningful employment in the skilled trades. Politicians are so solicitous of our acquisitive urge that they have made it even more difficult for the government to make sure that everyone is paying their proper taxes (Box 8.1).

Text Box 8.1 The Disappearing Tax Collector

The Internal Revenue Service budget is a plausible marker of our view of taxes. Since 2010, the IRS budget has been cut by 18 percent. It has lost 14 percent of its workforce. Only 53 percent of telephone calls from taxpayers to the IRS were answered in 2016—a drop from 74 percent in 2010. These declines in performance occurred while workloads increased. In 2016, the agency processed 10 million *more* returns than in 2010. In 2016, the agency identified almost 1 million fraudulent returns that prevented over $6.5 billion in refunds being distributed.

The enforcement budget has been cut by 20 percent, and the enforcement division has lost 25 percent of its staff since 2010. In 2010, the agency audited one of every 90 tax returns. In 2016, that proportion had fallen to one audit for every 140 returns.

High-income individuals with complex returns seem to have benefited from the budget cuts. In 2011, the audit rates for incomes over $1 million were 12.5 percent. By 2016, the rate had been cut in half (5.8 percent).

Politicians, embracing possessive individualism, show little interest in burdening us with the need to pay taxes.

Source: Brandon Debot, Emily Horton, and Chuck Marr. "Trump Budget Continues Multi-Year Assault on IRS Funding Despite Mnuchin's Call for More Resources." *Center on Budget and Policy Priorities*, March 16, 2017.

Economics is certainly about making choices. But the most fundamental choice is what fraction of disposable income will be devoted to culturally reinforced hedonism and what fraction will thereby be available for other-regarding commitments? These latter choices are odious under the grip of possessive individualism.

Our pleasure-yielding acquisitive habits are rationalized by appeals to our freedoms and our rights as individuals. We are free to choose, free to acquire, and free to satisfy our momentary whims. Our freedoms are part of our bundle of rights, including the right to do precisely as we wish. Standard political discourse in America, and not just on the 4th of July, is loaded with celebrations of our freedom. Freedom talk operates at two levels. First, there is an aggressive aspect that targets foreigners who wish to harm us. This trope was popular during the long Cold War, and it persists today as a strident warning to ISIS, al-Qaeda, random terrorists, bedraggled immigrants from afar, and an imagined list of other enemies. This conversation concerns a collective—a nationalist—aspect of our freedom. It has recently provided the fuel for a number of dubious politicians. In Europe, there is a similar emergence of xenophobic right-wing politics that is loaded with the same underlying notion of freedom from something unwanted.

For the United States, this language of freedom constitutes a central part of our creation story. While the quest for freedom did not work out so well for indigenous peoples, the language of freedom motivated millions of European immigrants who were "yearning to be free." In those early days, immigrants were symbols of our strength and our purpose. Their arrival served to validate the foundational account of America's manifest density. Now, with the ravages of possessive individualism on display, that aspect of freedom has been converted into a less noble idea. It now looks like aggressive self-interest. Our constant appeals to freedom seem motivated by the desire to make sure others do not have a chance at what we enjoy.

This brings us to the second idea of freedom—the acquisitive urge that rationalizes our individualized consumption. This version of freedom derives from the frequent illusion that markets and capitalism are logically necessary for democracy to exist—and that democracy is both necessary and sufficient for a capitalist market economy. Neither belief is true. But the deceit persists: we are free to choose stuff in the market, and we are free to choose who our political class shall be. In that choice of political leaders, we inevitably load both aspects of freedom on them. We chose them, and now they must preserve our freedoms to engage in market relations with the least possible "interference" in our freedom. We might call it the "election exchange." It cannot, therefore, be a surprise that most politicians, whether aspiring or ensconced, recapitulate our language of possessive individualism, of acquisitive excess, of hostility toward taxation, of wariness of regulating private firms, and of indifference toward collective action. This addiction to the misleading notion of freedom serves to corrode civic trust and engagement.

Under this cultural inspiration, it is useless to attack the self-dealing of the private firm under managerial capitalism when that assault would leave intact the primary source of their antisocial practices. Firms are able to get away with particular unwelcome behaviors because we—a society composed of steadfast possessive individualists—enable them in their practices. We allow them to behave in a manner that is consistent with our own hedonistic acquisitive commitments. And when they hold wages low, refuse to offer feasible fringe benefits to their workforce, or outsource certain jobs—the better to hold prices low—we continue to reward them with our custom. The lower their prices, the happier we are.

Firms are celebrated as "job creators," but the political class remains silent when firms close and move to China where they become job creators for a different population of hard-pressed eager workers. Those whose jobs are outsourced, and who thereby are economically dispossessed, feel betrayal and outrage. But they—and the politicians who remain silent—are unable to marshal a coherent response because they, too, are imprisoned by the manifest deceits that derive from rights talk and the alleged freedom that is granted to firms.

If firms were thought of not as job creators but as reliable centers of plausible livelihoods and meaningful engagement, then the story would differ. One cannot be both a job creator and a job denier. In an earlier chapter, I discussed the lavish financial inducements showered on firms that seek a new location for their alleged job-creating attributes. After a certain period of time, when those (or other) firms leave or close, there is never a reciprocated financial obligation for the stranded labor and destroyed livelihoods. Firms behave as we expect firms to behave. But it is nowhere written that firms possess the immutable right to disregard the social compact that binds citizens together. Like teenagers out alone at night, they behave in particular ways because they can.

It is here that the usual excuses will be lined up and deployed. Firms cannot possibly remain competitive if they must behave in certain ways. Prices will increase if firms are required to behave in new ways. Firms will disappear if they are made to do certain things they can now avoid. Firms will suffer "inefficiencies" if they are forced to do new things by meddlesome politicians. The list goes on. I return to Amartya Sen's observation that some of the foundational truths of economics can be rechristened as important parts of "The Revolutionary's Handbook." The Second Theorem of Welfare Economics teaches us that under any particular institutional setup, competitive markets will yield and sustain a Pareto Optimal configuration of prices and quantities that cannot be altered without harming some individual or group of individuals. And so the lodestar of economics—efficiency—turns out to be arbitrary all the way down. Economics offers no help. It is all "political." Or, more honestly, it is all about ethics. Whose interests shall society choose to ratify?

We come to an awkward pass. It might have been assumed that the private firm, yoked to managerial capitalism, stands as a central impediment to enhanced prospects for those whose livelihoods depend on labor. And of course, overcoming the presumptive autonomy of the private firm—thought to be endowed with special privileges under the cultural embrace of possessive individualism—will not be easy. But we now see that the unwanted excesses of possessive individualism are not confined to the owners of capital.

The vast majority of individuals in the metropolitan core seem mesmerized by the culture of possessive individualism in their comprehensive commitment to a consumerist society and by their affinity for incessant rights talk. Indeed, contemporary notions of freedom are presumed to entail a rather complete absence of duties to others and to society as a whole. Like the most

dedicated capitalist, a large number of citizens seem resistant to any institutional arrangements that they imagine will diminish their self-serving ideas
of liberty and freedom. Aggressive resistance to taxes so essential to a modern
nation-state is often worn as a badge of honor. With possessive individualism
standing as the reigning spirit of our time, many citizens are suspicious of,
and often hostile to, those who are less fortunate—immigrants, the unemployed, the homeless, and the mentally ill. Charity toward disaster victims in
far-off places remains intact, but charity toward those close at hand is often
grudging and resented.

Possessive individualism also infects the global economy. With improved
transportation, communications, and logistics, it was easy to assume that
distance would cease to be an important consideration in economic affairs.
As the world got smaller, differences in economic circumstances would
gradually be evened out. The tight interconnectivity would make it unlikely that stark differences across space would persist because all potential
gains from trade across regions could quickly be realized. Economic theory
suggested a convergence in prices, in costs, and ultimately in standards
of living.

We are observing precisely the opposite effects playing out. Advances in
communications, coupled with dramatically falling transportation costs,
have made it easier to manage and control far-flung economic operations
across the globe from a central location in the metropole. It is impossible to
overlook the enormous advantages—think of it as *economic momentum*—
associated with increasing returns to scale. Advanced communication
devices and management innovations are given extraordinary salience and
sway in global capitalism, such that standard notions of comparative advantage are now becoming irrelevant. The World Trade Organization, justified on the principle of comparative advantage and the unalloyed benefits
of unfettered trade, might now be an instrument to enhance not *comparative* advantage but *current* advantage. In a world of infinitely mobile capital, of instant communication, of ocean (and air freight) shipping costs that
continue to fall, and of any number of countries offering abundant and im-
mobile low-cost labor, it does not seem unreasonable to assume that the geography of the world's production and consumption patterns is now rather
locked in.

Fewer than 100 corporations now dominate production, finance, and
transportation for the majority of what the world's population is able to consume. Approximately two-thirds of the world's total net national income—a

reliable approximation of the world's total consumption capacity—is found in just 35 countries of the OECD core where only 17 percent of the world's inhabitants reside. Are there plausible forces at work that will diminish that share of total income and consumption in these 35 countries? This seems unlikely. Only a few years ago there was much excitement about the promise of the so-called emerging market economies—the five BRICS (Brazil, Russia, India, China, and South Africa). Brazil and India have reverted to type, Russia remains a marginalized supplier of low-priced carbon products in dubious demand, and China now seems intent on scaring or alienating its neighbors—and it has enough economic problems at home to cause considerable anxiety in the Politburo. South Africa remains a land of sweeping corruption, persistent economic misery, and unfulfilled promise. So much for "emerging markets."

It is not obvious that there are any feasible transformations in how the world's economy is now structured. This means that the economic relations we observe *within* countries of the metropolitan core are rather set in place. But there are profound differences in these two varieties of isolation. In Africa and the Middle East, it seems reasonable to expect continued economic despair, migration to large capital cities or national economic hot spots such as Abidjan, Johannesburg, and Lagos, but little comprehensive change. This also means that Europe will continue to be threatened by economic migrants coming north in search of employment. In the stressed countries of the metropolitan core—the United States, Britain, Belgium, France, Greece, Spain, and Italy—a similar pattern of rural outmigration to urban areas seems likely to persist. Rural areas will face continued aging and depopulation. Rural–urban migration—in both the poor isolated periphery and the metropolitan core—will bring down birth rates, as all such migrations do. Eventually, the demographic transition will stabilize, and the isolated periphery will likely settle into persistent economic marginalization to the larger world. The core-periphery dichotomy seems secure.

The nature of contemporary capitalism now appears to be the evolved emanation of several centuries of possessive individualism having been acquired, embraced, and gradually refined in the rich metropolitan core. Indeed, one might say that the full flowering of possessive individualism is a major component of an explanation as to why countries in the metropole are so rich. Politicians have embraced the program. But consistency demands that if possessive individualism is to be credited for making 17 percent of the world's population the fortunate recipients of 62 percent of the world's personal income, this particular cultural commitment must also bear the blame for the converse of that achievement: 83 percent of the world's population has access to just 38 percent of global income.

Some may resist the implication that the two are related. However, the earlier evidence offered by Jeffrey Williamson (2011) provides empirical support for this idea. While some economists will resist the dependency thesis of Raul Prebisch (1950), it seems reasonable to suggest that much of the isolated periphery is now economically irrelevant to the metropolitan core. To argue over whether this condition implies "dependence" does not seem worthwhile. Pessimism concerning much improvement in the economic prospects for most of Africa is reflected in a recent comprehensive assessment by Dani Rodrik (2018).

This situation of global social and economic differentiation—of enduring marginalization and despair—should not be considered an aberration. It is the quite expected outcome of the enduring and pervasive spirit of possessive individualism. While the harried foxes of the metropolitan core feel indignant toward the private firm under managerial capitalism, the above comments must be understood as insisting that the abundant failures of managerial capitalism do not start with owners of firms. Those unwanted failures rest squarely on the shoulders of the political class and their millions of enablers. In other words, we are responsible.

In the following section, we will see the results of this enabling behavior. I call it "willful inequality."

II. Willful Inequality

The standard historical account of income inequality has focused on those who receive income from ownership of capital versus those who receive income from their ownership of labor power. In that sense, inequality was easily traced to one's ownership of assets. One owned capital or one owned only their labor power. Ownership was destiny. The work of Karl Marx concerned little else. We see in Figure 8.1 that the share of total national income going to capital has increased for a subset of the world's rich countries since 1975, rising from about 20 percent to approximately 28 percent. Labor's share has fallen proportionately.

But there is another profound phenomenon that the comparison in Figure 8.1 does not capture. Specifically, inequality is no longer uniquely

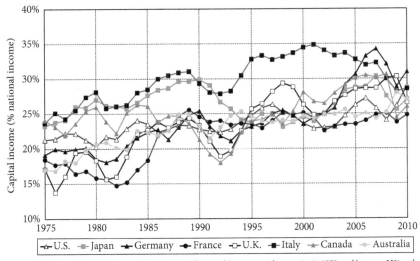

Capital income absorbs between 15% and 25% of national income in rich countries in 1970, and between 25% and 30% in 2000–2010. Sources and series: see piketty.pse.ens.fr/capital21c

Figure 8.1. The Capital Share in Rich Countries, 1975–2010
Source: Piketty, 2014 (Figure 6.5).

defined by the *source* of income received (capital versus labor) but rather by the *type of labor* income one receives. Does one's income arise from the receipt of wages and salary, or does it arise from professional advantages that bestow extraordinary compensation, including sizeable bonuses?

Recent data from the Luxembourg Income Study (www.lisdatacenter.org) tracks the evolution of earnings and finds that America's super-income earners are found in just three sectors—professional services, finance and insurance, and health care. The top 1 percent of income earners consists of (1) physicians; (2) executives, managers, sales supervisors, and analysts working in the financial sectors; and (3) professional and legal service industry executives, managers, lawyers, consultants and sales representatives. Part of this disparity is attributable to the gap between

> how much money its elite professionals earn relative to the median worker. Workers at the 90th percentile of the income distribution for professionals make 3.5 times the earnings of the typical (median) worker in all occupations in the United States. Only Mexico and Israel, which have very high inequality, compensate professionals so disproportionately. In Switzerland, the Netherlands, Finland and Denmark, the ratio is about 2 to 1.

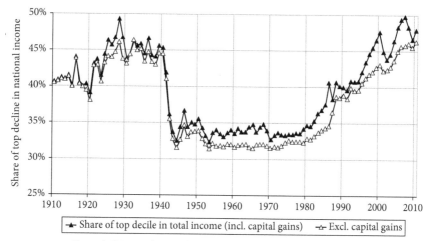

The top decile income share rose from less than 35% of total income in the 1970s to almost 50% in the 2000s–2010s. Sources and series: see piketty.pse.ens.fr/capital21c

Figure 8.2. Share of Top Decile in National Income: United States, 1910–2010
Source: Piketty, 2014 (Figure 8.5).

This ratio, the elite professions premium, is very highly correlated with income inequality across countries.[1]

Consider Figure 8.2. Here we see the trajectory of the share of the top decile in total U.S. incomes since 1910. Notice that capital-gains income has never figured too prominently in this trajectory, reaching modest proportions only after the dramatic drop in inequality brought on by World War II. The rather egalitarian postwar period ended around 1980 when we begin to see a dramatic increase in inequality—even surviving the financial crisis of 2007–2009.

The question worth asking is whether this steep rise in inequality is unique to the United States. In Figure 8.3 we see a trajectory for the four major Anglophone countries of the share of total income enjoyed by the top decile since 1910. The United States stands out as the most extreme, showing double the share for Australia.

In his definitive work on the subject, Thomas Piketty (2014) asks if the Anglophone countries differ in important ways from other rich countries. Figures 8.4 and 8.5 are clear indications that they do. While inequality in the Anglophone countries of Figure 8.3 started a strong rebound in the early 1980s, this pattern was *not* followed in France, Sweden, Germany, Japan, Denmark, Italy, or Spain. From this evidence, Piketty suggests that we are

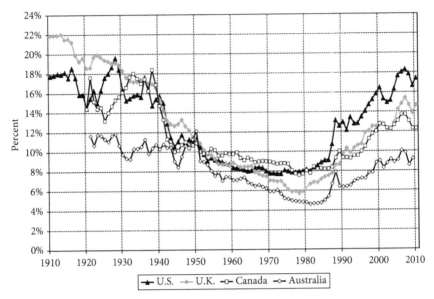

Figure 8.3. Share of Top Percentile in Total Income
Source: Piketty, 2014 (Figure 9.2).

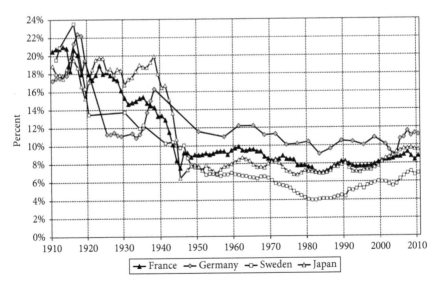

Figure 8.4. Share of Top Percentile in Total Income
Source: Piketty, 2014 (Figure 9.3).

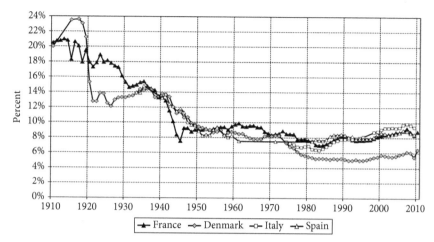

Figure 8.5. Share of Top Percentile in Total Income
Source: Piketty, 2014 (Figure 9.4).

not observing some *inherent structural* artifact of contemporary capitalism. Rather, the explanation is to be found in distinct ethical notions that pervade particular cultures. This is seen in the Luxembourg Income Study mentioned earlier. The political class in these four Anglophone countries reveals itself smitten by the profound disparities enabled and reinforced by possessive individualism.

The essential point here is that the American version of managerial capitalism, and to a lesser extent the variant of that found in the UK, Canada, and Australia, has acquired an extreme commitment to possessive individualism. The importance of this differential commitment warrants emphasis. A commitment to income inequality is revealed to be a differentially acquired cultural affliction. There is no inherent structural attribute of capitalism and its firms that can explain these disparate empirical findings. As above, it would be a mistake to launch an attack on the private firm while allowing the greater affliction of possessive individualism to remain intact in the population as a whole.

I wish not to be misunderstood here. The capitalist firm is—and must always be understood to be—a public trust. There is no private and inviolate space within the capitalist firm that can stand against the needs of the larger political community. But efforts to reform the capitalist firm in more socially beneficent ways will not succeed if the rest of us, as customers and employees, fail to reassess our cultural commitments to the pleasures of low prices, to the indifferent treatment of employees, and to the granting of all manner of financial inducements and side-payments to firms under the deceit that they are community-minded job creators.

The citizens of democratic market economies hold the behavior of firms in their hands. Firms can only get away with those behaviors that democratic societies allow them to. This means that the citizenry, compromised by the manifold deceits of possessive individualism, must abandon our affinity for rights talk and come to understand that full personhood—comprehensive citizenship—requires the acceptance of correlated obligations.

III. Recovering Obligation

[T]o get a valid theory of political obligation . . . one must be able to postulate that the individuals of whom the society is composed see themselves, or are capable of seeing themselves, as equal in some respect more fundamental than all the respects in which they are unequal. . . . This condition was fulfilled in the original possessive market society, . . . by the apparent inevitability of everyone's subordination to the laws of the market. So long as everyone was subject to the determination of a competitive market, and so long as this apparently equal subordination of individuals to the determination of the market was accepted as rightful, or inevitable, by virtually everybody, there was a sufficient basis for rational obligation of all men to a political authority which could maintain and enforce the only possible orderly human relations, namely, market relations. (Macpherson, 1962, pp. 272–73)

These sentiments draw an essential distinction that will now occupy our attention. The central idea of possessive individualism, the product of foundations laid down in the eighteenth century, is that we are both free and fully human by virtue of sole proprietorship of our person for which we owe nothing to society. Since to be human is to live free of the will of others, each individual's freedom can be limited only by such obligations as are necessary to secure the same freedom for others. All coherent market societies consist of a series of market-mediated relations, with the political aspect comprising rules to protect an individual's property in his or her person and possessions, thereby maintaining orderly relations of exchange between individuals regarded as free proprietors of themselves (Macpherson, 1962, p. 264).

With the many advantages of hindsight, we may now see just how naïve this vision would turn out to be. The Enlightenment vision was optimistic—even utopian—because it failed to grasp the rather inevitable dynamic nature of market relations as they evolved in democracies susceptible to capture by concentrated economic interests. We can gain insight into this process by focusing our attention on two key aspects of possessive individualism: (1) sole proprietorship over one's person; and (2) freedom consistent with, yet limited by, the freedom accorded to others.

A. Property in One's Person

Possessive individualism regards an individual as the sole proprietor (owner) of her personal capacities. This Lockean association of *personhood with property* offers a plausible explanation as to why, in the fullness of time, serious problems would emerge. Notice that if each individual is the owner of her personal capacities, then it follows that the individual is the proprietor of all *future value* associated with the use of those abilities. In other words, it is not just present action that is under the full control of the individual, but that control—that proprietorship—turns every present action into a potential future value that is under the exclusive proprietorship of the individual. This implies that attentive stewardship of one's person is an investment in future action and therefore future value. The rational individual will seek to maximize the present value of that discounted future stream of benefits. Notice that what is being called "property" is not a physical object such as land or a dwelling. Rather, as previously noted, *property is a value*—a benefit stream that runs into the future.

Possessive individualism means that the value of the asset at a particular moment is the discounted present value of all future uses to which that asset might be put. This is consistent with human capital theory, which sees schooling and job training as valuable investments in the embodied stock of human capital so as to enhance an individual's lifetime earnings profile and net worth. Possessive individualism is the underlying conceptual structure that enabled Karl Polanyi to identify labor as a "fictitious commodity" capable of being bought and sold for the purpose of creating new income and wealth (Polanyi, 2001). Polanyi would have been more correct to consider labor as a *fictitious asset*.

Human beings are economic assets, whether as slaves who are owned by others or as participants in labor markets where they alienate a portion of their daily capacities to owners of capital in exchange for a wage or salary. As we saw in Chapter 3, this idea of labor as an asset was appreciated by Henry George (1905), who observed that whether a single person owned all of the land (an asset) on an island or the other 99 men (a different asset) on that same island would make no difference to him or to them. But the sort of ownership George envisaged was a mere illustration of this basic point. Free individuals are proprietors of their own asset value, and as owners they are free to rent or sell their labor power to those who are owners of the means of labor—capitalists. Some of those human assets have great market value—perhaps as managers of hedge funds—while other human assets (unskilled workers) have precious little market value.

It is understood that in a market culture, one's social standing and esteem are related to the economic value of their bundle of assets—their stock of human capital. Proprietors of human capital in much of Africa gain social status by owning many cattle. Proprietors of human capital in metropolitan capitalism gain social status by a different form of accumulation—they are "ultra-high-net-worth" individuals. As Veblen pointed out, their several homes, their quiet cars, and their lavish vacations are constant reminders of their social worth. In 2016, the world's top *10* billionaires held approximately 13 percent of total global wealth, and Figure 8.6 reveals that the wealth of these 10 individuals exceeded the total Gross Domestic Product of nine nations. The "property value" of these 10 individuals is considerable in the extreme.

At the other extreme, the economies of the metropolitan core reveal a large number of individuals with very low net worth; their asset value as potential labor power is minimal. They are unemployable or have a market value that is inadequate to earn a plausible livelihood. A general embrace of possessive individualism as a cultural norm leads to a shared vision that such people need to pull themselves up and become contributing members of society. In certain political circles, such individuals are considered deserving of their miserable state, or they are seen as ingrates intent on extracting financial support from the public treasury. It seems that the good Parson Thomas Malthus survives in the public imagination.

Top 10 Billionaires versus World Gross Domestic Product, 2016

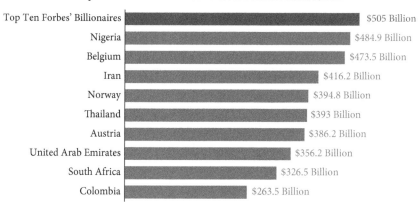

Top Ten Forbes' Billionaires	$505 Billion
Nigeria	$484.9 Billion
Belgium	$473.5 Billion
Iran	$416.2 Billion
Norway	$394.8 Billion
Thailand	$393 Billion
Austria	$386.2 Billion
United Arab Emirates	$356.2 Billion
South Africa	$326.5 Billion
Colombia	$263.5 Billion

Figure 8.6. Wealth of the 10 Richest Individuals Compared to GDP of 9 Countries
Source: https://inequality.org/facts/global-inequality, accessed November 19, 2017.

B. Reciprocated Freedom of Action:
On Functionings and Capabilities

The autonomy of an individual as owner of his own capacities requires a reciprocated presumption of autonomy of all others who also stand as owners of their assets and capacities. In addition to precluding the extraction of one's powers against their will, this condition might be thought of as the Hobbesian proviso that individuals as owners of their capacities are limited in their autonomy by the obvious autonomy of others. This condition of reciprocated freedom is intuitive and, as we have seen, implies immunity from unwanted encroachment by others. Macpherson considers this to be assurance against the imposition of extractive power by others. MacIntyre points out that this condition precludes individuals being made the instruments of the desires of others. As Hobbes showed, a civil society—one in which each individual is free from the intrusions of others—implies an authoritative agent (Leviathan) to guarantee the maximum liberty for each free person consistent with the maximum liberty for all other free persons. We have earlier seen that the elimination of horizontal violence by individuals under a coherent legal justice system is the sufficient means for realizing this condition. Moreover, Locke was concerned with controlling encroachment by governments on their citizens—an instance of vertical violence.

In this general vein, Amartya Sen and Martha Nussbaum, among many others, have devoted a great deal of time urging us to consider an individual's well-being in terms of his or her "capabilities" (Nussbaum, 2000, 2011; Sen, 1985a, 1985b, 1992, 2005). The basic argument in the capabilities approach is that the necessary freedom to achieve calls attention to what the individual is able to do. It is to have control over her own life prospects. The capabilities approach is sympathetic with my advocacy for the idea of recovering personhood under managerial capitalism. The notion of capabilities stresses a view of the individual as a participant in a social game and the capacity of that individual to succeed in whatever pursuit seems compelling. That is, the individual is considered fully human if she has the capacity to blossom and flourish to the full extent of her capabilities. We have seen that this is related to three varieties of freedom advanced by Sen: (1) autonomy; (2) immunity; and (3) opportunity. As indicated earlier, I regard this innovation to be an improvement over standard notions of freedom.

However, notice that an emphasis on capabilities—the capacity to choose, to be free from encroachment, and to achieve—retains the traditional notion of the individual as an autonomous hedonist "seeking to be free" from impediments and the extractive powers of others. That is, the capabilities approach appears to perpetuate a vision of the individual as an isolated entity pursuing opportunities to deploy his capabilities unimpeded—perhaps even uninfluenced—by others. Here is the idealized individual seeking to be free. This approach is consistent with the creation of the individual as wrought by the Enlightenment.

Unfortunately, the notion of an idealized "free individual" is problematic. The individual in any society is not an isolated automaton but has instead been shaped by a specific embeddedness in a very particular social setting. We come to learn what we want by coming to grips with what those around us consider to be socially valued. On this view, my interests and alleged "capabilities" are not really mine: I have picked them up, or they have been given to me by others. What I have become as a person is the end result of an unwitting collective effort that has given me what I have become (Bromley, 2006). Therefore, personhood is not the promised freedom and autonomy of democratic market capitalism. Rather, personhood is a gift of the way in which societies are constituted—how they choose to become under the influence of Dewey's Arc. *Full personhood is given to us by the actions of others.* Enlightenment thinkers failed to grasp this essential point.

The idea of *functionings* and *capabilities* appears to be a somewhat more pleasing account of the traditional focus on the centrality of the individual. By way of contrast, the concept of personhood recognizes the fluid and constructed nature of how sapient persons become. The point here is to argue that the Enlightenment and managerial capitalism have combined to give legitimacy to the widest scope for individual capabilities. But notice that those with more capabilities, or with capabilities that fetch greater rewards under managerial capitalism, are now "pulling away" from those with fewer (or less market-valorized) capabilities. The only trouble with a meritocracy is that those with more merit end up winning the game. Unless the political system has the capacity periodically to recalibrate the winnings—the "Jubilee" solution—possessive individualism is destined to produce the situation we now observe—an economy of many foxes and a few hedgehogs.

There is an additional danger in a focus on capabilities. Where, in this concern for the well-being of the individual, are we to locate any sense of the obligations that come with participation in a social milieu? Our lives are not mere experiential opportunities for bolstering our well-being. Living is also giving. A meaningful workplace is a realm of commitment and support. The precapitalist rural farmer in England was enmeshed in a web of both rights and obligations. And his social superiors—traditionally imagined to be omnipotent and ruthless—were likewise bound by a web of rights and responsibilities. Weberian "webs of significance" bound all together in a fraught but reciprocated community of expectations, rewards, defeats, pleasures, disappointments, and standoffs. It was an *energetic existence*. It required effort on all sides and obligations on all sides.

It would look rather grim to modern sensibilities. But one thing remains clear: those poor filthy illiterate farmers at the bottom of the heap could never be abandoned by their social betters. Everyone knew that the rich very much needed the poor. The reality of managerial capitalism is that this aspect of mutual dependence has been stripped away. Possessive individualism means there are no obligations. There is only empty talk about the manifold joys of rights and freedom.

IV. What We Owe to Others

[M]oral progress is not a matter of an increase of rationality—a gradual diminution of the influence of prejudice and superstition, permitting us to see our moral duty more clearly . . . it is best to think of moral progress as a matter of increasing sensitivity, increasing responsiveness to the needs of a larger and larger variety of people and things. (Rorty, 1999, p. 81)

We have two quite distinct ideas in play here. The first idea is about individuals as sole proprietors of their personhood being free to exercise, within the limits of an equal autonomy for others, complete freedom of movement, of thought, and of action. Ah, liberty. The other idea is about such liberated automatons interacting through market-mediated relations. It is necessary to notice that the usual conjunction of these two ideas is neither necessary nor logical. Recall the earlier discussion that markets are not necessary—nor are they sufficient—to bestow full personhood. Human societies can quite easily be organized on terms that have little to do with market relations. Indeed, human history reveals that the market fetish is no more than 300–400 years old in the Western world. The more profound clarification, therefore, concerns the idea of sole proprietorship of our person.

This principle is at the very core of the Enlightenment. The social legitimacy—the collective moral authority—of this idea was foundational to the liberation of the individual in the eighteenth century. Freedom from dependence on the will of others meant freedom from necessary relations with others except for those relations that the individual enters into voluntarily with a clear view of his own interests. In other words, the newly sapient individual was necessarily the proprietor of his own personhood and capacities for which he owed nothing to society. The idea was compelling. Since freedom from the will of others is what makes individuals completely human, each individual's freedom can be limited only by such obligations and social rules as are necessary to secure the same freedom for others. It followed that the humane society was a constructed realm of activity whose explicit purpose was the protection of each individual's "property" in his person and acquired possessions. Central here is the maintenance of orderly relations of market-mediated exchange between individuals who are regarded as proprietors of their own personhood (Macpherson, 1962).

As we have seen, however, the moral force of this notion of the individual as a self-proprietor necessarily rested on the perception of a cohesion of self-interest among those who have a voice in choosing political leaders. Underlying this cohesion of self-interest, we find an awkward problem. If the free individual must work in order that she might eat, and if she can only work if she is willing to subjugate proprietorship over her person to the will of another person—the owner of capital—then the most fundamental presumption of the Enlightenment is necessarily violated. It is logically impossible to be a free person and then be obligated to submit to the commands of another person in order to survive. The gradual emergence of a possessive market culture, under the claimed virtuous and salubrious—and freedom-enhancing—experience of thoroughgoing markets, turns out to be the fatal defect of the charming promise of the Enlightenment.

Sadly, the rupture is complete. We have arrived where we must pause. The central argument of the preceding chapters is that the evolutionary pathway of capitalism has been a gradual dispossession of those with only their labor power to acquire the means of life—nourishment. The historic presumption of a common cohesion of interest among all members of a polity is no longer tenable. One cannot consult the evidence contained in Figures 8.1–8.6 and draw encouraging inferences about some presumed cohesion—especially in the Anglophone world. The evidence is strongly against sanguinity. Too many wage-earning households have been reduced to nervous and anxious foxes. Ironically, it is the very agency granted by the Enlightenment that first legitimized the possessive individual to be the master of his own functionings and capabilities. But then, through the full emergence of a meritocratic system predicated on the exquisite refinement of possessive individualism, it is now apparent just how very isolating and precarious life can be in a full-blown market culture if an individual is the proprietor of a singularly limiting asset called "labor power."

The emergence of managerial capitalism—with the sharp-eyed diligent *wrangler* of highly liquid capital, unbound by any plausible emotional ties to owners of labor power—represents the denouement of this process of dispossession and disregard that has finally turned individual agency and opportunity into individual subservience and marginalization. But we must also notice that the emerging dispossession is not inherent—or preordained—in a society held together by market relations. The Danes, the Swedes, the Finns, and the Norwegians seem to have bolstered the proprietorship—the personhood—of their citizenry without at the same time sundering the cohesion of interests necessary to justify the perpetuation of an economy largely mediated by market relations. It bears mention that international surveys continue to reveal that the citizens of these four damp, cold, and often dark lands are the happiest in the world. Perhaps it is the abundance of aquavit.

Or perhaps the many varieties of herring. Or perhaps it is something more fundamental.

These interesting exceptions aside, the inherent tendencies in managerial capitalism, reifying and recapitulating the full measure of a market-predicated meritocracy, have given most countries in the metropole an economy in which the idea of a shared mutuality of interests between those who own and manage capital, and those who own only their labor power, has now become impossible to abide. That cohesion began to unravel in Britain in the 1800s as the Industrial Revolution progressed. However, the first aspect of possessive individualism—sole proprietorship—has flourished under the evolutionary trajectory of capitalism and now stands implicated as the logical explanation for the complete absence of a shared mutuality of interests. Rights talk is now the common theme of social discourse, and against this leitmotif, the idea of obligations falling on the liberated individual—relishing the supposition of full personhood—seems anachronistic. Everyone is in for themselves.

But some members of contemporary nation-states have a much greater capacity to exploit their possessive proprietorship. Those who control capital have scant interest in those with only their labor to sell. Members of this latter group may well imagine themselves empowered by their self-proprietorship, but it is of no comfort or solace in an economic environment where labor is seen by firms as an inconvenient cost. Those who are sole proprietors over an asset that is limited to labor—that must be sold to reticent owners of capital—increasingly find themselves with meager and dwindling market value. In the long evolutionary history of capitalism, individuals who found themselves similarly disadvantaged—makers of buggy whips, harnesses, wagons, kerosene lanterns, and candles—moved on to other lines of work because alternatives were in good supply. It is impossible to pay attention to the news and fail to notice a consensus that automation, global outsourcing, and general technical change in many ordinary labor-intensive tasks now pose a threat of unprecedented severity to those with rather ordinary and abundant manual skills.

It now seems that the presumptively beneficial effects of thoroughgoing market relations are under attack. Much of the frustration, anxiety, and resentment associated with Brexit, the rise of right-wing parties in Europe, and the election of Donald Trump have emerged precisely because of a shared sense that ubiquitous market relations no longer serve the interests of the citizenry. However, this is a flawed diagnosis of the problem. There is nothing necessarily perverse, unequal, or exploitative about an economy predicated on market relations. As mentioned earlier, the Scandinavians have found a way to tame the untoward excesses of market relations. Rather, as I stressed earlier, the serious flaw necessarily resides elsewhere.

This brings us to the alleged harmony of interests within society—that is, a harmony of interests sufficient to counteract the powerful centrifugal forces inherent in a possessive market society. Managerial capitalism stands as evidence of the dissolution of that essential aspect of the liberated individual. As we saw earlier, the primacy of rights and of rights talk leads to a shared idea that what we owe to others is—in a word—nothing. Those who labor owe nothing to those who own capital, and those who own capital are sure they owe nothing to those who seek work in order that they might eat. When ownership of property was a prerequisite to the franchise, it was easy to limit participation. Full democratization posed a threat to this class-based hegemony, and it took some time before the managerial class figured out how to exploit its advantageous position.

To reprise Matthew Arnold, the emergence of inequality materialized the upper class, vulgarized the middle class, and brutalized the lower class. It is reasonable to conclude—as we watch political turmoil across the metropole—that while the materialized upper class is now comfortable, the middle class is no longer capable of being vulgarized. Like the lower class, the vast middle class has now become brutalized.

It seems that managerial capitalism has anointed the minuscule upper class with illusions of entitlement; it has unnerved the shrinking salaried class by closing off any upward mobility; and it has rendered the bottom-trawling wage-earning class comprehensively dissolute in its haggard quest for secure livelihoods. Cohesion of interests—a necessary condition for the concept of social obligation to arise and be durable—is a distant memory. Macpherson notes the exquisite irony here. Modern society is trapped by its commitment to possessive individualism—material acquisitiveness—at the very time when capitalism no longer provides the necessary conditions for deducing a valid theory of political obligation that will prevent the continuation of a flawed social experiment.

The liberated individual, she who is free of any obligations other than to herself, is seen as fully human. And yet, that very personhood—driven by the presumptions of possessive individualism—prevents the crafting of any implicit contractual relations with other persons unless those relations are strictly self-serving. In a world where everyone is holding out for self-serving relations with others, interpersonal relations become scarce indeed. The reality of full personhood thrives as long as all personal interactions are confined to the realm of market relations. We are back to introductory economics: the individual is modeled as nothing but a consumer looking for the most utility for a given financial outlay. Is that all there is to life?

Obligation, because it is alien to possessive individualism, has become scarce. It is spotted only rarely, in fleeting moments in which the precepts of the flawed logic of personhood give way to the episodic lapses of nostalgia for a time when people seemed to care about others. The feeling quickly passes.

The choice is harsh: we either abandon the conceit of the Enlightenment in which each person is completely free from the will of others, or we turn our back on the world of thoroughgoing market relations. Macpherson avers that we cannot now create a valid theory of obligation to a liberal-democratic state in a possessive market society (Macpherson, 1962, p. 275). I am less pessimistic than Macpherson, and I have Scandinavia on my side. I also have history. The manifold problems of nonmarket economies—whether Mao's destructive, indeed lethal, communism, or the Soviet Union's comical planned and bloated state capitalism—offer ample evidence that however much one may despise many forms of market relations, the incentive properties inherent in a market economy are unimpeachable. The key, of course, is to make sure that all prices are reflective of social costs. This is no easy feat, but it can be worked on—and good progress is possible.

I have insisted that an economy is always in the process of becoming, and so the challenge is not to get all prices perfectly calibrated once and for all. Rather, the challenge is to acknowledge that an economy is like a favorite old automobile that requires constant tending and maintenance. Like the old family sedan, we know what a market economy is, and we know how to maintain it so that its performance is gently and constantly enhanced. Recall that the fundamental challenge in sticking with the market is to begin to wring out of it the enormous tendencies toward inequality. Again, the Scandinavians know how to do this.

We are left with a necessary strategy of a full-scale assault on the destructive conceit of the individual as the sole proprietor of his functionings and capabilities, unmediated by any concern for the interests of others. In the cold light of day, and long after the soaring exhilaration of the Enlightenment has shown its underside, it is somewhat embarrassing to admit that in a society defined on such selfish grounds, none of us bears any possible obligations to other individuals—or to the society that has given us life and liberty. How selfish.

Notice Richard Rorty's concept of moral progress as consisting in the granting of pertinence to the interests of an ever widening circle of others. Adhering to this idea would bring immediate scorn down on the current structure of managerial capitalism. It would delegitimize the metaphor of many foxes and a few well-served hedgehogs. Indeed, a diminishment in the prevalence of rights talk would at the same time raise the prominence of considering the obligations and interests of others. A market economy need not be an arena of privilege and despair—of alienation and superfluous consumption.

Given the choice of abandoning a market economy for Stalinist *dirigisme*, or reconstituting a market economy in the interest of greater equality and other-regarding behavior, there can be little doubt which option would be the dominant preference. It is well understood that societies that will not bend eventually break. Bending is better than breaking.

Note

1. Jonathan Rothwell, "The Myths of the 1 Percent, What Puts People at the Top," *The New York Times*, November 24, 2017.

References

Bromley, Daniel W. 2006. *Sufficient Reason: Volitional Pragmatism and the Meaning of Economic Institutions*, Princeton, NJ: Princeton University Press.

George, Henry. 1955 (1905). *Progress and Poverty*, New York: Doubleday, Page & Co.

Macpherson, C. B. 1962. *The Political Theory of Possessive Individualism*, Oxford: Clarendon Press.

Nussbaum, M. 2000. *Women and Human Development: The Capabilities Approach*, Cambridge: Cambridge University Press.

Nussbaum, Martha. 2011. *Creating Capabilities*, Cambridge, MA: Harvard University Press.

Piketty, Thomas. 2014. *Capital in the Twenty-First Century*, Cambridge, MA: Harvard University Press.

Polanyi, Karl. 2001. *The Great Transformation*, Boston: Beacon Press.

Prebisch, Raul. 1950. "The Economic Development of Latin America and Its Principal Problems, United Nations Department of Economic Affairs" (reprinted in *Economic Bulletin for Latin America*, 1962, Vol. 7, pp. 1–22).

Rodrik, Dani. 2018. "An African Growth Miracle?" *Journal of African Economies*, 27(1): 1–18.

Rorty, Richard. 1999. *Philosophy and Social Hope*, New York: Penguin.

Sen, Amartya. 1985a. *Commodities and Capabilities*, Amsterdam: North-Holland.

Sen, Amartya. 1985b. "Well-being, Agency and Freedom: The Dewey Lectures 1984," *Journal of Philosophy*, 82(4): 169–221.

Sen, Amartya. 1992. *Inequality Re-examined*, Oxford: Clarendon Press.

Sen, Amartya. 2005. "Human Rights and Capabilities," *Journal of Human Development*, 6(2): 151–66.

Williamson, Jeffrey G. 2011. *Trade and Poverty: When the Third World Fell Behind*, Cambridge, MA: MIT Press.

9

Recovering Personhood

Possessive individualism undermines the realization of full person-hood, and it enables the capitalist firm to shed any sense of obliga-tion to those who must rent or sell their labor power in order that they might eat. The fundamental crisis of capitalism is that the self-absorbed individual—and the self-dealing capitalist firm—are locked in a perverse contest in which their mutual dependence is both ac-knowledged and resented. Re-creating historic ideas of obligations—civic duties—seems impossible to imagine. A more plausible transition is to be found in the idea of loyalty: loyalty to others with whom we work, with whom we share social spaces, and with the community at large. Loyalty from the capitalist firm toward its workers would be a start. Loyalty from the acquisitive selfish individual would be helpful in restoring a shared and necessary sense of personhood.

I. Beyond the Self

A cause is good, not only for me, but for mankind, in so far, as it is essentially a "loyalty to loyalty," that is, an aid, and a furtherance of loyalty in my fellows. It is an evil cause in so far as, despite the loyalty that it arouses in me, it is destructive of loyalty in the world of my fellows. (Royce 1995 [1908], 56)

In his enduring classic *Exit, Voice, and Loyalty, Responses to Decline in Firms, Organizations, and States,* Albert Hirschman identified *loyalty* as a central aspect of the success of going concerns (1970). The importance of loyalty is found in the realization that it serves as a deterrent to exit—the dangerous loss of continued engagement by individuals in the affairs of the going con-cern. Exit—whether of disgruntled restaurant customers who never return, or dispirited citizens who lose faith and refrain from voting, or the superb employee who quits because of an abusive supervisor, or discerning and attentive parents who remove their children from indifferent schools—is a threat to the essential vitality of all going concerns. Loyalty is essential because it deters exit and enables the exercise of voice—whether to explain to the manager why the restaurant meal was disappointing, to continue to engage in political activity and to vote, to report the abusive supervisor so that the workplace becomes more civil for all employees, or to keep one's children in the problematic school and become engaged in an effort to help the school become better. Voice implies engagement, commitment, pushing back—caring about the larger realm of our being.

The philosopher Josiah Royce wrote an entire book on the idea of loyalty, and he anchored that idea in something beyond the individual. It seems that Royce recognized, early in the twentieth century, that America had become obsessed with individualism. Indeed, we are told that Royce was moved by the need to reject the celebrated "heroic individualism" associated with Walt Whitman, Ralph Waldo Emerson, and William James (Kegley, 2008). As we saw earlier, if there is anything that defines the spirit of the American experience, it is individualism. Contemporary economics is built around the individual as a mere consumer who seeks to maximize utility. And, as we saw in Chapter 3, the idea of the autonomous individual can be traced back to the early fifteenth century in England. The Anglo-American commitment to the individual is robust and much celebrated. But at what cost?

II. On Loyalty

My interest in the concept of loyalty is predicated on the possibility that the idea might prove useful as a means to meliorate the alienation that seems to have emerged from our enduring commitment to possessive individualism. Alienation concerns a feeling of separateness, of isolation, of apartness. We saw that to psychologists, alienation speaks to a sense of separation between the imagined self and the world out there that seems unattainable. Alienation thrives in a world where loyalty is absent.

Consider the discussion in Chapter 1 of a time when horizontal violence was the accepted approach to dispensing with justice. Individuals who had suffered at the hands of others took it upon themselves to exact what was called justice but what was, in fact, retribution. This violence among individual members of a nation-state was gradually supplanted by official protocols in which police and judges and lawyers assumed the role of dispensers of justice. We can think of this transition as a reassuring one to individuals who could now see that the government took an interest in their suffering at the hands of others and that it was prepared to offer protections—justice—to all.

It is possible to read into this transition an emerging sense of loyalty by governments to their citizens. Here is recognition of the sense of community and the need for social protection. And it is reasonable to infer that this grant of responsibility for the citizenry gradually produced an attitude of reciprocated loyalty on the part of the citizenry toward their government as a protector and arbiter of a just society. This is part of the idea of the "citizenship exchange" that is often missing in the notional states of Africa. There, individuals pay little to their government in the way of taxes, and their government in return offers very little in the way of support or protection. Criminal "justice"—such as it is—often remains a private affair.

But what if this welcome participation by the government in protecting the individual has gradually fostered a perception that each of us is *owed* a variety of such protections and that little is expected of us in return? As citizens, we have come to revere our bundle of claimed "rights," and it is the government's job to assure us of the sweep and nature of those rights. Perhaps our devotion to possessive individualism has fostered a perverse reliance on government as a reliable protector of our much-prized rights. But what if this sense of assured protection has also worked to absolve us of any sense of loyalty to other individuals? Has it become too easy to see other individuals as threats to our prized individualism? After all, they get in our way on the roads and byways, they clog up our walking and bicycle paths, they crowd in on our pursuit of solitude, and they talk—or use their cell phones—in movie theaters. Personal confrontations remain troubling, whether in the workplace or in the checkout line.

There are plausible reasons to conclude that those of us in the grip of possessive individualism are aware that something is not quite right. In his book *Being Mortal*, the noted public intellectual on health care—Dr. Atul Gawande—writes about the end-of-life travails in an assortment of dreary and clinically sanitized nursing homes and assisted living facilities (2014). He calls attention to the isolation, alienation, indifference, and evident sadness that seems to pervade such places; all the while residents are surrounded by the hustle and bustle of nurses, exercise coaches, religious messengers, janitors, visiting relatives, and the long hallways lined with hunched-over nappers secured to their wheelchairs by a restraining blanket. Little communication takes place; blank stares are the norm. Into this waste-land, Gawande writes about an innovator—Bill Thomas—who entered Chase Memorial Nursing Home in New Berlin, New York as the new di-rector. Before long, the facility was alive with several dogs (a greyhound and a lapdog), four cats, and approximately 100 parakeets. And then there were real live plants—not plastic substitutes—in every room. The staff and residents were initially stunned as the chaos of these "intruders" upset the comfortable serene boredom.

The professional staff—mostly nurses—revolted. They were hired to take care of people, not to scoop up dog waste in the hallway. In a scene reminiscent of *One Flew Over the Cuckoo's Nest*, residents soon took the side of the cats and dogs and enjoyed watching the nurses slowly adapt. Gawande writes:

> Gradually people [the staff] started to accept that filling [the facility] with life was everyone's task. And they did so not because of any rational set of arguments or compromises but because the effect on residents soon became impossible to ignore; the residents began to wake up and come to life. . . . " People who we had believed weren't able to speak started speaking," Thomas said. "People who had been completely withdrawn and non-ambulatory started coming to the nurses' station and saying, 'I'll take the dog for a walk.'" All the parakeets were adopted and named by the residents. The lights turned back on in people's eyes. (Gawande, 2014, p. 122)

Gawande reports that a few years later there are still 100 parakeets, four dogs, two cats, a colony of rabbits, and a flock of laying hens. There are still hundreds of indoor plants and a thriving vegetable and flower garden. There is an on-site child-care facility for the staff, as well as an after-school program. The nursing home was reconstituted from a place for dying into a place for living. The gradual appearance of loyalty—to parakeets, to plants, to dogs, to the nursing staff, but most importantly to the other residents—seems to have rescued everyone from their sullen and focused individualism and created for them a community. The essence of community is to communicate, to no-tice and care for others. There is little "rights talk" on display; everyone is loyal to something beyond themselves.

Gawande's account focuses on the transformative experience for the residents. All plausible indicators would judge these changes to be successful innovations. However, I now want to change our focus a little and turn attention away from the residents. It is time to think about this facility in terms of the individuals who work there—nurses, clinical aids, receptionists, and maintenance staff. In view of the initial hostility to the changes introduced by Bill Thomas, we can infer a rather standard workplace. The nursing staff was engaged in an unpleasant daily contest with sullen residents to counter the inevitable sorrow associated with such places. The staff showed up, did what was expected of them, and somehow dealt with the apparent desperation of many of those whom they attended. Those of us who have ushered parents and grandparents into such places have no idea how the people who work there maintain their spirit and equilibrium. Gawande's account of their immediate hostility to cleaning up dog waste is a humorous reminder of the quotidian grind. And we know that wages in such places are not princely. An assembly-line worker can become bored snapping on hubcaps at a Ford plant. But a daily routine of attending to the dying requires a different order of devotion.

I want to focus on the nursing staff in order to revisit the issue of vertical violence inside of firms. In an earlier chapter, I noted that Locke and other Enlightenment philosophers had argued that true liberty demanded restraint on the authority of ruling sovereigns to inflict harm on their subjects. The emergence of civil rights writ large is a reflection of that important transformation. And so today the individual citizen in most nations enjoys considerable protection against arbitrary action by officers of the state. However, in an ironic reflection of the early warnings of Adolf Berle and Gardiner Means, the modern corporation—under the exacting tyranny of managerial capitalism—now stands as the apparent source of violence against employees. The findings of dissatisfaction in the workplace reported in Chapter 4 are reflective of this problem. Efforts to bring about greater protection for workers and improve working conditions are resisted with great resolve. Owners and managers and supervisors are equally susceptible to possessive individualism. Workers bring it into the workplace.

Recall the account of efforts to certify a union to represent Nissan workers in Mississippi. The necessity of an election, which seems to offer all of the benefits of democracy, actually pits workers against each other and reinforces the centrifugal forces of possessive individualism. But such divisive forces are not limited to the modern corporation. Efforts are being made to strip public employees, particularly school teachers, of union protection. Certification campaigns are expensive, divisive, and difficult to mount. There can be little surprise that teachers' unions have become rare. One might even see this situation as a return to an earlier time when the official power of governments was a force bearing down on the individual. After all, these restrictions on worker protection were not forced on teachers by the captains of industry. But there is more to the story. We might usefully think of it as the *rise of resentment* (Cramer, 2016).

The assault on teachers and public workers in general has become a favorite cause of conservative politicians fueled by the rise of resentment. This growing culture of resentment is animated by the realization that public employees have long enjoyed a suite of workplace benefits not available to workers in the private sector. Over the past several decades, public-sector workers have exchanged modest salary increases for a set of vacation and health-care benefits that seem generous when compared to those offered in the private sector. The political response to this situation—animated by resentment—has not been a rush to provide similar benefits for workers in the private sector. On the contrary, conservative politicians have decided to *take away* such benefits from public employees. After all, if government workers enjoy such benefits, workers in the private sector might soon get the dangerous idea that they ought to have similar benefits. We see here an explicit effort to demonize workers with union protections and to turn them into harried foxes.

It is one thing to resist making life more pleasant for workers, and quite another to take aggressive steps to make life worse for workers. But the current political climate seems to encourage just that behavior. Many voters have supported these retrograde policies despite the implications for workers in general. Is this what possessive individualism has wrought—resentment? Political scientists seem puzzled that so many individuals would vote against their economic interest. Perhaps the experts underestimate just how possessive individualism has encouraged the demise of other-regarding behavior. Does possessive individualism explain the rise of resentment?

III. On Familiarity

I have devoted a great deal of attention to the problems associated with possessive individualism. At a practical level, many of those problems seem to emanate from the dominant spirit of the age captured by Mary Ann Glendon's "rights talk." We are all quite clear about the nature and extent of our rights. We are also clear that as liberated individuals we have few, if any, obligations—except, that is, to ourselves. After all, it is quite enough to shoulder the burden of a suite of obligations to the acquisition and enjoyment of those aspects of life that are implied by our inchoate "rights." Given our imagined self-worth as individuals, we are *obligated* to the task of assuring that we get into the very best universities (and only three or four are worthy of that mark), that we quickly purchase the latest technical gizmos, that we have the most alluring possessions, and that our children—if we decide to have any—participate in the best sports, school plays, and social celebrations. And that they, too, in due time, will enroll in the very best universities. The meritocratic circle continues.

Our obligations, it seems, are to ourselves. The idea of obligations to others or to the general "good" is a difficult sell. We have a hard enough time attending to our own obligatory pursuits. Few individuals have the time or inclination to bother with obligations or duties to others. That seems like an impossible burden to carry through life. Everywhere one looks there are people in need. If I am obliged to do something for them, there would be no time or money for my own obliged needs.

And so it seems useful to consider a different strategy. Imagine a world in which we give up on the idea of obligations or duties to others and instead embrace the more compelling idea of *loyalty*. What if loyalty might gradually emerge to serve as a companion to our preoccupation with our imagined rights? As we noted earlier, Royce advanced the idea of loyalty to loyalty. Imagine a worker coming to the aid of a distressed colleague—not out of any obligation to that individual, but out of loyalty to a colleague and to the going concern. We see that loyalty acknowledges a slight tinge of self-interest, but that it also signals an interest in the community of which both individuals are a part. If I am loyal to my organization, then an extension of help to a distressed colleague is beneficial to the organization, and it is beneficial to me. That is, if the distress of a colleague undermines the going concern, then loyalty—not obligation—authorizes an expression of concern and commitment to that colleague, as well as to the going concern. Who knows, someday I might very well be in need of support from a colleague.

We see that the mutuality of interests, exemplified by other-regarding behavior, strengthens an organization and serves to turn it into a real community. The workplace is not just a place of work. The workplace is a community. Loyalty is not an obligation. Loyalty is an offer of concern and commitment to something beyond the individual. Loyalty undermines the corrosive hedonism of possessive individualism.

Apparently, before Bill Thomas arrived, Chase Memorial Nursing Home was a place quite devoid of loyalty. In fact, it was a place that seemed to possess little emotion at all. Residents came there and soon died. They were transient, and thus long-term personal engagements were difficult and therefore best avoided. Nursing staff showed up each day, did a plausible job of what was expected of them, and went home at the end of their shift—inspired or distressed by their work. But there seemed to be precious little loyalty in the air. I would be surprised if the staff felt great loyalty to each other or to the going concern. Notice how a staff member immediately rejected the idea of cleaning up after a dog—despite the high probability that this employee had happily provided a dog for his or her children. A dog for one's children was expected. But a little extra dog-related effort at work for the benefit of death-bound individuals was an unwanted nuisance. Loyalty seemed in very short supply. And yet, once the cacophony subsided, and the nursing staff observed the profound change in the distressed residents, attitudes changed.

This positive change did not arise, I am quite sure, out of a sense of some new *obligation* to the nursing home or to its residents. That change arose, it might be argued, from a new and surprising sense of commitment to the residents and to other coworkers. This emergent commitment can quite easily be understood as a new sense of loyalty to the going concern and its residents. The burst of energy and attentiveness among the desperately ill then seems, in turn, to have inspired the lethargic nursing staff. As Dewey would say, the introduction of animals and plants and gardens and child-care facilities constituted a *trying*. And before long, everyone inside that facility was engaged in a surprising *undergoing*. Staff and residents alike became something new and different. In their newness they evinced a nascent feeling we might as well call loyalty: loyalty to their colleagues, loyalty to the sick and dying residents, and loyalty to the long-run well-being of the facility that provided them employment and a paycheck. That is not a bad outcome. We might think of it as a new awareness of shared *familiarity* with the lifeworld of the nursing home. Perhaps a workplace became a community.

Although it is dangerous to make too much of an imagined past, it is not unreasonable to suggest that in the early days of industrial capitalism there was a sense of *familiarity* between workers and their bosses, including those who were owners of capital. There were obvious struggles and differences of viewpoints, to be sure. The aggressive hostility to workplace reform in Britain in the late 1800s and subsequent battles over unions in the United

States are certainly unpleasant reminders of the enduring tensions between workers and capitalists. And yet there are many instances in which workers and their superiors interacted with civility and an understanding of mutual dependence. The fact that so many families could rise into so-called middle-class status attests to the implicit bargain that existed in the 1950s and early 1960s. But things started to go off the rails in the late 1960s. It was then that American society rather fell apart.

Street battles over the Vietnam War, civil rights marches and demonstrations, campus protests, assassinations, and various political hostilities all seem to have bubbled over, and they continued into the 1970s. Then serious inflation from the deficit-financed war in Vietnam set in, and soon Ronald Reagan was ridiculing "welfare queens" allegedly driving around in Cadillacs. This racist taunt was accompanied by a new attitude of hostility to the government. Reagan became famous for his attack on the role of government—and on public employees—when he joked that the most feared sentence in America was: "Hello, I am from the government and I am here to help you." Soon, public employees were subject to ridicule. As we saw earlier, Reagan's hostility to the idea of a community of citizens and their government was overmatched by Britain's Margaret Thatcher who confidently announced that there is "no such thing as society—there is only the individual."

Something happened to democratic capitalism in that troubled era. And then, just when many people were feeling abandoned by their government, along came the harsh reality of financial capitalism, the savings and loan crisis, followed in the 1990s by globalization. There was the famous Enron scandal. Trust in the traditional verities was destroyed. New protests followed as young people—and many workers—sensed that they were being left behind. The correlated loss of manufacturing jobs, the growth of outsourcing, and governmental austerity programs combined to leave many households with a new level of insecurity. Fox-like behavior emerged.

Something also happened to the sense of community and thus to the idea of loyalty to anything beyond the immediate self. Possessive individualism triumphed. Both ideas of violence, horizontal and vertical, reemerged in the aftermath of these problematic years. Workers became fragmented and isolated in the wake of sustained political and corporate attacks on unions. And of course millions of nonunionized workers understood all too well what was in store for them. The emergence of globalization and multinational trade arrangements, fostered by the World Trade Organization, encouraged the consolidation of firms to take advantage of the enormous promise of increasing returns to scale. Mergers and acquisitions under financial capitalism placed more physical and emotional distance between management and labor. The ongoing transition into managerial capitalism has compounded that problem. Familiarity gave way to sullen resentment. Alienation became a governing strategy.

IV. On Transcendence

> My doctrine starts from the obvious fact that a moral individual, a person with rights and duties, is not born, but made. He is the product of a long process of social adjustment and of inner consciousness. . . . His moral freedom, his private judgment, his rights, his conscience is not the root, not the source, it is rather the result, the flower of his moral life. He is not born self-conscious. Not at birth is he free, or dutiful, or conscientious. He wins these qualities, if at all, only through the aid of a long social training. On the other hand, no social training can make a moral personality, unless, at each step in the process, the embryonic moral individual himself cooperates in the process—becomes, as they say, <u>self-active</u>, takes over the moral motives and makes them his own—wins individuality through somehow coming into a voluntarily chosen unity with his <u>social world</u>. (Royce, 1908, pp. 13–14; emphasis in original)

Recovering personhood will require a rediscovery of familiarity with colleagues, with overlings and underlings, and with a wide range of assorted others. Openness to familiarity is a necessary precursor to a willingness to give loyalty a chance. And once loyalty takes hold, full personhood and community will not be far behind. The plague of world disorder could use a little more community. As that happens, habituated notions of personhood—contaminated by several centuries of possessive individualism—will require careful reconsideration. This brings us to the idea of transcendence. Transcendence was a topic of considerable interest to Royce and also to the profoundly transformative notion of being (*Dasein*) developed by the German philosopher Martin Heidegger in his *Being and Time* (1962).

Royce understood transcendence in two senses. To be fully human requires: (1) the intense development of our capacities to respond to the world around us—to maintain as much openness to that world as possible;

and (2) recognition that truth and reality are not given to us but are always to be discovered (Kegley. 2008). The quest for self-actualization as an ideal, the very thought of loyalty to a cause, requires transcendence. The first condition for what Royce considered "sin" was therefore an unresponsiveness to the larger world out there, and an inordinate responsiveness to self-interests. As we saw earlier in the transformation at Chase Memorial Nursing Home, Royce believed that a "social life" helps us toward self-transcendence. Kegley notes that the social order can lead an individual to give into the collective will—to become a mere part of the crowd—a "they." Here we refuse to take responsibility for our own existence. The other danger is that we fall into egoism—the sufficiency of the individual. The only escape is loyalty through transcendence. Royce's inspiration comes from his understanding of the realm of grace ascribed to the biblical Paul.

One need not invoke deep theological implications here. The profound and timeless importance of openness, attentiveness, caring, and loyalty are evidence of the transcendent quality of a fully moral person. These are the qualities that appear to be endangered by possessive individualism. Heidegger's transcendence, to the extent that I grasp the full implications of his writing, is consistent with Royce.

V. On Burdened Loyalty to Community

There was a time, not very long ago, when the term *community* referred to a geographic place—a town or perhaps a section of a large metropolitan area. The Latin Quarter in Paris was a community, the Bronx in New York City was a community, and the French Quarter in New Orleans was a community. Haight-Asbury in San Francisco, too, was a community. Individuals who lived in such places or who visited there understood what the idea of community implied. If one has paid attention to public discourse in the early days of the twenty-first century, it will be evident that there is now a different sense of the word. Now we see that the idea of "community" pertains to Latinos, or to lesbians, or to immigrants, or to those confused about their exact gender, or to Evangelical Christians, or to those upset with current politics. The word *community* has become a subtle way to slice and dice all of us into separated "silos" or distinct identities. The triumph of this new meaning for the word is found in the way that political commentators have managed to legitimize the idea of "identity politics." An obvious corollary of this trend is that most everyone complains about how individuals have now sorted themselves into these micro-clusters of nearly identical traits and inclinations. The social media exacerbate this tendency by making it easy to identify and to name (to "friend") those most like us. And then everyone seems to complain about something called "cocooning."

Royce's advocacy for loyalty is elaborated by what he calls burdened loyalty to loyalty. Loyalty is the essence of commitment to a cause. A cause is something beyond the safe comfort of the isolated self. Extending one's awareness and consciousness beyond the ego-bound self requires effort. It is a chore, it can be unsettling, and it can take work to initiate it—and to sustain it. Being conscious of others is a burden, and burdens require commitment. Commitment is evidence of loyalty to something beyond the ego—beyond familiarity, beyond comfort. Indeed, loyalty requires the extension of familiarity to the unfamiliar. More importantly, the extension of the realm of familiarity beyond the self is not as easy as becoming familiar with a garden or a sunset. Expanding one's domain of familiarity—Deweyan *trying*—is enriching to the self only if that effort constitutes an *undergoing*. And this requires that the new realm of familiarity must be an active participant in the trying and undergoing. Gardens and sunsets may inspire, but they do not try and they do not undergo. Dewey's Arc reaches back and alters us. And in that alteration, we expend and receive transcendence.

The residents of Chase Memorial Nursing Home transcended their isolation because they could not help themselves. The introduction of dogs, cats, plants, parakeets, gardens, and a child-care facility required that they undergo change. And change is a burden. More importantly, the subsequent burden of speaking to fellow residents, of engaging nurses, of watering plants, of walking dogs, and of trying to nap over the cacophony required what we might call *rewarded burdens*. Full personhood is found in rewarded burdens—often unwillingly endured. But it is the undergoing, as Dewey understood, that comprises the practice of living. Without undergoing, there is no life. *Full personhood is burdened loyalty to loyalty.* Personhood requires a community that demands acknowledgment and contending. Personhood is energetic.

Possessive individualism, reinforced by the full flowering of managerial capitalism, denies the relevance of community, and it therefore deprives all of us the opportunity to undergo burdened loyalty to loyalty.

The crisis of our time is that managerial capitalism does not need to wait for the full automation of the workplace by steel and plastic and rubber and sensors and computer chips. Managerial capitalism is well on the road to "automation" by other means. Mindless and numb workers—peripatetic foxes—have now become the new automation.

References

Cramer, Katherine J. 2016. *The Politics of Resentment: Rural Consciousness in Wisconsin and the Rise of Scott Walker*, Chicago: University of Chicago Press.

Gawande, Atul. 2014. *Being Mortal*, New York: Henry Holt.

Glendon, Mary Ann. 1991. *Rights Talk*, Cambridge, MA: Harvard University Press.

Heidegger, Martin. 1962. *Being and Time*, New York: Harper and Row.

Hirschman, Albert O. 1970. *Exit, Voice, and Loyalty: Responses to Decline in Firms, Organizations, and States*, Cambridge, MA: Harvard University Press.

Kegley, Jacquelyn A. 2008. *Josiah Royce in Focus*, Bloomington: Indiana University Press.

Royce, Josiah. 1908. *The Philosophy of Loyalty*, New York: Macmillan. (long quote on page 391 from Pittsburgh Lectures on the Doctrine of Loyalty, 1980, HARP, Folio 82, 13–14).

Index